The Drillmaster of Valley Forge

Smithsonian Books

COLLINS
An Imprint of HarperCollins Publishers

Albany

New York

Pennsylvania

Hudson (North)

Fishkill

Susquehanna River

New York City

Schuylkill River

Germantown

Valley Forge

Lancaster

Philadelphia

Delaware River

York

Chadds Ford

New Jersey

The Drillmaster of Valley Forge

The Baron de Steuben *and the* Making
of the American Army

PAUL LOCKHART

THE DRILLMASTER OF VALLEY FORGE.
Copyright © 2008 by Paul Lockhart. All rights reserved.
Printed in the United States of America.
No part of this book may be used or reproduced in any manner whatsoever
without written permission except in the case of brief quotations
embodied in critical articles and reviews.
For information, address HarperCollins Publishers,
10 East 53rd Street, New York, NY 10022.

HarperCollins books may be purchased for educational, business,
or sales promotional use. For information, please write:
Special Markets Department, HarperCollins Publishers,
10 East 53rd Street, New York, NY 10022.

FIRST EDITION

Designed by Kate Nichols
Maps © Mr. Daniel W. Studebaker, West Milton, Ohio

Library of Congress Cataloging-in-Publication Data
Lockhart, Paul Douglas, 1963–
   The drillmaster of Valley Forge : the Baron de Steuben and the
making of the American Army / Paul Douglas Lockhart.—1st ed.
      p.   cm.
   Includes bibliographical references.
   ISBN-13: 978-0-06-145163-8 (alk. paper)
   ISBN-10: 0-06-145163-0 (alk. paper)
1. Steuben, Friedrich Wilhelm Ludolf Gerhard Augustin, Baron von,
1730–1794—Military leadership.   2. United States. Continental Army—Drill and
tactics.   3. Military art and science—United States—History—18th century.   4.
Valley Forge (Pa.)—History, Military—18th century.   5. United States—History—
Revolution, 1775–1783—Campaigns.   6. Generals—United States—Biography.   7.
United States. Continental Army—Biography.   8. Prussians—United States—Biography.   9. United States—History—Revolution, 1775–1783—Participation, Prussian.   I. Title.
E207.S8L63   2008   2008013761
973.3'341—dc22

08 09 10 11 12 OV/RRD 10 9 8 7 6 5 4 3 2 1

To my dearest Jo Anna

I miss you more than I can say

Acknowledgments

A LTHOUGH MY ACADEMIC CAREER has diverted me from my long-standing interest in military history of the American Revolution, this is a book that I have longed to write for more than two decades. I owe a great deal to my early mentors who encouraged my fascination with the period and especially my curiosity about the intersection of European and American military history: Walter R. Weitzmann, Arthur L. Johnson, and the late Jim Levitt, all of SUNY/Potsdam College; and the late Gunther E. Rothenberg, my *Doktorvater* at Purdue University, who above all else taught me the valuable lesson that American military history must be studied within a broader European context, and that knowledge of European languages is fundamentally necessary to achieve that end.

From the time I finally decided to tackle this project and over the past three years, a number of individuals helped me in all sorts of ways. Ms. Diana Kaylor, Interlibrary Loan librarian at Wright State University, has been, as always, remarkably resourceful, allowing me to get my hands on all the published works I needed for the book. Many others, including Professor Ed Melton of Wright State, and author-historians Thomas Fleming and David McCullough provided me with sage advice at various points in the writing process. Herr Henning-Hubertus von Steuben, of Natendorf, Germany, provided invaluable assistance in tracking down illustrations of his ancestor the Baron;

Mr. Daniel W. Studebaker, a good friend and talented draftsman, composed the maps on very short notice. The staff of the Chicago Historical Society, where the Anton Kalkhorst collection of Steubeniana is deposited, did their best to ensure that my stay in their library was pleasant and productive.

I owe more than I can say to my agent, Will Lippincott, for his kind and patient guidance over the past two years. Will recognized something of interest in the Baron's story, and taught me a great deal about writing outside the narrow strictures generally imposed by the academic world. Much the same can be said of my equally patient editor, Elisabeth Kallick Dyssegaard. Elisabeth's vision of the book considerably improved my writing of it. *Tak skal du ha',* Elisabeth!

I should point out, however, that any errors of fact or substance that might appear in this book are entirely my own. All translations from French or German manuscripts are mine.

My gratitude, also, to friends and family, whose enthusiasm for this project kept me going at every turn: my brother, Keith Lockhart; my parents, Newton and Marilyn Lockhart; and my brother-in-law and mother-in-law, Ralph C. Beach III and Maria Beach. My grown children, Kate, Nicholas, Paige, and Philip, all encouraged me with their expressions of interest in what I've been doing for the past three years; my youngest, Alexander, is incapable of articulating that level of interest but has kept me from sinking into despair at difficult moments, as only a baby can.

Finally, I am indebted beyond words to my wife and partner, Jo Anna Lockhart. Sadly, she passed away shortly after the completion of this book. For the past thirteen years, she has been my love, my best friend, and my muse. This book simply could not have been written without her.

Kettering, Ohio
May 2008

Contents

List of Maps and Figures

The Drillmaster of
Valley Forge

CHAPTER I

The Finest School of Warfare in the World

[1730—63]

If there is a war, I promise you, at the end of the second campaign, that your friend will either be in Hades, or at the head of a regiment.

STEUBEN TO COUNT HENKEL VON DONNERSMARK,
JUNE 4, 1754[1]

IN THE MAJESTIC but stark interior of Magdeburg's Reformed Church, one-week-old Friedrich Wilhelm Ludolf Gerhard Augustin von Steuben was christened on September 24, 1730. It was a simple ceremony—everything the Calvinists did in church was simple, stripped of pomp—but it was noteworthy for reasons other than its liturgical plainness. Two of the men surrounding the preacher at the carved stone baptismal font that stood before the nearly bare altar wore the uniform of the Royal Prussian Army—hardly unusual, since Magdeburg was a garrison town, one of the largest in this part of the kingdom of Prussia. Yet these were distinguished soldiers with considerable social ties. The baby's given name reflected the exalted station and honorable life into which he had been born. He was named after his godfathers: Ludolf von Lüderitz, royal forester in Magdeburg; Gerhard Cornelius von

Walrave, colonel of artillery, a Catholic of Dutch birth who would shortly become the highest-ranking engineer officer in the entire army; and Augustin von Steuben, the infant's paternal grandfather and patriarch of the Steuben clan, a prominent theologian.

These three men, and two noblewomen, stood close to young Friedrich's parents, who had been married only one year before, in this same church. The fourth godfather, however, was noticeable primarily by his absence. No one expected that this final sponsor would actually show up for something so mundane as a baptism. He didn't have to. Just the fact that he had agreed to list himself as a godfather, and to allow the boy to be named after him, spoke volumes about the ranking of the Steuben family.

That man was Friedrich Wilhelm I, king in Prussia, the living head of the Hohenzollern dynasty. Friedrich Wilhelm—who loved his army more than he loved his own children, more than anything other than his serious and vengeful God—would not have agreed to stand in as godfather to just *anyone*. His doing so for this baby that day showed that the Steuben family was high in his favor, that Friedrich's father was on his way up in the world, and that baby Friedrich would not have an ordinary life. Should he survive into manhood, he would grow up to be a soldier, too, and great things would be expected of him. What no one present that day could have anticipated was that Friedrich von Steuben would win his fame not on the battlefields of central Europe, but in distant America.

F RIEDRICH VON STEUBEN WAS, and is, frequently described as "German" or, more specifically, "Prussian." He was both and neither, though he rarely was so specific in identifying his homeland. Steuben proudly acknowledged his service in the Prussian army, which began early in his life, but he always referred to his origins, his family, and his pretended landownership as "European." This lack of affinity to a particular place might appear odd to modern minds, but it made perfect sense to Steuben. It reflected the political realities of eighteenth-century Germany and the peculiar circumstances of Steuben's life in Europe.

"Germany" per se did not exist before Otto von Bismarck created it with blood and iron in 1871, and in Steuben's time the word was a mere geographical expression, referring to the German-speaking lands of the old Holy Roman Empire. Before Napoléon Bonaparte forced its dissolution at bayonet point in 1806, the Empire was a strange conglomeration of some three hundred quasi-independent "territorial states." These states varied dramatically in size, power, and prestige, and were ruled by an equally wide variety of titled nobles—electors, princes, dukes, counts, margraves, landgraves, and so forth. At their head stood the emperor, an elected sovereign, and invariably a member of the ancient Habsburg dynasty. The emperor wielded little real power over the Empire's constituent members; he was more akin to the president of a contentious federation. The individual German princes retained almost total authority over their respective subjects. They maintained their own armies, levied their own taxes, enforced their own laws, and minted their own coin. The princes obeyed the emperor when doing so suited their interests. By the time young Friedrich von Steuben reached adolescence, the princes of the Empire had polarized, coalescing around two rival power centers: to the south, Catholic Austria and the emperor's court at Vienna; to the north, the upstart Protestant kingdom of Prussia.

Prussia was the great political and military success story of eighteenth-century Europe. In the previous century, as the Electorate of Brandenburg, it had been politically influential but poor and sparsely populated, cursed with some of the worst farmland in all Germany. The Thirty Years' War of 1618 to 1648 had all but destroyed the impoverished territory, as marauding armies, economic distress, and plague laid waste to entire villages. In the second half of the seventeenth century, however, clever statecraft on the part of its rulers—the Hohenzollern dynasty, the very same family that would produce the German emperor Wilhelm II, the infamous Kaiser of First World War notoriety—allowed Brandenburg not only to recover from the devastation wrought by the Thirty Years' War but even to expand its territories and build up a respectable army.

In Steuben's day, the Hohenzollern ruled over a scattered but vast collection of territories, stretching eastward from the Rhine valley to East Prussia. Now it was known as Brandenburg-Prussia, or simply "Prussia." Its rulers proudly bore the title of king, a distinction unique among all of the German princes. The second king and Steuben's god-father, Friedrich Wilhelm I (1713–40), single-handedly transformed Prussia into a major military power. Through scrimping and saving, Friedrich Wilhelm created a modern and very large army—disproportionately large, given the modest size of his subject population. Plain-living, coarse, and unimaginative, Friedrich Wilhelm shunned the refinements of fashionable French culture, but he made his beloved army the centerpiece of his regime. He attracted much international attention for his personal bodyguard, a regiment of "giant" grenadiers, each of whom exceeded six feet in height. Yet for all that, he was a peaceful ruler. His son and successor, Friedrich II—better known to posterity as "Frederick the Great"—would not show the same restraint.[2]

Prussia's was a thoroughly militarized society, in which everything was geared toward the needs of the army. It was, in Mirabeau's biting words, an army with a country and not the other way around. Nearly 80 percent of the state budget was earmarked for the use of the army, which was the fourth largest in Europe, even though the kingdom ranked tenth in territorial size and thirteenth in population. All Prussian males, without exception, were registered for conscription at birth. Still, Prussian manpower was a precious national resource, so in order to spare the economy the loss of so much valuable labor, the Prussian kings relied heavily on foreign recruits to fill out the ranks of the army. Roughly two thirds of Prussian soldiers in the eighteenth century were foreigners.[3]

It was on its officer corps that Prussia placed its heaviest demands. Officers were recruited almost exclusively from the lesser nobility, the Junker class. Military service was not required of the Junker, but it was certainly expected. For a poorer nobleman, a career as an army officer was most honorable, as the Prussian kings cultivated an intimate bond between themselves and their officers, no matter how lowly in rank. Unlike in other European armies, all commissioned officers had direct access to the king, who in turn proudly displayed his solidarity with them by wearing the same plain blue uniforms they wore. The conditions of service were not pleasant—promotion was slow and the pay inadequate, and officers faced the bleak prospect of a quick death in battle or an impoverished old age—but there was no greater honor than to be able to say that one had been even a mere lieutenant in the army of "Old Fritz," as Frederick the Great came to be known. Military service, in short, was a way of life for the Prussian nobility, and Prussian officers held greater prestige—at home and abroad—than their counterparts in the Austrian, French, Russian, or British armies.[4]

It was into this latter-day Sparta that Friedrich von Steuben was born on a Sunday evening, September 17, 1730. His lineage was distinguished but unremarkable, a typical Prussian military family of the Junker class. His grandfather, the theologian and Reformed preacher Augustin von Steuben, married Charlotte Dorothea von Effern, daughter of the Count of Effern and the Countess of Waldeck. Four of their sons pursued military careers. The youngest of these, Wilhelm August von Steuben, followed the conventional path to his Prussian officer's commission. After a brief education at the university town of Halle, sixteen-year-old Wilhelm August entered Prussian military service as an officer-cadet (*Fahnenjunker*) in a cavalry regiment in 1715. His promotion through the ranks was slow but steady, typical for a man of his class. By the time of his marriage to a woman from a prominent Junker family, Maria Justina Dorothea von Jagow, in 1729, he had been promoted to lieutenant of engineers. Wilhelm August and Maria had been stationed at the bustling garrison town of Magdeburg only very briefly when their firstborn, Friedrich, came into the world.[5]

Much about Friedrich von Steuben's youth is shrouded in mystery. He would write and say very little about his childhood, which was unstable and possibly unpleasant. One aspect of his origins, however, is very clear, though historians have needlessly made it a point of controversy: his social status. Friedrich von Steuben was nobly born.

In eighteenth-century Europe, "noble" was hardly synonymous with "wealthy." The Prussian Junker, who dominated the officer corps, were little better off than peasants. Nobility derived from bloodline, not from ownership of vast landed estates.[6]

The controversy over Steuben's claim to noble status centers on his theologian grandfather, Augustin von Steuben. Until very recently, German historians believed that Augustin was the grandson of a humble miller named "Steube"; in order to seek preferment, Augustin falsely claimed descent from a defunct branch of the noble lineage, "von Steuben." Research in Steuben genealogy, however, has uncovered a great deal of evidence indicating that Augustin was indeed nobly born. Moreover, as a favorite preacher of the king of Prussia, he was much too visible to have effected such a blatant deception. His marriage to a woman of unimpeachable aristocratic credentials could not have taken place if Augustin had not been noble. Four of Augustin's eight children got married, each into prominent Junker families; all eight of those children were sponsored at baptism by high-ranking German nobles.[7]

Young Friedrich's mother and both of his maternal grandparents came from established Junker families; his paternal grandmother stemmed from an even more refined aristocratic line; the details of his paternal grandfather's lineage may be unclear, but they were *definitely* noble. Measured by any yardstick, Friedrich von Steuben was indeed a nobleman.*

Yet Friedrich was no ordinary Junker. His baptismal tie to the king signalled that.

That bond with the king was a great boon to Friedrich's father, allowing him to rise to a captaincy at a relatively young age. But that

---

*Some writers have asserted that Steuben claimed status as "German aristocrat"—namely, a member of the higher levels of the noble estate. Steuben never said such a thing. When writing about his social origins, he never claimed to be anything other than a "poor Junker" or a "Baron" (see chapter 2), both of which were indeed correct.

did not mean his life would be any easier. Quite the contrary: since Wilhelm August had talent, his services were very much in demand, but the minuscule size of the Prussian engineering arm meant that there were few opportunities for advancement beyond the rank of captain. He would be denied even the simple pleasure of raising his family in Magdeburg. In 1731, before Friedrich had celebrated his first birthday, the king sent Wilhelm August to Russia with a small group of handpicked officers to help the tsarina Anna rebuild her army. It was a great personal honor for Captain Steuben, who accompanied the Russian army on campaign against the Turks and earned a citation for bravery in the War of the Polish Succession (1733–38).

Life for line officers in the Prussian army was hard work, dull and unprofitable. It was doubly so for their families, and the Steuben family had it harder than most. They were not entirely isolated, for there were plenty of Germans near them—German-born officers made up a large proportion of Tsarina Anna's officer corps, and in fact German was the common language of command in the Russian army. But the Steubens were far, far away from their relations, some of whom they would never see again: both of Wilhelm August's parents would pass away while their son served in Russia. Nor did the Steubens have the luxury of settling down in one place for very long. Wilhelm August's duties took him from Cronstadt, to St. Petersburg, to the Livonian port of Riga. The family grew during these years, but the harsh climate claimed the lives of most of the new additions. Altogether, the Steubens buried five of their children in Russian soil.[8]

The king recalled Wilhelm August to Prussia in 1739. It was a welcome change for the homesick officer and his dependents. It did not mean, however, that they could get back to the relative comfort of peacetime garrison life. In 1740, Friedrich Wilhelm I died, to be succeeded by his very different son, Friedrich II. Frederick the Great was refined and erudite, as cultured as his father was boorish, but he inherited his father's love for the military life. And he had an edge that his father lacked. The new king was eager to test the mettle of the army that his father had nurtured. Only six months after ascending to the throne, Frederick launched his kingdom into the first of several acts of outright aggression that would earn him undying fame on the battle-field. In December 1740, his army invaded the Austrian province of Silesia, hoping to wrest the territory from the grip of the young and untried new Habsburg empress Maria Theresa.

The First Silesian War (1740–42), the opening salvo of the conti-nent-wide War of the Austrian Succession (1740–48), first demon-strated to the world the power of Prussia's army, and made King Frederick's name a household word throughout Europe. It was also a momentous event for the Steuben family. Wilhelm August was awarded the coveted order *Pour le mérite*—the "Blue Max"—for his role in the siege of Neisse in 1741, and immediately after the conclu-sion of peace in 1742, he was promoted to the rank of major. In an army in which fifty-year-old lieutenants were commonplace, such a promotion at age forty-three was a rare honor. And since the Prussian engineer corps was so small, this rank placed Wilhelm August near the very top of the chain of command. The elder Steuben had paid his dues and been suitably rewarded. Decent income was the most obvious perquisite, but there were others. The Steuben family could count on a moderately sedentary lifestyle, and if any of their sons chose to follow in his father's footsteps, the path to high rank would be all the easier.[9]

THE END OF THE FIRST SILESIAN WAR marks the point at which Friedrich von Steuben emerges as an individual, no longer a face-less component of the family. His father was stationed in newly con-quered Silesia, first in Neisse and then in the fortress town of Breslau (Wroclaw in present-day Poland). In these two towns, Breslau espe-cially, Friedrich would receive all of his admittedly minimal education.

Breslau was a pleasant town, provincial and comfortable. It was thoroughly Catholic, though that did not constrain the locals from fraternizing with their new, nominally Protestant Prussian overlords. "Our Silesian women," one Breslauer wryly remarked, "were excited with such passion [for the Prussian soldiers] that many of them must have been left with a little Brandenburger." Breslau was also home to a fine university, and here Friedrich von Steuben—just entering his teens—had the chance to study with Jesuit priests, renowned throughout Europe as the best educators on the Continent. Time and circumstance, however, precluded even a thorough grounding in the basics, and kept his parents from giving young Steuben "any better education than that which a poor young nobleman in Prussia always receives."[10]

Friedrich was nearing the age at which he would begin his military education, and as the eldest son of a military family, he did not have many options. His first taste of military life came in August 1744, when Frederick the Great decided to renew his struggle with Maria Theresa. Prussian troops battered their way through Saxony and into Habsburg Bohemia, precipitating the Second Silesian War. Wilhelm August von Steuben was once again called to the field of battle.

The elder Steuben's exalted rank entitled him to bring family members along on campaign. He took Friedrich with him. The boy was just about at the right age to begin a military apprenticeship: he celebrated his fourteenth birthday while observing his father at work directing the Prussian engineers as they laid siege to the ancient Bohemian capital at Prague.

According to Major von Steuben's directions, blue-clad engineer troops carved carefully mapped parallel trenches with pick and spade, zigzagging rough concentric circles around the Austrian outerworks; artillery commanders sited their mortars and heavy siege cannon. Young Friedrich was hooked—by the smoke and the noise and the excitement, by the respect that his father's office carried, and by the great responsibility that his father bore for the king. There was no doubt that he wanted all this for himself, but the engineering service was not enough to satisfy his already considerable ambition. One could rise only so far in the so-called "technical" branches, the engineers and the artillery. The real glory, and the real chance for advancement, lay instead in the infantry.

So that was the path he chose. Friedrich von Steuben's military career began almost as soon as the war was over. In the autumn of

1746, right around the time of his sixteenth birthday, he donned the blue coat with rose-colored cuffs, white waistcoat, and skimpily cut white breeches of the Infantry Regiment von Lestwitz (Regiment Nr. 31), one of the units that made up the Breslau garrison. Like all aspiring officers in the Prussian army, Friedrich had to serve time in the ranks before he could qualify for his commission. He started out as an officer cadet (called *Gefreiten-korporal* or *Freikorporal* in the infantry). Officer cadets were in an uncomfortable position. They were considered NCOs while on duty, carried the company colors when on maneuvers, and had to demonstrate thorough familiarity with drill and military routine. Though not yet officers, they were nonetheless discouraged from fraternizing with other enlisted men. After two and a half years as an officer cadet, Steuben was promoted to ensign (*Fähnrich*), "a strange intermediate rank which offered many of the burdens but few of the privileges of a full officer." Not until he was twenty-two did Steuben rise to the lowest fully commissioned rank, that of lieutenant.[11]

The Prussian system of promotion and training was doubtless one of the more intimidating conditions of service for young officers. Yet it had its advantages, chief among them that it helped to cultivate the mixture of reserve and care with which Prussian officers were expected to treat the rank and file entrusted to them. Several years spent in the nebulous space between officers and enlisted men taught the officer cadets and the ensigns to appreciate the burdens of a private soldier's life. An officer was responsible for the physical welfare of each of the men under his command, and could not shirk his duty of training them. High-ranking officers would conduct daily drills themselves, even at the battalion level, a feature of the Prussian army that foreign observers found both strange and admirable. Even King Frederick did not consider himself above this duty. He frequently led troops in drill, without any pomp, wearing his plain black hat and unadorned regimental coat, cuffs encrusted with the snuff he perpetually indulged in. Leadership, perhaps, cannot be taught, but the Prussian system came closer to doing just that than any other method of officer training used in a European army during that period.[12]

For the ten years that followed his enlistment in 1746, Friedrich von Steuben remained stuck in the garrison at Breslau. As an infantry lieutenant, he was kept perpetually busy. A captain commanded each infantry company, but the lieutenants were the real workhorses. Steuben's daily activities included leading his company in hours of drill, keeping a watchful eye on the discipline and cleanliness of his men, maintaining the company's accounts and other paperwork, supervising the distribution and cooking of rations, and all of the other elements of the stultifying but necessary routine that made up life in the peacetime army.

Steuben's life in the army was not all work. He loved the theater, and attended plays when time and budget permitted, but mainly he devoted his off-duty hours to study. While most of his comrades whiled away their little free time in gambling, drinking, and frequenting brothels, he taught himself basic arithmetic and mastered French. The latter was a vital discipline for an ambitious man in his line of work. A man—or woman—in mid-eighteenth-century Europe could not claim to be truly cultured unless he or she read, wrote, and spoke French, for that was the language of learned Europeans and of those muckraking, troublemaking social critics of the Enlightenment, the philosophes. It was also, curiously, the language of the Prussian king and his court. Any officer who aspired to great things in the Prussian army would have to be fluent in French. Steuben felt perfectly at home with the language, though his own French prose would always be inelegant and workmanlike.

Lieutenant von Steuben was popular with his fellow officers and loved hearing of their comical misadventures with prostitutes and tavernkeepers, but he rarely partook of the same. Next to his soldierly duties, reading was his chief joy, and his tastes in literature were quite broad. Although raised a Calvinist, he spent little or no time with the Bible or devotional works, and he was sufficiently open-minded to admit that he found Catholicism more sophisticated and intellectually engaging than his own creed. He read widely in military science, but he enjoyed philosophical works and fiction equally. He acquired a vast and detailed knowledge of ancient Greek and Roman history, and he steeped himself in the latest writings of the French philosophes, especially Montesquieu. His favorite author was Cervantes, *Don Quixote* his favorite book.[13]

If young Steuben had a significant flaw, it was carelessness in financial matters, which could be a serious problem for a poorly paid officer. His regimental commander noted that while he was "clever," he was "not capable as a manager"—a verdict that would be equally applicable to him in his later years. But this did not compromise his performance as a leader of men. Evident early on was the tender concern with which he treated the soldiers under his command and his conviction that a good officer should share the hardships and perils the enlisted men had to suffer. In the summer of 1754, his company was detailed to dig trenches through an actively used cemetery outside the city walls of Breslau. As his men toiled in the oppressive heat, choked by the noisome stench of recently disinterred bodies, Steuben fretted over their health. "I fear for my poor soldiers," he confided to a friend. "As yet I have no sick [men], but I fear the month of July. In order not to alarm them, I am continually at work, notwithstanding my disgust for this abominable occupation."[14]

He was also ambitious, and he ached for action. He would not have to wait long, for in the south, war was brewing. Empress Maria Theresa had been biding her time, waiting for the chance to avenge herself on Prussia and reconquer the lost province of Silesia. After Austria concluded a defensive pact with Prussia's former ally France, in May 1756, King Frederick decided that the time had come to take preemptive action before his enemies could mobilize. That August, he sent sixty-three thousand troops crashing across Prussia's southern frontier and into neutral Saxony. The strike eliminated a potential threat, but inevitably sparked war with Austria. Prussia's act of overt aggression also alienated nearly all of Europe except Britain. By the spring of

1757, Russia, France, Sweden, and many of the German states had rallied to Austria's side.

The ensuing conflict, the Seven Years' War (1756–63), was no mere dynastic squabble over titles and scraps of land. Maria Theresa and her allies, fearful that Frederick the Great had become a loose cannon whose continued existence threatened the delicate balance of power in Europe, aimed at nothing less than the defeat, humiliation, and dismemberment of Prussia. For Prussia, the war was a struggle for the very survival of the kingdom; for the army of Old Fritz, it would be the ultimate test of its abilities.[15]

As an officer in the Lestwitz Regiment, stationed close to the theater of war, Friedrich von Steuben would soon be part of that life-and-death struggle. Hoping to knock Austria out of the war with a single crushing blow before France and Russia could come to its aid, King Frederick pushed more than one hundred thousand troops from Saxony into Austrian-held Bohemia. Stunned, Austrian forces fell back to the heavily fortified city of Prague, where Frederick and most of his army struck them on the morning of May 6, 1757.

The Lestwitz Regiment, including twenty-six-year-old Lieutenant von Steuben, was part of the initial Prussian assault on the thickly defended Austrian center. The attack, launched across a treacherous and boggy no-man's-land, was bloody and fruitless, but the superior generalship of King Frederick and his lieutenants allowed the Prussians to exploit a widening gap on the Austrian left. As the Austrian army reeled from the swiftly delivered and unexpected blow, the solid remainder of Frederick's crack infantry battalions rolled up the Austrian right flank and pushed the enemy back in disarray to shelter behind the city walls of Prague.

Steuben had seen his first real action—coincidentally, on the very same fields where he had so intently watched his father at work nearly thirteen years before—and his baptism by fire could not have been more terrifying. Overall the Prussians lost more than 20 percent of their strength on the sodden ground at Prague that May morning. Steuben's regiment suffered more than most. As the young lieutenant strode, sword in hand, before the neatly dressed ranks of his company, urging them forward during the first assault, his regiment practically melted into the ground behind him. Austrian musketry claimed 50 percent of Lestwitz's men in the attack. Among them, seriously wounded but still alive, was Friedrich von Steuben.

***

Historians of the American Revolution frequently assert that Washington and his Continentals faced, in the British army, the greatest army in the world. It has become part of the mythos of the Revolution, for it underscores the unlikelihood of American victory: that citizen-soldiers ultimately defeated not just a large and powerful foe, but *the* largest and most powerful foe. To contemporary observers, however, there could be no doubt: the single greatest fighting force in Europe was the Prussian army under Frederick the Great. Its brilliant victories in the War of the Austrian Succession and the Seven Years' War, often against incredible odds, inspired admiration from friend and foe alike, and military thinkers all over Europe sought desperately to unlock the secrets to Frederick's success. The British, like the French, the Austrians, and the Russians, had fallen under the spell of the warrior-king of Potsdam.

The Prussian army was not without its shortcomings. It was not the largest army in Europe; its weaponry was not the most technologically advanced; and the kingdom provided for its soldiers in a most ungenerous fashion. King Frederick's miserliness was legendary: Prussian uniforms were skimpy and poorly made; rations, even in peacetime, were barely adequate. Few if any armies paid their soldiers more poorly than did Prussia's. Only in corporal punishment, administered in liberal doses to disobedient soldiers, could the Prussian army be described as generous. Mostly because of its size, the army counted nearly as many major defeats as it did victories, and in the end, Prussia survived the Seven Years' War mostly because its most dangerous enemy, Russia, defected in 1762.

Yet the Prussian army was great in spite of all these failings. Its greatness came from its professionalism, its hardiness, and the machine-like precision with which it could maneuver on the battlefield. It wasn't that there was anything remarkable about the raw material from which the army was fashioned. Taken individually, Prussian soldiers were no better or worse than their peers in other armies. It was the quality of leadership that mattered, and Prussian officers were, on the whole, dedicated professionals devoted to their craft and to their arbitrary, often misanthropic, king. Ultimately, credit for the success of the Prussian army must be given to Old Fritz. The king took a keen interest in the most minute details of tactics and maneuvers, and in the education of his officer corps. He insisted upon constant drill and exercise for all branches of the service. The cavalry arm improved immeasurably under his tutelage, as did the artillery—undoubtedly the best in Europe at the time. The infantry, however, was the heart and soul of the army, and it was upon his foot soldiers that Frederick lavished his greatest attentions.

In the "linear tactics" employed by eighteenth-century armies, success depended on two qualities in the infantry: first, the ability of individual soldiers to load and fire their muskets quickly and efficiently, combined with the restraint to withhold their fire until commanded to unleash it by their officers (a concept known as "fire discipline"); second, the ability of the infantry battalions to change formations precisely and without losing cohesion, even in the heat and fury of battle. The latter quality was necessary for an army to change from column of march to line of battle, even in the face of the enemy. Speed of fire allowed the Prussian infantry to maintain something resembling a continuous rolling thunder of musketry. Prussian infantrymen were trained to load and fire not only in stationary lines, three ranks deep, but also while marching rapidly forward or in retreat—no small feat, given the limitations of the flintlock musket. A musketeer in the Prussian army was expected to be able to load his weapon in the space of eleven seconds, enabling him to keep up a rate of fire (counting the time it took to aim the musket and pull the trigger) of at least four rounds per minute.

Things rarely went as smoothly on the battlefield as they did on the parade grounds of Potsdam, but still the Prussian infantry excelled both at speed of fire and at skill in maneuvering. No European army could approach the precision with which Frederick's infantry moved on the battlefield. One British observer noted, with gape-mouthed admiration, that while Prussian troops appeared slow and methodical to the untrained eye, "yet they are so accurate that no time being lost in dressing or correcting distances, they arrive sooner at their object than any others, and at the instant of forming they are in perfect order to make the attack." The remarkable discipline of his infantry made it possible for Frederick to pull off amazing tactical feats. At the battle of Leuthen (December 5, 1757), the king's army of thirty-five thousand men managed to outmaneuver, outflank, and ultimately crush a well-fortified Austrian army three times its size.[16]

FRIEDRICH VON STEUBEN'S CAREER PATH after Prague was anything but conventional. After his convalescence, he volunteered for a post as a staff officer in one of the king's new light infantry units, the so-called "Free Battalions" (*Freibataillone*). The Free Battalions were not used as line infantry, but rather for scouting, reconnaissance, and raiding. Ill-disciplined and prone to riotous behavior, they were notoriously difficult to command; the men of one of the Free Battalions murdered their commanding officer in 1761 and then the battalion defected en masse to the enemy. By serving as adjutant of Free Battalion No. 2 (under General Johann von Mayr), Steuben risked both his reputation and his life. But he did well. A fellow officer in the unit later saluted him as "an able and pleasant officer."[17]

It was in the Free Battalion that Steuben experienced his second major battle. While holding off the Austrian and Russian armies to the east with a small screening force, Frederick's main army—only around twenty-two thousand strong—lunged west, making a forced march of almost two hundred miles in less than two weeks, to confront an allied force of French troops and Imperial levies (the *Reichs-*

armee). The French had a numerical advantage of almost two to one, but Frederick's generalship made up the difference. At the village of Rossbach, on November 5, 1757, Frederick's cavalry hit the French cavalry hard, driving them from the field, while the Prussian infantry deployed quickly into line of battle and hurled themselves at the Franco-Imperial infantry while the latter were still in marching columns. The French and Imperial troops, caught in a vicious crossfire, panicked and fled in confusion, while Frederick's rear guard— including the Mayr Free Battalion—mopped up the shattered survivors. It was one of Frederick's tactical masterpieces, and the casualties told the story: the Prussians suffered fewer than five hundred casualties altogether, while the Franco-Imperial army lost five thousand killed or wounded and nearly as many taken prisoner.

Steuben remained with Mayr's Free Battalion until sometime in 1759, and from there his star rose rapidly. General J. D. von Hülsen, commanding a brigade in the army of Frederick's brother, Prince Henry, selected the now-veteran lieutenant to serve on his staff as a *Brigade-Offizier*, a sure sign that Steuben had by now attracted the attention of senior commanders. The staff appointment was a flattering mark of recognition, but it did not remove him from danger. Far from it. Two more battles faced him—in fact, two of the worst bloodbaths in the glorious history of the Prussian army: Kay, on July 23, 1759, and Kunersdorf, on August 12, 1759. In both cases, the Prussians, severely weakened by heavy losses from fighting three major armies simultaneously during three years of constant campaigning, were mauled by combined Austro-Russian armies. The action at Kunersdorf very nearly resulted in the complete destruction of the main Prussian army, the capture of King Frederick, and the loss of Berlin. Here Steuben received yet another wound, as did both his king and his general, Hülsen. At least he was rewarded for his pains with a promotion to the rank of first lieutenant in November 1759.

At Hülsen's side, Lieutenant von Steuben fought in at least two more desperate battles against the Austrians (Liegnitz, on August 15, 1760, and Torgau, November 3, 1760), but by then his administrative abilities, physical courage, and good nature had brought him to the attention of Prince Henry, who was always on the lookout for new talent—especially, it was rumored, if that talent came in the form of a handsome young officer. Whatever the nature of their relationship, it paid immediate dividends for Steuben. In May 1761, the lieutenant was officially transferred from the muster rolls of the Lestwitz Regiment to what was called the "Royal Suite," the king's personal headquarters, and given temporary duty as a *Quartiermeister-Lieutenant*. In this capacity, he would assist King Frederick and his staff with intelligence and strategic planning. It was a dream job for a thirty-year-old company officer.

But the army was suffering from an acute dearth of experienced officers. The campaigns of 1757–60 had claimed an unspeakable toll in officers and men. While losses in the rank and file could be made good from more intensive recruiting within Prussia, officers were much harder to replace. Regardless of his personal preferences, Steuben would have to go where he was needed, and so his tenure in the Royal Suite was soon over. Later, in the summer of 1761, the king assigned him to the staff of General J. von Platen, commanding the ill-fated Prussian forces fighting against the Russians in the northeastern theater of operations. That didn't last long, either. When Platen's army, outmanned and in sorry shape, surrendered to superior Russian forces at Treptow in October 1761, Steuben marched with his fellow officers into captivity at St. Petersburg.

Even as a prisoner of war, however, Steuben found that his luck had not run out. As an officer with high-ranking connections, he was entitled to comfortable accommodation and a great deal of freedom while in Russia. He turned this to his advantage, and aided by the speaking knowledge of Russian he had acquired during his childhood in the realm of the tsars, he made powerful friends—not the least of whom was Karl Peter Ulrich, Duke of Holstein-Gottorp and heir to the throne of Russia. The duke was not a likeable man, his personality being as unattractive as his smallpox-scarred face, but he had an affinity for all things Prussian. Steuben thought it a friendship worth cultivating, and his instincts proved correct. When the duke's aunt, Tsarina Elisabeth, died in January 1762, Steuben wasted no time. He wrote in haste to King Frederick's foreign minister with news that was almost too good to be true: Karl Peter Ulrich, now Tsar Peter III, was eager to discuss peace terms with his personal idol the Prussian king. Old Fritz was delighted with this unexpected development, for Russian troops occupied a large chunk of Prussian territory and held the capital at Berlin. A lenient peace settlement with the new tsar could well prove to be the difference between life and death for Prussia.

Steuben found that it was not a bad thing to be the bearer of good tidings. Frederick wrote to him personally to thank him for his unofficial diplomatic efforts. When Frederick's emissary to Tsar Peter arrived in St. Petersburg, Steuben stayed on as his assistant. The mission was an unqualified success. Tsar Peter made peace with Frederick, pulled his troops out of Prussia, and Frederick's most dangerous enemy was out of the war for good. With Russia gone, Austria and France could not keep up their war against Prussia for very long. The peace was a godsend for Prussia. And it worked out well for Steuben, too. He had exchanged several letters with the king himself and had played a personal role in saving Prussia from what seemed at the time to be certain destruction. When he returned to Prussia in May 1762, the king received him in person. It is hard to imagine a more fortuitous turn of events for an ambitious junior officer. The Fates would surely favor him now.[18]

And they did . . . for a while. The war with Russia was over; the wars with Austria and France, drawing to a close. King Frederick had some much-needed breathing space, and to make up for the wartime loss of so many talented generals, he decided to devote some of his time to the making of new ones. He did this through the creation of a rudimentary staff school—the "Special Class on the Art of War" (*Spezialklasse der Kriegskunst*)—an intensive course in generalship that he himself would teach. Thirteen students were carefully selected from the up-and-coming leaders of the army, to be schooled in the higher levels of strategic planning and army leadership. And Steuben, just recently promoted to captain, was one of them. At thirty-one, he was being groomed for a general's rank, with the greatest soldier of the age as his personal tutor.

But something went horribly wrong. Steuben ran afoul of a classmate: as he himself put it, he had earned the "rancor" of an "implacable enemy." Most likely Captain von Steuben was referring to General Wilhelmi von Anhalt, a jealous, vindictive, and brutal misanthrope, who for some perverse reason stood high in the king's favor. Anhalt had gained a justly deserved reputation for wrecking the careers of officers for whom he had taken a dislike—and there were many of them. Whatever or whoever authored Steuben's fall from grace, it happened in the blink of an eye. Steuben finished the staff school around the time the war with Austria ended, in February 1763, and found himself almost immediately demoted. He was assigned to a company command in the Infantry Regiment von Salmuth (No. 48), stationed at Wesel, on the far western edge of the kingdom, a humble post in a mediocre regiment, and at a remote location. It was clearly *not* a mark of royal favor. Only a couple of months later, he was dismissed from the service entirely. After residing for a while in Berlin, he left Prussia sometime before the end of 1763.

It is still impossible to determine exactly what happened to the promising career of Captain von Steuben. He did not blame his misfortune on the king, whom he still mentioned years later with the purest reverence. It is true that the king radically pared back the size of the army upon the conclusion of peace in 1763, as a matter of economy, and so it is possible that Steuben was the victim of nothing more insidious than "downsizing." Yet that does not seem to be a logical explanation. Even as he mused over his life during his twilight years, Steuben found the events of 1763 almost too painful to contemplate, much less to discuss in writing.

"Of my service in the Seven Years' War, I have no reason to be ashamed," Steuben proclaimed many years later. Indeed, he could be—and was—quite proud of it. After his arrival in America more than fourteen years later, he would frequently tell his new acquaintances that he had studied war in the finest school in the world. He didn't just mean the king's *Spezialklasse*, but the entire range of experiences that the Prussian army had bequeathed to him. He had been an NCO, a company commander, an adjutant, a general in training, and a junior diplomat. He had trained raw recruits, led an infantry company into battle, and served on staffs at the battalion, regimental, brigade, and army levels. He had watched his men die, and in turn he had been wounded in battle twice, so he knew what it was like to fall in combat.

But what set Steuben apart from his contemporaries was his schooling under Frederick the Great, Prince Henry, and a dozen other general officers. He had learned from the best soldiers in the world how to gather and assess intelligence, how to read and exploit terrain, how to plan marches, camps, battles, and entire campaigns. He gleaned more from his seventeen years in the Prussian military than most professional soldiers would in a lifetime. In the Seven Years' War alone, he built up a record of professional education that none of his future comrades in the Continental Army—Horatio Gates, Charles Lee, the Baron Johann de Kalb, and Lafayette included—could match.

But in the summer of 1763, Captain von Steuben, of course, was unaware of any future use to which his extensive education and considerable talents might be put. All he knew then was that he had given his all to the army. He had known no other world. Perhaps it would have been more merciful if he had remained a company commander all his life. Instead, he had been given a taste, just a taste, of a glorious future in the service of his king, only to have it taken away from him just at the moment when that future looked most promising. Since his paper credentials did not match his actual experience, he was just another mediocrity, just another minor officer who had been cast aside by the fortunes of war. At age thirty-three, Steuben's life appeared to be over.

CHAPTER 2

Courtier and Supplicant

[1763—1777]

> I am a good soldier, a poor courtier and
> a miserable lawyer.
>
> STEUBEN, JUNE 16, 1764[1]

WITHOUT THE ARMY, Friedrich von Steuben was lost.

The Prussian army had practically owned him from birth. It had consumed his childhood and his adolescence. As soon as he was physically able, he had joined it, for he knew no other life, and because that's what young Prussian noblemen did. And when the army had finished with him, it spat him out ungratefully.

When, in his declining years, Steuben recounted, for posterity and Congress, the events of his life in Europe, he downplayed his desperate condition in 1763. He had all sorts of options, he said: he could have retired to a life of ease on his estates in southwestern Germany; he could have accepted a commission in the army of Piedmont-Sardinia. He settled, instead, for the cushy life of a courtier.

In reality, Steuben's life followed a much different course. The truth was that he had no estates, in southwestern Germany or elsewhere; he owned nothing and had no prospects.

"My adverse fate," he once admitted in a rare unguarded moment, "forced me to leave my fatherland, my friends, and my support, and perhaps renounce them for life."[2] He was adrift in a Europe at peace, where his calling counted for little, and he was willing to pounce on any job that his honor would permit him to take. After wandering aimlessly for the better part of a year—just how he got by is anyone's guess—he finally found such a job: in the autumn of 1764, he took the post of court chamberlain (*Hofmarschall*) to the sovereign prince of Hohenzollern-Hechingen.

That summer, his travels took him to Wildbad, a picturesque little town nestled in the northern portion of the Black Forest, remote but highly popular with the powerful and well-to-do in southwestern Germany, who were drawn to the healing properties of its springs. Most likely, that was what drew Steuben there—not the spa itself, but its fashionable clientèle, who that fall included an old friend from the Prussian army, Prince Friedrich Eugen of Württemberg, one of Frederick's generals. Accompanying the duke was his consort, Margravine Friederike Dorothea, twenty-seven-year-old niece of the Prussian king. A beautiful, vivacious, and learned woman, she was also quite lonely, so the presence of the courtly Steuben provided her with a pleasant diversion. The two hit it off immediately. Soon she introduced him to another guest at Wildbad: Josef Friedrich Wilhelm, the Catholic prince of a tiny German territory called Hohenzollern-Hechingen, a small portion of the original ancestral lands of Prussia's ruling dynasty. With Friederike's help, and bearing a testimonial from Prince Henry of Prussia, Steuben persuaded Prince Josef to hire him as chamberlain for his modest residence at the town of Hechingen.[3]

The post came as a great relief to Steuben. It wasn't much, but it was infinitely better than nothing at all. Hohenzollern-Hechingen was a genuinely minuscule German state. Its capital, the town of Hechingen, was small, slow-paced, and pretty; the prince's palace, the Altes Schloss, was a modest whitewashed structure that might have been mistaken for a city hall in a larger German town. Steuben's position there was not a demanding one. A *Hofmarschall* was not a political figure but rather a member of the prince's personal staff, a sort of social secretary and manager of the princely household. He supervised the daily administration of the court and its personnel, advising his master on matters of economy and personal finance, and was responsible for the education and rearing of the prince's children. For Steuben, who loved parties, being at the center of the social scene at court was no small attraction.

He fit in well, fast becoming a trusted member of the prince's family. And he made friends, many friends, foremost among them the prince's ranking minister, Chancellor Daniel Marianus Frank. Because of his central position in the household, Steuben soon came to know influential men from neighboring courts as well. Yet he was never quite comfortable there. The duties bored him, and being fully aware of his ineptitude in handling his own money, he was reluctant to watch over the prince's finances. After Chancellor Frank asked him repeatedly to take over the management of the court accounts, Steuben stubbornly refused. "You know full well, my dearest friend," he wrote Frank, "and I do not conceal it from anybody, that in the management of my own affairs I have always been . . . careless. . . . It would be ridiculous to load upon my shoulders the management of another, and by far more considerable, household."[4]

Not that there was much for him to manage. The prince was so heavily saddled with debt that in late 1771, he decided to dissolve his household temporarily. Chancellor Frank would watch over affairs in Hechingen, while the prince, his family, and his chamberlain would take a brief sojourn in southern France. There they would live, incognito, as private citizens, unencumbered by the burden of hospitality.

For the next three and a half years, Steuben and the princely family would live in self-imposed fiscal exile, first at Strasbourg and then at Montpellier. It was a disaster, at least from a financial standpoint. The prince was unable to hide his identity for long, and therefore was still compelled to entertain innumerable dinner guests with all due ceremony and munificence. "Our incognito," Steuben reported to Chancellor Frank in dismay, "is a laughable masquerade."[5] The chamberlain didn't mind Strasbourg all that much, for it was both a university town and a fortress with a large garrison. In between chaperoning the young princess and shopping, he found the time to strike up friendships with prominent French officers in the Strasbourg garrison.

Montpellier should have been equally alluring. Nestled between the Alps, the Pyrénées, and the Mediterranean, it was a popular resort for the Parisian elite seeking to escape the grayness of the Île-de-France in wintertime. But Steuben did not enjoy it—though not for lack of trying. He attended the Comedy almost nightly, or as often as his money and his duties would allow. Yet the city, by his estimation, was overcrowded and dirty. Good seafood was plentiful and cheap, but he craved "good beef and sauerkraut," which, like most essentials, were either unavailable or too expensive. "I cannot understand," he wrote, "how this place has acquired such great renown in half of Europe."[6]

Though he loved his surrogate princely family, Steuben soon wearied of the effort required to keep the household together and within budget. Chaperoning the young princess and trying to make sure she had an adequate education, looking for affordable housing, purchasing daily necessaries for the household—these were challenging chores when in Hechingen, but logistically much more difficult when away from home. "The happiest hour of my life," Steuben intimated to Chancellor Frank, "will be when . . . I shall be able to embrace you, my dearest friend. After that I shall be ready to die at Hechingen."[7]

His employers agreed. What little money they had ran out, and the prince grew increasingly despondent. In the summer of 1775—just as, far away across the Atlantic, George Washington was engaged in a struggle of his own, trying to cobble together an army to fight the British—the exiles returned to Hechingen dejected and chastened.

AT HECHINGEN, we first get a glimpse of Steuben's personal appearance. Sometime around 1769, he had his portrait painted. Since he was not a wealthy man, that in itself was a sign of high social standing, for Prince Josef undoubtedly commissioned the portrait.

The Freiherr von Steuben. The only known portrait of Steuben in civilian clothes, probably painted between 1769 and 1772. The insignia of the Order of Fidelity, bestowed upon him along with the title *Freiherr* (Baron), is visible on the left breast of his coat. Despite the claims of later historians, Steuben was both a nobleman and a genuine baron. *(Private Collection)*

The insignia of the Order of Fidelity (*Hausorden der Treue*). The honor was bestowed upon Steuben by the margrave of Baden-Durlach, a German prince of middling significance, in 1769. He never claimed it was a gift from Frederick the Great, although some scholars mistakenly believe that he did. *(Private Collection)*

Roughly age thirty-nine at the time, courtier Steuben only vaguely resembles the distinguished baron who has come down to us from the more familiar portraits painted by the American artists Ralph Earl and Charles Willson Peale. With a long nose on a longer face and closely set eyes looking impossibly large beneath dark eyebrows, he stares back at the viewer in a half-serious, almost playful way, with his small mouth upturned in a partial smile. He hardly looks as if he could have been a soldier: his light brown hair is neither powdered nor queued, but hangs in long, soft curls about his ears and neck. There is, however, a hint of the lush about him, not only in the expression on his face but also in the informal posture, and the weight that was already beginning to show beneath his prominent chin. His fondness for fine clothing is obvious, too. He wears an elegantly ruffled shirt with a lace collar, surmounted by a waistcoat and a collarless frock coat of figured green silk, garments that should have been beyond his modest means. And on the frock coat, peeking out from under his left arm, almost as if he were indifferent to its presence, is an eight-pointed star.

That star was his pride, the emblem of the elevated social status he had achieved at Hechingen. He owed it to his patroness and protector, Princess Friederike. She had not forgotten him. More than four years after their meeting at Wildbad in 1764, the princess nominated him for a knighthood—not in her own land of Württemberg, nor in Hechingen, but in nearby Baden-Durlach, where Steuben was also well known and well liked. At Friederike's request, the ruling margrave of Baden-Durlach elevated Steuben into the Order of Fidelity (*Hausorden der Treue*), a chivalric order founded more than five decades before. In a ceremony held at Wildbad in June 1769, the princess herself pinned upon Steuben's chest the distinctive insignia of the order, a Maltese cross mounted on an eight-pointed silver star emblazoned with the motto *Fidelitas*.

Chivalric orders were a prominent feature of noble life in eighteenth-century Europe. They had changed a great deal from their inception at the time of the Crusades. Then, they had served to sanctify and mobilize those who went to the Holy Land to fight against the infidel in the name of Christ. By Steuben's day, however, such orders were almost purely honorific, a means by which European monarchs could reward their subjects for faithful service, outstanding achievements, or high moral character. In this regard, they did not differ much from British knighthoods today. Yet the orders served other important purposes. Rulers could use knighthoods to show their solidarity with their nobles. Though membership in some orders could translate into preferential treatment—such as the Prussian *Pour le Mérite*, which Steuben's father had received—in general it did not entail material reward. Nobles still coveted such distinctions regardless. In a society in which social rank was more important than wealth, and honor more important than life, elevation into a chivalric order was a badge of prestige.

Another, more enduring, honor, came to Steuben with his induction into the order: the title of *Freiherr*. Like the medal of fidelity, this title would become part of his permanent identity. When life took him away from Germany, first to France, then to the United States, he rendered the title into its nearest French-language equivalent, a version that would be instantly recognizable to French and American audiences alike. The rough translation of *Freiherr*—literally, "free lord"—was "baron" and hence the name by which he would become known, the name he would use himself, while in America: not the Germanic "Freiherr von Steuben," but the Gallic "Baron de Steuben."*

Steuben's use of the title "baron," like his claim to noble status, would later become a matter of some controversy, just one of many pieces of evidence that he was a self-promoting fraud. A fraud indeed he was, but not because of the title, a title he was granted eight years before he even thought of coming to America. The German title *Freiherr* was not an inherited one, and did not imply landownership or wealth. It was a purely honorary distinction, one frequently bestowed

---

* Although American authors tend to refer to him as the "Baron von Steuben," Steuben never styled himself in this fashion, so I have eschewed this in favor of his preference for the "Baron de Steuben."

by German princes upon deserving subjects of noble birth, and nothing more.* But in one other way, harmlessly, the newly minted *Freiherr* did change his identity. Until 1769, he was known by his Christian name, the one given to him at baptism in 1730: Friedrich Wilhelm Ludolf Gerhard Augustin von Steuben. For some reason, when he forwarded his family tree to the court of Baden-Durlach, he rendered his name differently. From that point on he would be known as Friedrich Wilhelm August Heinrich Ferdinand von Steuben. He never gave a reason for doing so; perhaps he was seeking to make a symbolic break with the past, to sever his ties with a time and place he longed to forget.

Titles and knighthoods were not enough to keep Steuben at Hechingen. After the family's return from Montpellier, his paltry salary shrank, and he pined for the life of a soldier. So, in 1775, Freiherr von Steuben began to look for military employment.

Actually, he had already started to look for an army that would have him. During a brief stay in Lyons he made the acquaintance of a prominent Englishman, Philip Howard of Corby Castle, who promised to find him a job in the army of the British East India Company. That fell through—the East India Company, Steuben found, was not interested in hiring foreign-born officers—but the experience encouraged him to cast his net wide. More promising leads followed. A high-ranking officer in the Strasbourg garrison offered him a colonelcy if he could persuade Prince Josef to raise an infantry regiment for service in the French army. That, too, came to nothing, even though it initially had the backing of the French crown.

---

* Almost without exception, American historians have agreed that Steuben was not a legitimate baron. Others have asserted that Steuben claimed to be a "Baron of the Empire." Baron of the Empire (*Reichsfreiherr*) was a title granted by the Holy Roman Empire; Steuben *never* claimed to be a *Reichsfreiherr*. He claimed only to be a *Freiherr*, which was a very commonly held distinction among the Junker class. *That* title was legitimately held, being granted along with the Order of Fidelity in 1769. He did not claim the title before that date. Its first appearance in the surviving archival material is in a *Ranglist* (list of court personnel) for the court at Hechingen, dated 1771. And given the close ties among the lesser princes of southwestern Germany, Steuben could not possibly have made such a claim without justification.

Undeterred, Steuben turned to Prussia's other great adversary, Austria. One of many influential friends he had made while in France was none other than Charles-Joseph, Prince de Ligne, a soldier, diplomat, and personal companion of Emperor Josef II. Like so many of Steuben's casual acquaintances—men he met at elegant soirées or in raucous, smoke-filled taverns—the Prince de Ligne was instantly taken by the chatty Prussian with his obvious knowledge of military theory and practice. The prince, one of the most celebrated military authors of his day, was no mean judge of martial talent, and he considered Steuben a prime catch for the Austrian service. But he was unable to arrange a personal meeting between Steuben and the emperor, or to sway the leading Austrian generals in Steuben's favor, and so that opportunity also proved to be illusory. An appeal to the Margrave of Baden, the same man who had decorated Steuben with the Order of Fidelity, likewise yielded nothing concrete.[8]

First Britain, then France, then Austria, then Baden—all dead ends. It was not that Steuben had failed to impress. Quite the contrary. The French officer at Strasbourg who had offered him a colonel's rank was so distraught when their proposed arrangement came to nothing that he tried to broker a marriage between Steuben and a young woman from a prominent local family, hoping that he could at least solve his new friend's financial problems. The Prince de Ligne saluted Steuben unsolicited: "When I heard you speak of military affairs with the talent that distinguishes a pupil of the hero [i.e., Frederick the Great] from whom you have learned so much . . . I believed that it would be very fortunate for our service to have you amongst us."[9] But admiration did not translate into employment.

When Freiherr von Steuben did come across a legitimate opportunity—*the* opportunity—it came not through the good offices of one of his friends, but from a complete stranger.

While visiting Karlsruhe in May 1777, Steuben struck up a conversation with another visitor, one Peter Burdett, an English cartographer in the margrave's employ. Burdett gave the *Freiherr* a detailed lesson on the current political situation in Britain's rebellious colonies. The

Briton knew the topic well, making it clear that his sympathies lay with the rebels and not with his own king. Unbeknownst to Steuben, Burdett was also an agent in American pay, one of many informants working for the newly arrived American commissioner in Paris, Benjamin Franklin.

Franklin and his partner Silas Deane, Burdett revealed, were actively scouting for battle-hardened military leaders. There was no shortage of European officers willing to risk their all for fame, glory, and riches fighting for the American cause, but precious few of them had any significant experience in the higher levels of military leadership and organization. Steuben's eyes widened as he listened. Coyly, he indicated to Burdett that he himself might be interested, if a position were truly available, and he gave Burdett an account of his own exploits in the service of Old Fritz.

Burdett was suitably impressed, and Steuben was hooked. He would go to Paris to meet with Burdett's friend Franklin. Burdett wrote immediately to Franklin; receiving no reply that month, he penned another letter for Steuben to take directly to the American's hands.

> The Bearer [of this letter] is Baron Steuben of whom I had the honor to write to you by the hands of a Friend about a month since. He is a Gentleman of Family, Merit and great experience, well known to some of the First Personages in Europe, and hereby gives you sir a strong proof of his Ambition to make the Acquaintance of Docter Franklin in actualy performing a Journey from Germany to Paris for that Purpose.[10]

Steuben was jaded from so many abortive offers of employment, and this one sounded no more or no less promising than the others. It also entailed greater risk, a much longer journey, and therefore a greater outlay of his own cash. But there was something about Burdett's sales pitch that drew him in, and he wasted no time. The *Freiherr* immediately took to the road and headed for Paris, with virtually no money to his name. He paused only briefly at Strasbourg to have a new suit of clothes made for the occasion—it would not do to present himself in that glittering city while dressed in travel-worn clothing. It would not be the last time he would overspend on sartorial splendor.

Thus dazzlingly attired, freshly unemployed, and again in debt, Freiherr von Steuben set out alone from Strasbourg for Paris.

S TEUBEN WAS SUPREMELY CONFIDENT that a commission in the American army was his for the asking. Still, he had no idea what he was getting himself into. He may have been a more worldly man than most Prussian officers of his grade, but he had never been in a city the size of Paris before. Here he was an innocent.

Paris in the age of the Enlightenment was a city of stark contrasts: of great wealth and great poverty, of rigid noble privilege and egalitarian ideals, where the last great bastion of ancien régime monarchy in western Europe clashed with the radical social and political ideas of the philosophes, the prophets of the Age of Reason. And in Paris, the American rebellion was all the talk, at least among the intellectual elite and in the salons of its well-to-do citizens. To them, even those who admired Britain's parliamentary monarchy as the most freedom-loving and progressive government in Europe, the American rebellion was a noble experiment, a chance to see if a nation founded on the concepts of civil liberties and representative government could survive.

The rebellion was being closely watched at court, too, but for reasons that had more to do with realpolitik than concerns over liberty and inalienable human rights. Young Louis XVI, then not quite twenty-three, had been king for only three years, having inherited a country that still smarted from the drubbing it had suffered at the hands of Britain and Prussia in the last war. That defeat had robbed France of much of its colonial empire, devastated its national pride, and, worse still, left the kingdom with a huge national debt. The American rebellion offered the chance to set at least some of that right. By backing the rebels, France could slake its thirst for vengeance, weakening the British empire, while simultaneously gaining a loyal and lucrative trading partner in North America. But its involvement would also result in open war with Britain, and that in turn meant higher taxes and even greater debts. Would it be worth the price?

Some of the most important decision makers at Versailles thought so. The foreign minister, the Comte de Vergennes, pushed for active confrontation with Britain, and public opinion in Paris backed him up. But there were also naysayers, who pointed to the forbidding costs of renewed war with Britain. The king was torn: like any self-respecting monarch, he found it difficult to sympathize with those who would take up arms against their God-anointed sovereign, but he also ached for revenge on the rival nation that had humbled his father and his kingdom in 1763.

It clearly would not do to rush into war with Britain. For the time being, the hawks at court were content to provide the Americans with covert aid until the moment was right to throw off the thin mask of official neutrality. Money and muskets could be sent overseas, so long as it was done without the king's official involvement. War would come soon enough, but the fictitious neutrality of the crown would allow breathing space so that the nation could gird itself for war.

On the other side of the Atlantic there was a dilemma of a slightly different sort. Within the Continental Congress there were some who harbored an abiding distrust of France, and others who feared any kind of foreign partnership. Material support from a major European state or two would be helpful, so long as there were no strings attached, and therefore a genuinely reciprocal alliance was out of the question. This sentiment changed as the war dragged on and defeats outnumbered victories. The idea of a French or Franco-Spanish alliance grew increasingly alluring—but only if it did not amount to trading one European master for another.

Of all the European powers, however, only France welcomed American diplomats as emissaries of a sovereign state. Congress sent Silas Deane of Connecticut to Paris in early 1776 to represent American interests there; Benjamin Franklin joined him near the end of the year. Deane negotiated the first, unofficial, shipments of arms and other supplies from France to America, but Franklin quickly overshadowed him. The aging Franklin, disarmingly unpretentious and yet learned and courtly, became an instant celebrity in Paris.[11]

Working from Franklin's residence—a pretty little garden house at the Hôtel de Valentinois, in the village of Passy, immediately outside Paris—Franklin and Deane did their best to present the case for French intervention in the American war. They also acted as employment brokers for the Continental Army. Steuben was hardly the first European soldier-adventurer to see in the American rebellion an opportunity for career advancement. Some, like Steuben, were unemployed and down on their luck. Others, mostly officers of line rank—captains, lieutenants, subalterns—knew full well the bleak calculus of their career trajectories in peacetime Europe: without war there were no casualties, and without casualties their chances for promotion and advancement were slim.

They hounded Franklin and Deane incessantly. "I am well nigh harrassed to death with applications of officers to go to America," Deane griped to Congress in November 1776. Franklin was more explicit: "You can have no Conception," he wrote, "of the Arts and Interest made use of to recommend and engage me to recommend very indifferent Persons. The Importunity is boundless . . . the Numbers we refuse incredible."[12] The two commissioners, who knew little of the art of war, were ill equipped for the task, and undoubtedly passed along some undeserving candidates to Congress, but Congress as a body was even less capable of discerning the qualities that made a good officer. It was all too easy to be fooled by a neatly tailored uniform and a haughty manner. Congress handed out commissions in the Continental Army with reckless abandon.

That is not to say that Deane and Franklin could not find any talented officers. Deane himself had given the green light to the likes of the Marquis de Lafayette and Johann de Kalb, the giant Bavarian who had proven himself in the French army during two wars. But these were rare exceptions. Regardless, the flood of foreign volunteers demanding, and receiving, Continental commissions could not help but kindle resentment among American-born officers, who felt no less entitled to rank in their own army. By the middle of 1777, the two Americans at the French court were under a great deal of pressure to choke off the flow of foreign officers to America.

It was at this point that Steuben chose to come to Paris to ask for a commission. Had he made the trip just a few months earlier, he could have expected a warm welcome and an easy commission—maybe even a quick promotion to major-general, such as Lafayette and the Baron de Kalb had recently been granted. Rather, Steuben arrived at the worst possible moment, when Franklin and Deane were still smarting from the rebukes of Congress for being so generous to foreign applicants.

Steuben did not go directly to the Valentinois, thereby denying the Americans the chance to turn him down flat. Desperate and impatient though he may have been, Steuben had been a supplicant before, and he knew better than to rush blindly into such an important interview. He would need a testimonial or two, preferably from someone the American commissioners knew and trusted. Fortunately, he did have just such a friend: Claude-Louis, Comte de St. Germain, former field marshal in the French army and currently minister of war to Louis XVI.

Steuben and St. Germain had known each other for some time. Actually, they had been enemies at Rossbach in 1757, though neither would have known this. Their first face-to-face meeting took place in Hamburg

in 1763 or 1764. St. Germain was not then in French pay. He had made a name for himself in the War of the Austrian Succession and the Seven Years' War as a capable but blunt and sharp-tongued French

Benjamin Franklin. History has ascribed to the colorful Franklin the credit for recruiting Steuben, but the truth is that he did not give Steuben much encouragement. *(Library of Congress)*

Caron de Beaumarchais. French playwright and advocate of the American
cause. He befriended Steuben when
the latter was in Paris, and introduced
him to Deane and Franklin. *(Emmet
Collection, Miriam and Ira D. Wallach Division of Art, Prints and Photographs, The New
York Public Library, Astor, Lenox and Tilden
Foundations)*

commander, but his undisguised
admiration for the Prussians,
combined with his tactless criticisms of his mediocre superiors,
led to his forced resignation in
1760. The king of Denmark clev-
erly grabbed him, gave him high
rank, and set him to reforming the Danish army along Prussian lines.
Upon becoming French minister of war in 1775, he urged the adoption of
Prussian-like reforms in his native land. The idea was no more popular
then than it had been in 1760; the backlash from the officer corps was one
of the factors that would lead to his resignation near the end of 1777.[13]

Their shared regard for the Prussian army drew Steuben and St.
Germain together. It proved to be the vital connection, for it opened to
Steuben avenues that would have been closed to him otherwise. When
Steuben arrived in Paris in June 1777, St. Germain was still a man
with much political clout. He was happy to see Steuben, and happier
still to help him. Without hesitation, he granted the Prussian an audience, penned a glowing reference for him, and then introduced him to
even more influential men: first the Comte de Vergennes, Louis's foreign minister, and then the famous—some might say infamous—busi-
nessman and playwright Pierre-Augustin Caron de Beaumarchais.

Beaumarchais was the most ardent advocate of American independence then living in France; certainly he was the oddest. Just a couple of
years younger than Steuben, Beaumarchais—whose irreverent play *The*

Barber of Seville brought him instant notoriety—was the founder of Roderigue Hortalez et Compagnie, an export firm that secretly sold munitions to the American rebels with the clandestine blessing of the French crown. As a highly literate man, and a friend of Voltaire and other men of letters, he was a perfect match for Steuben; and since he was on friendly terms with Silas Deane, he was an invaluable professional contact. Steuben and Beaumarchais hit it off immediately. Before long, Steuben made his temporary residence at Beaumarchais's house on the Left Bank. The Baron now had three substantial allies: St. Germain, Vergennes, and Beaumarchais. How could the Americans refuse him?[14]

Beaumarchais arranged for Steuben to meet the American commissioners at Franklin's Passy residence on June 25, 1777. Steuben had been in Paris for about two weeks when he strode that evening along the picturesque garden walk, between rows of elegant statuary, that led to the front door of the house at the Valentinois—unless he was ushered quickly and quietly into the partially hidden back entrance. The Americans were primed for the meeting by Beaumarchais's enthusiastic endorsements. Deane, a frequent visitor at Beaumarchais's house, had already met the Baron, albeit briefly. The three men made an odd group as they sat together in Franklin's salon. Steuben, now forty-six, was beginning to show signs of middle age, growing heavy in the face and the midriff, yet was still energetic, almost fidgety, resplendent in his new finery; Deane, the slave-owning Yankee aristocrat, was slim and serious, every inch the diplomat; and bespectacled Dr. Franklin, the oldest of the three by a quarter century, was dressed in the plain, almost peasantlike frock that had drawn so much comment at

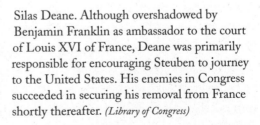

Silas Deane. Although overshadowed by Benjamin Franklin as ambassador to the court of Louis XVI of France, Deane was primarily responsible for encouraging Steuben to journey to the United States. His enemies in Congress succeeded in securing his removal from France shortly thereafter. *(Library of Congress)*

The Comte de Vergennes. Minister of foreign affairs under Louis XVI of France, Vergennes collaborated with Deane, Franklin, Beaumarchais, and the war minister St. Germain to get Steuben to America. At the end of the war, he refused to honor St. Germain's promise to find Steuben a place in the French army. *(Library of Congress)*

court. They chatted for a while in French, though Deane was still halting and uncomfortable with the language.[15]

Silas Deane took the lead. Unlike Franklin, who would have preferred not to act as talent scout for the Continental Army, Deane saw the task of feeding military experts into the American war machine as a vital part of his duties. He also took Beaumarchais seriously—again, unlike Franklin, who referred disparagingly to the womanizing, sometimes flippant Frenchman as "Monsieur Figaro." Beaumarchais, in turn, set great store by Deane. "I have found a great difference between the honest deputy Deane, with whom I have negotiated, and the insidious politician [Arthur] Lee and the taciturn Dr. Franklin," he lamented to Vergennes after Congress recalled Deane from his post in November 1777.[16]

Deane conducted the interview with Steuben while Franklin sat by quietly. "I . . . could not bring the Doctor to pay the least attention to him, or to give the Baron any encouragement," Deane later recounted. Deane knew what his Prussian guest wanted; he did not question Steuben's qualities and character, nor did he doubt for a moment that Steuben had a great deal to contribute to the Continental Army. But he still did not dare to promise Steuben a commission, let alone put him on the Continental Army payroll. Congress would not tolerate it.

Henry Laurens, president of Congress and no friend of Deane's, had already complained that Deane was incapable of "say[ing] nay to any Frenchman who called himself Count or Chevalier."[17] Deane also knew that, regardless of Vergennes's and St. Germain's support, the French crown would do little or nothing to help Steuben without being pushed to do so.

The crafty Deane took another tack: he told Steuben *not* to go to America.

> I candidly and impartially stated to the Baron the situation of our affairs in America, and our unfavorable prospects in France, and told him that unless the Court of France had resolved to give us effectual aid it would, in my opinion, be to no purpose for him to run the risques of a voyage, and the loss of his time and other prospects, in going to America; for it was extremely probable that without such assistance America must make the best terms in her power.

It was a ruse. Deane suspected that since government spies were everywhere, a private conversation at the Valentinois would be anything but private, and very soon Vergennes would know precisely what advice Deane had given to Steuben, word for word. Deane's hope was that his talk with Steuben would lead the cautious Vergennes to believe that the American rebels were on the verge of making peace with Britain, and therefore into pushing harder for a greater French commitment to Steuben and to the American cause.[18]

Steuben, however, was not privy to Deane's subtle game. He was disappointed by the diplomat's counsel, but as yet undeterred. He was ready to run the risk of rejection in America. As soon as the esteemed commissioners could get him a berth aboard a westbound ship, he would be packed and ready to leave.

But then came the crushing blow. Steuben asked only for funds to cover his voyage to America. "Mr. Deane made no kind of difficulty," the Baron noted. "But Doctor Franklin started a great many." Franklin refused even to pay Steuben's travel expenses, and his voice would be the deciding one. He tried to placate his guest, who was obviously taken aback by Franklin's inflexibility. Perhaps Congress, Franklin conceded, might see its way to reimburse Steuben with a grant of land deep in the American wilderness, but even this could not be guaranteed. Beyond that, Franklin could do nothing. He stated brusquely that "he was not empowered to make any [cash advances], & that he could not even enter into the least engagement with any Officer whatever."

Steuben did not know, could not have known, the fetters that bound the hands of Deane and Franklin. He knew little of American politics or the scope of the commissioners' powers. To him, it seemed that he had been betrayed, or at least misled, and the offer was nothing short of insulting. It was not even an offer, really. To travel to America at his own expense, with no firm prospect awaiting him at the end of the journey? Why, anyone could do the very same thing, with or without military experience or recommendations from the chief ministers of the French crown. Anyone, that is, with the money to buy a passage overseas, and that Steuben did not have. Franklin's tone of voice, which Steuben found condescending—"he told me that with an Air & Manner to which I was then little accustomed"—repelled him. Infuriated, he ended the interview. Stomping out of the house, he mounted his horse and, with scarcely a look backward, rode back to Beaumarchais's residence on the Rue de Condé.[19]

JUST AS HE WAS PREPARING to leave Paris for good, Steuben received welcome news: he was wanted in Karlsruhe, at the court of the Margrave of Baden.

The margrave had been as good as his word. A vacancy had opened in his army, and he was holding it for Steuben. Steuben would be a fool not to seize it. Employment with the margrave would be a substantial prize. Baden was not Prussia or Austria, but it was of respectable size, with a respectable budget. The margrave could offer a much more generous salary, and far greater prestige, than the prince of Hechingen had. Steuben left Paris, but in leisure, confident that he had finally found a guaranteed position. The margrave knew him well; the Baron would not have to prove himself.

But Steuben never got that far, for what he found waiting for him at Karlsruhe was not an officer's commission, but a rumor—a horrible, vicious rumor. Someone at Hechingen had lodged a foul accusation against the former chamberlain: that while at Prince Josef's court, Friedrich von Steuben had "taken familiarities with young boys" in his charge. This was a serious allegation. In the self-consciously masculine society of the Prussian army, homosexuality was not an issue of grave concern, nor was it an absolute taboo. Prince Henry's more than professional interest in handsome young officers was a matter of public knowledge; the great Frederick himself was widely rumored to be homosexual, a notion that the king did little to discourage. In Europe in general, however, homosexuality was not acceptable, and even open-minded and progressive intellectuals such as Voltaire considered it to be a great moral failing. And pederasty, because it involved innocent youths, was doubly reprehensible.

The allegations concerning Steuben's behavior were never proven, but they were no less damning than if they had been. Most of his friends at Hechingen, with the notable exception of Chancellor Frank, distanced themselves from him. The charges effectively killed Steuben's chances for employment in Baden. As a friend at Karlsruhe noted, the rumors would have to be disproven or "declared calumnious" before the margrave could even think of taking Steuben into his service. The burden of proof would therefore be on the Baron himself.[20]

Coming on the heels of the failed interview at Passy, this new development was devastating. Steuben was trapped: he dared not show his face at Hechingen, and a continued stay at Karlsruhe would have been unimaginably awkward. Broke, aging, and an accused pederast to boot, he had few options. He was unemployed and unemployable. The matter would never surface again—Steuben himself never mentioned it in his correspondence, and made only a vague reference to it later in life—but it clearly was the greatest crisis of his life.

Just at that very moment he was offered a way out of his predicament. While he was at Karlsruhe, considering his next move, letters arrived for him from France. Beaumarchais and St. Germain had written to him in great urgency: he *must* return to Paris, and at once. Without pausing to reflect on the meaning of this ambiguous summons, Steuben fled to Paris. He had little choice. The path to his salvation would have to lead through Passy to America.

HE ARRIVED IN PARIS sometime in mid-August 1777, where he visited Franklin and Deane once again at the Valentinois. Franklin, he found, had not changed his tune, but Beaumarchais and St. Germain had put their heads together and come up with a new plan. Steuben would still proceed to America as a volunteer, nothing more, with no commission in hand and no promise that he would get one upon arrival. He would proceed to Pennsylvania and meet with the Continental Congress, bearing written endorsements from the American commissioners. But Beaumarchais would underwrite the costs of his travel with a personal loan. Steuben would set sail from France as a guest of Roderigue Hortalez et Compagnie.

There may have been an additional incentive to entice Steuben. A British agent in Paris reported that the "Baron Steinben" had worked out a secret, lucrative deal with St. Germain: once he had served three years in America, he would return to France and receive a commission in the king's army. There was never any written confirmation of such an arrangement, but if true, then it helps to explain much about Steuben's subsequent conduct: why, for example, he was so eager to reconsider the American offer, and why, when he later grew disenchanted with the Continental Army, he was so confident that the French would take him back in a heartbeat.[21]

Beaumarchais and St. Germain were not simply going out of their way to help their mutual friend. Assisting Steuben was also in their best interests, and France's, too. If the Prussian proved to be half as useful as they thought he might be, he would fill an obvious gap in

American military leadership: the lack of officers experienced in the areas of army organization, logistics, training, and planning—all Steuben's strong suits. No one expected him to be a military savior, the man who would enable the Americans to win, but then, that wasn't their intention. St. Germain and Vergennes did not want the rebels to achieve independence on their own. They wanted America to need France, to be indebted to France for their very existence. The Americans would just have to be capable of holding on until France was ready to jump with both feet into the fray. If Steuben could be placed in a position of authority, perhaps he could help the Continental Army do just that. He would help Vergennes and his allies achieve their aims—while France got the credit. Steuben would be their gift to the Revolution.

The problem was that Steuben was essentially a nobody. Other foreigners already in the American army could boast of much loftier ranks and greater honors. Steuben, on the other hand, had been nothing more than a humble captain. Although his abilities were the kind that would quickly have become apparent to another military man after a few moments of conversation, they did not come across on paper. If Freiherr von Steuben were to find favor with Congress, his qualities would have to be made obvious to civilians unfamiliar with the language of war.

If Steuben was ever a fraud, he became one at Passy. Up until this moment, he had not publicly misrepresented himself or his credentials. But in August 1777, he would lay claim to distinctions and experiences that were not actually his.

The act of deception was not actually Steuben's but, rather, a team effort in which all of his promoters—Vergennes, St. Germain, Beaumarchais, Deane, and Franklin—took part. Deane and Beaumarchais were the principal conspirators. In the first days of September 1777, they composed their promotional materials for the *Freiherr*: a series of letters to be carried by Steuben and delivered in person to General Washington and to leading personages in Congress. The recipients were carefully chosen. Silas Deane wrote to

Robert Morris, the Philadelphia financier whose vast personal wealth and fiscal acumen gave him tremendous influence in Congress; Deane and Franklin wrote to Washington jointly; Louis de L'Estarjette, Deane's secretary, wrote to Henry Laurens of South Carolina, president of the Continental Congress.[22]

All three letters made roughly the same claims on Steuben's behalf. He was, they wrote, a "Lieutenant General in the Prussian army" and had "seen more than Twenty Years Service under the King of Prussia," "whom he attended in all his Campaigns." For a portion of that time he had served the king in person as "Quarter Master General" and another portion as "Aid de Camp" to the king. Steuben bore written testimonials from Prince Henry and "other great Personages"; he was also "warmly recommended by the Ministry here who are acquainted with his Person, & Character." His "distinguished character and known abilities" were attested to by "two of the best Judges of military Merit in this Country," namely Vergennes and St. Germain, "who have long been personally acquainted with him."

As if these accolades were not enough, their authors waxed poetic over Steuben's motives. He was travelling to America "with a true Zeal for our Cause & a View of engaging in & rendering it all the Service in his Power." He "goes over to America upon no other motive than to render himself useful in our good Cause, and [to] humble our Enemies." Steuben's ardor was reportedly so great that he had turned down "a very important and lucrative Post in one of the German Courts" in order to serve Congress. Congress could not possibly turn away such a talented soldier, whose "20 Years Study & Practice in the Prussian School may be of great Use to our Armies." Congress would be remiss in its duties if it did not accept such a great gift, freely given.

Nearly every statement was falsified or exaggerated, every detail— about Steuben's rank and experience—deliberately misrepresented.

If there were any doubts that the American commissioners were behind the charade, Silas Deane readily implicated himself. When he wrote to Robert Morris, he went out of his way to explain why it was that Steuben had nothing on paper to verify his military rank and experience. The Baron, he admitted freely, had come to Paris nearly three months earlier, but had left when he could not be guaranteed a place in the Continental Army. He returned to Paris only "after some of Our Freinds here . . . generously defrayed the Expences of his Voyage." Steuben had been in such a hurry to get to Paris this second time, however, that he carelessly left his personal papers behind in Karlsruhe. Deane was not overly concerned, he related to Morris, for he had already seen written proof that Steuben was who he purported to be, so when Steuben suggested that he arrange for his papers to be delivered to Paris, Deane stopped him. "I advised him not to delay his setting out. . . . I thought it would be only The Loss of Time." Steuben, in other words, had not hoodwinked Deane. Instead, the American knowingly covered for Steuben, hoping that Washington and Congress would simply forget about the specifics of his past.

The arrangements were made. The Baron de Steuben, late lieutenant-general, quartermaster-general, and aide-de-camp to Frederick of Prussia, would set out on the first available ship that Beaumarchais had at his disposal, and then make his triumphal entry into the United States.

CHAPTER 3

This Illustrious Stranger

[SEPTEMBER 1777—FEBRUARY 1778]

If I am Possessor of some talents in the Art of War,
they should be much dearer to me, if I could employ
them in the service of a Republick such as I hope soon
to see America.

STEUBEN TO THE CONTINENTAL CONGRESS,
DECEMBER 6, 1777[1]

DEANE, Beaumarchais, and the others had taken the
first steps in selling the Baron de Steuben, packaging
him neatly in flashy titles that would temporarily
substitute for manifest ability. Since it would be next to impossible to convey, in a few pithy phrases that anyone could understand, what it was that made Steuben worthy of attention,
superficial qualities would have to do for now. Deane and the
rest could get the Baron to Congress's doorstep; once there,
Steuben would be on his own.

In America he would be completely out of his element, so he
would have to prepare carefully while in France. First he would
need to assemble a retinue. No self-respecting general could travel
without a personal staff, whether he was on active duty or not.
Like any gentleman of high birth, he had to have at least a servant
or two to help him dress, to cook and clean for him, to perform

all of the routine daily tasks that no nobleman should have to do for himself. But he would also need a few literate junior officers to assist him with military and administrative responsibilities: a secretary to handle his correspondence perhaps, and a couple of aides-de-camp, protégés who could run errands for him and with whom he could consult.

Steuben's staff would serve an obvious practical purpose—since the Baron did not know English, and few Americans spoke either French or German, he could not get by without a couple of assistants who could translate for him. But a staff would also give Steuben an air of importance that he would lack if he travelled alone. Just as wearing the proper attire could convey the appropriate impression of professionalism, being surrounded by a busy staff of professional soldiers would show that he took his craft seriously, and that he was bred to command. And it expressed something that the Baron considered just as important: an appearance of nonchalance. For if he could afford to maintain a staff even while he was unemployed, he was clearly a man of considerable means. It meant that he did not *need* anything from the Americans, and the Baron did not want to look needy. Doing so would compromise his newly fashioned persona.

Beaumarchais, who had a personal stake in Steuben's future, was glad to help select a few men who served his own purposes as well as the Baron's. First there was Jean-Baptiste Lazare Theveneau de Francy, who was not to be officially attached to Steuben but would travel with him anyway. Francy was assigned to act as an agent for Roderigue Hortalez et Cie., representing Beaumarchais's business interests in America. "A handsome man, and what was called a beau in those days," Francy spoke English passably well but could not write it.[2] Beaumarchais's nephew, twenty-year-old Augustin François Des Epiniers, came with Francy. Beaumarchais thought his nephew spoiled and inept, but perhaps a tour in the Continental Army might make a man of him. Silas Deane had already given Francy a commission as captain of engineers nearly nine months before. A lieutenant in the French army, Louis de Ponthière, was hired as the Baron's personal aide-de-camp.

The fourth member of the little entourage would become the most vital member of the Baron's military family. Pierre-Étienne Duponceau was a fixture in Beaumarchais's Left Bank household and the playwright's unofficial student. A dreamy-eyed, nearsighted, and hopelessly scholarly boy of seventeen, Duponceau was possessed of an insatiable academic curiosity. For all that, he was tougher than he appeared at first glance, with his pale complexion and tall, lanky frame, exaggerated by adolescent awkwardness. He had a gift for languages—during the long sea voyage to America, he sketched out his ideas for a "universal language and alphabet," presaging Esperanto by more than a century—and in this regard he was particularly useful to Steuben, for he was fluent in English. After the Revolution, he would settle down to a legal career in Philadelphia, become a leading light in Franklin's American Philosophical Society, and earn a name for himself as a pioneering linguist and student of Native American tongues.[3]

Much less is known about the two remaining members of the Baron's group. Steuben had a young German manservant, one Carl Vogel, who was so unremarkable that even Duponceau's detailed diary scarcely mentions the man. And then there was Azor, the Baron's dog, who stayed at his master's side from Paris until after the end of the War for Independence. By all accounts, Azor was a large dog with a gargantuan appetite; Duponceau described him as an "Italian greyhound."* Steuben loved and indulged Azor without reservation. A few years later, while he and one of his aides traveled by coach down a muddy New York road, Azor—who had been trotting alongside—took advantage of a pause in the journey to leap through the coach's open window and right onto the laps of the two men. The Baron and his aide were wearing brand-new uniforms that Steuben had just purchased at great expense only a couple of days before. Azor's huge paws tracked clods of mud all over the Baron's immaculate white breeches as he nestled himself in the man's lap.

---

*Historians have described Azor's breed as anything from an Irish wolfhound to a mastiff. The only one of Steuben's circle to give particulars on Azor was Duponceau, and he consistently referred to him as an "Italian greyhound." Since the modern breed is characteristically small, and Azor was remembered for being quite large, a specific identification of Azor's pedigree remains elusive.

Steuben was fussy about his appearance, but he just couldn't bring himself to be angry with his dog. Instead, he laughingly tugged on Azor's ears and called him a "damned rascal."[4]

The Baron and his impromptu staff set out from Paris on September 5, 1777. The journey, which lasted nineteen days, took the party southward along the valley of the Rhône to their destination, the ancient Mediterranean port of Marseilles. Their French benefactors made a halfhearted attempt to shroud Steuben's progress in secrecy, but to no avail. The Baron had purchased new uniforms for his staff—including fine black hats in the French bicorn style, replete with plumes and cockades—but not knowing the colors of American uniforms, he ordered coats made of brilliant scarlet cloth with blue facings. They were just too obvious to escape detection, and British agents in France were not fooled. Still, to obscure the purpose of his trip, the Baron assumed a pseudonym. He would be the Monsieur de Franck, agent of Roderigue Hortalez et Cie., bearing dispatches for the governor of French Martinique.

Waiting for them at Marseilles was the ship-rigged merchantman *Flamand*, bound for the West Indies with a cargo of wine, miscellaneous vegetables, and sulphur. But, like Steuben's assumed name, this was a guise. In reality, *Flamand* was the French naval frigate *L'Heureux*, 360 tons, carrying a formidable battery of twenty-eight guns and a huge cargo of contraband: muskets and carbines by the thousands, several dozen cannons and mortars, and hundreds of barrels of gunpowder.

On Friday, September 26, 1777, *Flamand*'s crew cast off the mooring lines and made sail, the frigate passing between the two ancient forts that stood watch over the harbor entrance and into the open waters of the Mediterranean beyond. The Baron de Steuben was on his way to America.[5]

EVEN IN THE LAST QUARTER of the eighteenth century, when transatlantic travel was almost routine, it took a hardy soul to brave the passage from Europe to North America. Steuben's two-month passage was treacherous and very uncomfortable, and not without its moments of sheer terror. *Flamand* weathered two major storms during the crossing; there were also three fires aboard ship, always a potential horror, but even more so when the ship was practically packed to the gunwhales with explosives. There was the danger, too, of interception by a British warship off the American coast. Despite the falsified papers and the ship's reported destination, it would have been difficult to disguise the massive quantity of ordnance stockpiled in *Flamand*'s hold. A run-in with a British ship of the line could have resulted in a very ugly incident.

But *Flamand* managed to evade these perils. Steuben himself seemed to be wholly unconcerned by the prospects. His mind focused on what lay ahead, and regardless of his trepidation at his uncertain prospects in America, his spirits were more buoyant than they had been in a very long time. Duponceau's boyish enthusiasm helped. He undertook to give voice lessons to the ship's captain, Pierre Landais of the French Royal Navy. Landais had determination but little talent, and his off-key caterwauling kept everyone amused—everyone, that is, except Azor, who took offense at Landais's vocal endeavors and howled piteously whenever the captain took it in his head to sing.[6]

The Baron did not need diversion to occupy his time. He was on his way to a country and a people he knew absolutely nothing about, so for much of the voyage he tried to learn what he could. He studied intently the few books on America he had been able to scrape together before sailing from Marseilles, principally the Abbé Raynal's popular treatise on European settlements in the Americas. He also interviewed Captain Landais at length, for Landais had accompanied the explorer Louis-Antoine de Bougainville on his celebrated circumnavigation of the globe in 1766–69. When Steuben found the time, he tried to pick up a few words of spoken English from Duponceau, and with his secretary's help he composed a personal memoir chronicling his life in Europe.[7]

The ship's lookouts finally sighted the rocky New England coastline at the very end of November. The ship dropped anchor in the calm seas just off Portsmouth, New Hampshire, on Monday, December 1,

1777. The day was unseasonably warm and sunny, adding to the usual sense of euphoria that came at the end of a long and arduous voyage. A landing party—including Duponceau, who sprang nimbly into the party's longboat as it cleared *Flamand*'s davits—determined that the town was not in British hands, though the people they met ashore were initially a bit confused by Duponceau's red coat. Portsmouth's most prominent citizen, the merchant and former congressional delegate John Langdon, accompanied the group back to *Flamand*, and then escorted Steuben, his staff, and Landais to the town.

They were treated to a hero's welcome. Throngs of citizens came out to stare, gape-mouthed, at the oddly dressed Prussian and his French companions, and many of the locals followed the procession to John Langdon's opulent residence when the well-to-do merchant invited the foreigners to dine with him. "All the inhabitants of the place crowded together as if to look at a rhinoceros," an amused Steuben reported to his old friend Daniel Marianus Frank.[8]

At Langdon's dinner table, the Baron learned in detail of the progress of the rebellion thus far, and the news was encouraging. Although Philadelphia had fallen to the British, in upstate New York a truly grand thing had transpired. Maj. Gen. Horatio Gates and the Northern Army had defeated Maj. Gen. John Burgoyne in twin battles near Saratoga, capturing an entire British field army intact and throwing British strategy into disarray. Surely France would act now, and then victory would not be far off. The war, at any rate, was not yet over. Steuben could still make his mark.

After a stay of ten uneventful days in Portsmouth, Steuben and his party set out for Boston by carriage, where they arrived two days later. Newspapers across New England had already spread the word that a great Prussian hero had arrived on their shores, so as at Portsmouth the local elite turned out in force to meet their odd but distinguished visitor. The Baron made a favorable impression on the Bostonians. Boston had seen its share of foreigners and noblemen, but Steuben was different: not French and Catholic, but German and Protestant, an important distinction in a town of Boston's Puritan heritage. Unlike many of the French officers who had passed through recently, Steuben was down to earth, affable, and gregarious. And he and his companions were just so novel. "Only fancy to yourself," Duponceau recalled, "an old German Baron, with a large brilliant star on his breast, three French aides-de-camp and a large, spoiled Italian dog, [and] none of all that company could speak a word of English."[9]

Steuben was jobless and living on borrowed funds, but Boston's welcome did wonders for his deflated ego. He did not have to seek out John Hancock, as Langdon had suggested, for Hancock sought *him* out and fêted him as an honored guest. The former president of Congress hosted at least one dinner party in Steuben's honor, attended by all the luminaries of Boston Patriot society. Steuben bonded instantly with crusty Sam Adams, the two chatting amiably over military affairs and European politics. Adams, who liked neither Washington nor the idea of a professional army, was moved to write to Horatio Gates and his friends in Congress about this "Gentleman of great Merit."[10]

Duponceau had a grand time in Boston. As the only member of the Baron's staff who could speak English well, he could flirt with the local girls while Ponthière and Des Epiniers could do little more than point and grunt. In his enthusiasm, he committed a social gaffe or two—at John Hancock's house one evening he made the great mistake of addressing Sam Adams as "Mr. John Adams," earning a gruff rebuke from the offended Adams—but this failed to discourage his high spirits.[11]

To Steuben, on the other hand, life in Boston quickly became tiresome and exasperating. He had been led to expect that he would be taken care of, but he was very much on his own. The Baron had been in America for less than a month and already he was in debt, "having brought no money with him," as he complained, awkwardly and in the third person, to John Hancock, "upon the positive Assurance . . . that he should be supplied with every thing." No one offered him a place to stay, or even helped him to find lodgings. The town was too expensive for his tastes; the people of Boston were, in his view, tightfisted and unfriendly. He and his staff took up residence in two cramped rooms in a boarding house owned by one Mrs. Downe. The cost of firewood to heat the rooms amounted to some sixty dollars over three weeks, and the final bill for lodging there was far higher than the Baron was prepared to pay. It included additional charges for Azor and for the "trouble" the party had caused to their long-suffering hostess. Duponceau thought the charges were quite fair—the dog "ate as much as anyone of us"—yet they enraged Steuben, who threw his hands to his head and repeatedly exclaimed, *Der Teufel!* ("The devil!"), as he perused the itemized bill.[12]

The Baron confided his disappointment to William Gordon, a local pastor and friend of Samuel Adams. He believed that he "had been by some means neglected so as not to meet with the civilities that might justly be expected," Gordon noted, and "felt strongly the disappointment of the expectations he had formed of the manners of the people in this quarter."[13]

Steuben blamed his predicament on the leadership of the town, who were "almost as lackadaisical as certain people at Versailles," he wrote in disgust to Beaumarchais. "I still do not understand what they did to get where they are today." But he also worried about the attitude of Congress and of General Washington. Steuben had written to them from Portsmouth and still had not heard a word, welcoming or otherwise. His sense of dejection worsened when he and Francy encountered a handful of younger French officers who had been sent to America a year before by Beaumarchais and Deane. They had not received even the slightest encouragement from Congress. Humiliated and penniless, they awaited the first ship that could take them back to France. Steuben commiserated with them, and tried to persuade them to stay, but deep down he took their situation as an ill omen. If Congress was so bullheaded as to let these talented professionals go, then what kind of treatment could he expect?[14]

Had the Baron exercised a little more forbearance, though, he would have found some encouragement. Congress and George Washington had already replied to Steuben's letters from Portsmouth. Both were delighted to hear of his arrival, and in fact Congress was prepared to pay all of his expenses.

But the news did not reach Boston fast enough. Having heard nothing, and with his funds and his patience tapped out after five weeks in town, Steuben prepared to proceed directly to the seat of government in York, Pennsylvania. John Hancock and the state of Connecticut forwarded him some cash to defray further travel expenses. After purchasing fresh horses, a wagon, some supplies, and new blue-and-buff uniforms for his assistants, the Baron set out from Boston on the morning of January 14, 1778. Ahead of him lay a four-hundred-mile trip in the dead of winter.

D URING THE COURSE of the Revolutionary War, the cause of American independence would endure more dark times than happy ones. The winter of 1777–78 was no exception, and though there were worse winters in many regards, that of '77–78 probably deserves the epithet "gloomy" more than any other. It was not just the uncertainty of the hoped-for French alliance, nor the disagreeable weather, nor the desperate shortage of willing manpower to fill the dwindling ranks of the army. The thing that infused the season with despair was the conflict within—not that between Patriot and Tory, but among those who should have been united, the rebel leadership itself. The Revolution appeared to be tearing itself apart from the inside.

Because of Washington's almost miraculous victories at Trenton and Princeton, the previous year had commenced with a healthy measure of hope. But the British were not about the allow the rebels any respite, and so they would take to the field again in 1777 with a vengeance. Lord William Howe, commanding the main British force in New York, would move on Philadelphia, wresting that symbol of rebellion out of Patriot hands. Meanwhile, a three-pronged invasion of New York State would, if successful, amputate New England from the rest of the colonies. The latter enterprise proved to be a spectacular failure. Maj. Gen. Horatio Gates—sometimes unkindly called "Granny" for his matronly appearance and fussy demeanor—stopped the south-ward advance of General Burgoyne's army at Freeman's Farm, and then thoroughly trounced Burgoyne at Bemis Heights, two separate actions collectively called the Battle of Saratoga. To add to this shame, a makeshift band of New England militia forces ambushed a portion of Burgoyne's army at Bennington, near the present-day border of New York and Vermont. The victories were almost as reinvigorating as Trenton and Princeton had been, and more valuable in some ways, for they provided Vergennes with proof that the war was winnable and therefore deserving of French support.

Not far south, things were going much worse for George Washington. In June 1777, Howe launched his assault on Philadelphia after British transports carried his army from New York by sea and up the Chesapeake Bay. Disembarking at Head of Elk, Maryland, the British moved north by land to menace the capital. As Howe had predicted, Washington would not give up the city without a fight. The two armies clashed on the Brandywine Creek, near Chadds Ford, Pennsylvania, on September 11. The Continentals fought bravely but were overwhelmed by superior numbers. With Washington's army bruised and bleeding, Howe was free to march directly on Philadelphia, and on September 26 the British took possession of the town. Congress fled, first to Lancaster, then to York, where they would remain until the following summer.

Washington refused to give up just yet. Barely a week after the British paraded in triumph on Philadelphia's streets, he hatched a plan to drive Howe out. On October 4, at Germantown, just a few miles north of Philadelphia, the Continentals tried to envelop and crush the outnumbered British garrison. Washington's men fought well, and at first had the advantage of surprise, but the Redcoats quickly recovered, and ultimately the Americans were driven off in defeat.

The disappointing outcome of the Philadelphia campaign of 1777 somewhat dampened the jubilation over Saratoga, but the defeat's significance went well beyond its impact on American morale. Brandywine and Germantown spoke volumes about the martial qualities of the Continental Army. The men fought like demons at both battles; they had a tenacity and spirit that even their opponents acknowledged. But they lacked the ability to maneuver and change formation quickly, and the restraint that would allow them to deliver devastating volleys of musketry at close range against an advancing enemy. Nor were they comfortable with the use of the bayonet, and in eighteenth-century warfare that weapon still have a very real tactical value. The Continentals wanted, in short, the training that would permit them to fight the British in the conventional European fashion.

Brandywine and Germantown did not destroy the morale of the common soldiers in the ranks. But in the upper echelons of command, at Washington's headquarters and in the halls of Congress, the defeats around Philadelphia had a toxic effect. That campaign, coupled with the humiliating loss of the capital city, emboldened Washington's critics. A growing chorus of voices, secretive but unmistakable, questioned his leadership abilities and his commitment to the cause of independence. In the closing months of 1777, the general became convinced that there was a plot afoot to seek his downfall and replacement. He was right.

From the very first day that Washington assumed command of the army in 1775, he had had his detractors. Other, more experienced, soldiers, such as Horatio Gates and Charles Lee, felt themselves far more qualified to lead. Washington's elevation to supreme command especially rankled Lee. A professional soldier who had held a commission in the British army and a generalship in the Polish army, Lee had genuinely expected to be offered the position that was given to Washington. Lee served under Washington anyway, as a major general in command of a full division, but he never attempted to hide his disdain for his superior. At times, particularly during the unfortunate New York campaign of 1776, Lee's contempt manifested itself in conduct that bordered on outright insubordination.

Lee could not do much harm to Washington at the end of 1777—he had been taken prisoner by the British in December 1776—but there were plenty of others who mirrored his sentiments. Lee's fellow

British veteran Horatio Gates—an unimaginative man perhaps, but ambitious and self-righteous—thought poorly of Washington, too. The Baron de Kalb dubbed Washington "the weakest general" he had ever known.

What made this small group of disaffected generals dangerous was that they had political backing in Congress. The most vocal congressional opposition to Washington came from that faction known as the "true Whigs," radical revolutionaries who firmly believed that a sense of patriotic duty—civic virtue—was in itself sufficient to guarantee victory over the British. Men such as Thomas Mifflin and Dr. Benjamin Rush of Pennsylvania, and Sam Adams and James Lovell of Massachusetts, eschewed any measure that played to self-interest, convinced that virtue would lead all true patriots—military or civilian—to do the right thing. It was an impractical stance, to be sure, but in wartime it was dangerous, too. As a rule, the Whigs did not like the idea of a standing professional army, which they saw as a necessary evil at best; they far preferred reliance upon a militia of virtuous citizens. Washington represented everything they opposed, for he was both the commander and chief advocate of America's standing army. Worse still, he had been unwilling to risk the destruction of the Continental Army to save Philadelphia. He lacked the kind of virtue they were looking for in a patriotic general.

As 1777 drew to a close, the anti-Washington elements in Congress and within the army command coalesced into a coordinated plot to have the general-in-chief removed from command and replaced by Horatio Gates, the darling of the true Whigs. In Congress, the newly constituted Board of War, created in November 1777 to take over primary direction of the war effort, was slanted from the beginning against Washington. Three of its four active members—Gates, Mifflin, and Timothy Pickering of Massachusetts—were inimical to the commander. Soon one of Washington's own generals—the Irish-born Thomas Conway, a veteran of the French army—expressed the utmost disdain for Washington. "Heaven has been determined to save your Country," Conway carped to Gates, "or a weak General and bad Councellors would have ruind it." Washington and his supporters caught wind of this irresponsible talk, and the fight was on.

The resulting power struggle, which has come down through history as the "Conway Cabal," reached its peak in January–February 1778. Even as Washington and his allies moved decisively to squelch it that winter—Washington proved to be a much more agile political opponent than any of the true Whigs had anticipated—its poisonous effects could not help but trickle down into the army itself. When added to the fall of Philadelphia, the imminent expiration of enlistment terms in the army, and the rigors of the Valley Forge winter, it cast a pall over the Cause as 1778 dawned. Both the army and the Cause were sick, and they would need a strong dose of stern medicine if they were to survive the winter and face their opponents in the next campaign with any hope of success.[15]

THE BARON DE STEUBEN knew something of the situation into which he was headed. His hosts in Boston had not been able to hide the fact that there was was something amiss in Pennsylvania that winter. "Our army (if army it might be called) were encamped at Valley Forge," Duponceau noted tersely, "destitute . . . of every thing but courage and patriotism; and what was worse than all, disaffection was spreading through the land."[16]

Steuben knew, too, that he was not guaranteed a warm handshake from Congress or from Washington, for as he suspected, the sentiment in both quarters had turned against foreign officers. Not six months before, the Marquis de Lafayette—already in possession of a major general's commission, signed by Silas Deane—had met with an icy reception in Philadelphia. James Lovell, the sharp-tongued Whig from Massachusetts, had harangued him loudly and in public on the steps of Independence Hall, telling the astonished marquis that his services were not needed.[17]

Things had been going even worse for the foreigners since then. Almost on the very day that Steuben and company had departed Paris,

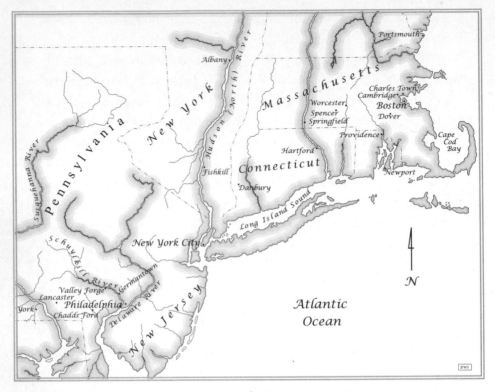

Map of the northeastern United States, 1777

Congress had decreed that all commissions given out by Silas Deane—
"this weak or roguish man," as Lovell called him—be nullified. In
November 1777, Congress recalled Deane from his post. Even more
unsettling was the fact that Deane's most vocal enemies in Congress,
the brothers Richard Henry Lee and Arthur Lee, were on good terms
with the current president, Henry Laurens of South Carolina. Washington was under pressure to stifle foreign intrusion into the officer
corps. When Lafayette and the Baron de Kalb were given general-
ships, it unleashed a storm of protest from envious American-born officers. Washington could not abide that kind of grousing, especially
when he agreed with the general tone of it. Steuben, as a foreigner and
one of Deane's creatures, did not appear to have much of a chance.

First, Steuben would have to get to York. In January 1778, that was easier said than done. With at most an additional servant or two to accompany them, and a guide provided by Hancock, the group—Steuben, Francy, Duponceau, Des Epiniers, Ponthière, Carl Vogel, and Azor—trudged along the roads that took them west through Massachusetts, into western Connecticut and to the Hudson Valley and beyond. They made remarkably good time, given the difficulties of winter travel in eighteenth-century New England and the special precautions they had to take. John Hancock had warned them to be on their guard for Loyalists en route. Tories were thick in the Massachusetts backcountry, and British successes in recent months had emboldened them.

Steuben's group encountered at least one Loyalist. One miserable night in late January they were passing through the village of Spencer, not far west from Worcester, Massachusetts. The snow was piling up fast around them, making further travel impossible, so they sought refuge in the only tavern nearby. Its proprietor, a man named Whittmore, was well known for his Tory sympathies, but they had little choice. The party entered the tavern, stomping the snow from their boots and brushing it off their woolen cloaks in big clumps. The innkeeper gave them a cold greeting. He informed them abruptly that he had neither food nor lodgings to offer them. Duponceau and Francy pleaded with the man as best they could, but to no avail, until Steuben caught wind of what was going on. Although he was not yet conversant in English, he knew enough to grasp the situation, and he instantly flew into a rage. He called out to Vogel: *"Pistolen!"* The manservant disappeared into the night, only to reemerge in moments bearing one of the Baron's gigantic horse pistols, which he had fetched from a pommel holster attached to his saddle. Steuben seized the pistol, drew back the hammer to full cock, and pushed its yawning black muzzle directly into the proprietor's face. He barked a few unintelligible curses, and then asked—still shouting, and in German—if the innkeeper might reconsider; did he or did he not have food, drink, and beds to spare? The innkeeper did not wait for a translation. He recalled that he did indeed have plenty of each, adding that he would be happy to oblige his guests. Steuben and his staff stayed up well into the night eating, drinking, and talking around the hearth, with the innkeeper waiting patiently on the group as if nothing unpleasant had happened.[18]

On they rode, through Springfield and Hartford, and into New York, where they crossed the Hudson by ferry near Fishkill. The trip was an unusual experience for all of the Europeans in the party. Steuben was, to say the least, an accomplished traveler. He had journeyed far and wide in the lands of the Empire, in Russia, and through much of France, and now he was venturing across the northern half of the American landscape, from New Hampshire to Pennsylvania. But this was not like travel in Europe. Places to stop and rest were relatively few and far between, and on many days the group was on the road from sunrise to dusk without encountering a single hamlet in between.

Duponceau found the whole thing fascinating. He jotted down the name of every village they passed through, every tavern that lodged them, every proprietor or proprietress who took them in—and, in the latter case, if the hostess were pretty or not. He was especially taken by the names of the establishments where they stayed: the General Wolfe, the Liberty Tree, the Sign of the White Bowl. The fare was not worthy of comment, except at one inn in New Jersey. "There was neither bread nor milk, nor any beverage except Whiskey," which curiosity impelled him to try.[19]

The Baron pushed on as if he had a pressing deadline to meet, taking only a single day to rest at Fishkill before crossing the Hudson. He allowed himself to relax a bit as they made their way through the towns west of Philadelphia, a region heavily populated with fellow Germans. Duponceau noticed Steuben's mood lighten as they passed tavern after tavern bearing the "Sign of the King of Prussia." The party stopped for a meal at one such inn in the village of Manheim. Nailed to a wall inside the tavern was a "paltry engraving . . . on which was represented a Prussian knocking down a Frenchman in great style," accompanied by the inscription "A Frenchman to a Prussian is no more than a mosquito." Steuben noticed it and "enjoyed it exceedingly"; he grabbed Duponceau and pointed it out excitedly to the teenage secretary, flashing him a sly and knowing smile.[20]

It was at Manheim that Steuben also had his first encounter with a serving member of Congress. Robert Morris, a portly and exceedingly wealthy Philadelphia merchant, came out to greet the Baron, accompanied by Continental postmaster-general Richard Bache. Bache, Ben Franklin's son-in-law, already knew Steuben by reputation. The three men had a cordial meeting over dinner, with both Bache and Morris adding their own written references to the growing pile of testimonials the Baron carried in his portfolio.[21]

Steuben must have felt as if he were walking straight into a lion's den as he and his friends approached York. A face-to-face meeting with Congress was an intimidating prospect. The Baron was by now well aware of the collective skepticism about foreign officers that prevailed at York, and about the rifts caused by the Conway Cabal—all of which made for a delicate situation. A careless word or unthinking gesture on Steuben's part could easily set one faction or another against him, inadvertently making enemies, and destroying his career before it had even begun.

But he was well prepared for his meeting with Congress, whether he knew it or not. Having been coached, he knew what Congress wanted to hear and what they definitely did *not* want to hear. When he wrote to Washington, Henry Laurens, and Congress right after his landfall in Portsmouth, he had said just the right things. He emphasized, modestly, the sacrifices he had made to come to America, and referred obliquely to his military experience in Prussia. He asserted that his highest goal was to use what talents he had "in the service of a Republick"—a key phrase, since he made no overblown statements about his devotion to America, but rather to republican principles, an eminently plausible claim. Most important, he made no demands. "I have made no condition with your Deputies in France, nor shall I make any with you," he informed Congress. With Washington, he was careful to address the officer corps' resentment of foreign officers in such a way as to allay any fears that Steuben would contribute to that resentment: "If the distinguished ranks in which I have Served in Europe should be an Obstacle, I had rather serve under your Excellency as a Volunteer, than to be a subject of Discontent to such deserving Officers as have already distinguished themselves amongst you."[22]

Thus the Baron, with much outside assistance from his American friends, deftly skirted the dark pit into which so many European hopefuls had fallen. He danced just as skillfully around the ongoing Conway controversy. At this point, Conway and Mifflin had already been largely marginalized, but Horatio Gates was not, and as president of the Board of War, he was not a man to be casually shunted aside. Prudently, Steuben made an effort to cultivate Gates. At Sam Adams's urging, he wrote to the general from Boston shortly after Christmas:

> I must express the esteem I have for you, and the eagerness I have to make the personal acquaintance of the man who vanquished Mr. Burgoyne. Your operations in the last campaign (of which Mr. de Malmidy has given me a written account) earn you the admiration of all those who practice the profession of arms, and although I have studied that profession for twenty-two years in a very good school, I will keep [that written account] for myself as a valuable lesson.[23]

It was a very politic gesture, to flatter the notoriously vain Gates. By contacting the general directly, Steuben ensured that he would not be seen as a partisan of Washington before he had his day with Congress.

———

CONGRESS WAS NOT ONLY READY for Steuben but also eagerly anticipating his arrival. His letters from Portsmouth had worked their intended effect. Two days after receiving his letter in mid-January, Congress resolved to present the Baron with the thanks of a grateful nation, and to "cheerfully accept of his service as a volunteer in the army of these states." Since that time, newspapers across the States heralded his progress from Boston, and men who had met the Baron along the way bombarded their friends in Congress with effusive praise for this selfless warrior of great renown. Congress was sold on him before he even set foot in York.

Steuben rode into the capital on February 5 accompanied by Duponceau and Ponthière; Francy and Des Epiniers had since headed off on their own to visit the army at Valley Forge. It was an exceptionally cold day in a winter that was otherwise not remarkable for its severity. The Susquehanna River was already choked with ice. Although the members of the Baron's party were not caked with dust or spattered with mud—the sole advantage, perhaps, of travelling on frozen roads—they had ridden four hundred miles in twenty-two days, a jolting pace, and it showed. They were bedraggled, saddlesore, and very tired, and their new uniforms were showing signs of premature wear and tear.

York was a small and unattractive town, with less than two thousand inhabitants, yet this makeshift capital of the United States was nonetheless a welcome sight for the weary travellers. They would have the chance to relax before Congress expected anything from them. Horatio Gates came out to greet them as soon as they arrived, offering the Baron the use of his personal residence. Steuben graciously declined. There was no sense in attaching himself *too* closely to Gates. Instead, he and his companions took quarters in a house that John Hancock had once used.[24]

Congress was not exactly an intimidating audience. Its move from Philadelphia and the winter weather had thinned its ranks. Less than two dozen delegates convened each day in their meeting place, the second floor of the town's new brick courthouse, and five of them had recently gone to Valley Forge to observe the army. It came as a great shock to Steuben that the domestic affairs of an entire nation and the conduct of a war against one of Europe's great powers would be directed by a mere handful of men. While the Baron took a day to recover from his journey, Congress appointed a four-man committee to meet with him, informally, in his own chambers. That committee—John Henry of Maryland, Thomas McKean of Delaware, Francis Lightfoot Lee of Virginia, and the president of the College of New Jersey (later Princeton), Dr. John Witherspoon—had no particular claim to military expertise, but then, judging Steuben's qualifications was not their purpose. They wanted only to know what motivated this man, what had driven him to America, and what he wanted from them.

Witherspoon, the only ordained clergyman in Congress, conducted the interview, his spoken French tinged by his broad Scots brogue. Steuben answered in French equally colored by his Brandenburg German accent, while the other three men sat in silence, listening intently but waiting for Witherspoon's translation. The Baron put on a performance worthy of a great actor. He asserted that he had never been promised a Continental commission, not by Deane or Franklin or anyone; he did not ask for one now, and in fact he pointedly refused to accept any for the time being. Nor did he "require or desire any command of a particular Corps or Division." His only ambition was to serve Washington as needed "and be subject to his orders." He had learned, "before he left France, of the dissatisfaction of the Americans with the promotion of foreign officers, [and] therefore makes no terms, nor will accept any thing but with [the] general approbation and particularly that of General Washington." Although in coming to America he had been compelled to give up a substantial income and several political posts in the Holy Roman Empire, he would not accept any pay, only the reimbursement of professional expenses he might incur in Continental service.

The last statement was a lie, of course, but it was an attractive lie, one that appealed to a money-conscious Congress while demonstrating that Steuben was not like the other foreigners. He added only one condition: if, once the war was over and independence gained, Congress should determine that he had contributed something of real value to the victory, then he should be reimbursed for his travel to America and be given an annual salary of six hundred gold guineas, paid retroactively from the summer of 1777, with interest. Congress would continue to pay him this same salary from the end of hostilities until his death. Six hundred guineas, coincidentally, was precisely the amount of the annual income he claimed to have given up in Europe.

Witherspoon and his colleagues couldn't have been more delighted. They weren't going to get something for nothing, but here was an offer that was the very definition of accountability. It was easy to promise a salary that wouldn't have to be paid until some time in the remote future. Steuben's demeanor, his spirit of cooperation and sacrifice—or the appearance of such—were the qualities that Congress had hoped to find in a foreign military expert, and except in the case of Lafayette, they had so far been disappointed. The committee reported back to Congress the very same day: Steuben was the genuine article and should be given every encouragement.

The committee was not yet through with Steuben. They met once more, four days later, but only to iron out a few minor matters. This time, Steuben was in control of the meeting and would name his terms. He requested, and received, captain's commissions for Des Epiniers and Ponthière. Duponceau would be given the brevet rank of captain and the appropriate salary. The Baron also asked that two of the disaffected French officers he had befriended in Boston be recalled to serve with him: François Adrien de Romanet, to be appointed as his aide-de-camp with the rank of major, and Pierre Charles L'Enfant, a talented young artist and brilliant engineer. In L'Enfant, he made a fortuitous choice, not only because the French engineer would in due time become an invaluable asset to the Continental Army but also because of his great contribution to the new republic when the war was over: it was L'Enfant who would draw up the first plans for the construction of the national capital on the Potomac at the end of the century.[25]

All the committee required of Steuben in return was that he accept the temporary rank of captain. He tried to refuse, but without success. Without a commission, Witherspoon pointed out, he would be a foreign national without any formal connection to the American army. If, God forbid, he should fall into British hands without the appropriate paperwork, it could prove highly embarrassing to Congress and painful for the Baron. He grudgingly conceded the point, and ironically he was Captain Steuben once again.[26]

Congress was elated with the Baron and with the deal they had struck with him. The delegates hosted a celebratory "entertainment" in his honor, something they had not done for any foreign officer before. He was treated, in the words of Richard Peters, member of the Board of War, "with every mark of distinction . . . [with] more particular attention . . . than I had known given to any foreigner."[27]

And Steuben, for his part, felt that he was well on his way to a brilliant military career. If his stay in Boston had left him feeling unappreciated, the reaction of Congress acted as a tonic on his ailing spirits. In the few days he tarried in York before setting off for Valley Forge, he penned letters full of gratitude to his mentors in Boston, Sam Adams and John Hancock. This time he wrote in his own inelegant words, as translated by Duponceau. "My journey has been extremely painful," he confided to Hancock, "but the kind reception I have met with from Congress and G. Gates at my arrival here have made me Soon forget those past incommodities. Now Sir I am an American and an American for life; your Nation has become as dear to me as your Cause already was."[28]

Acting on behalf of the Board of War, without waiting for congressional approval, General Gates granted the Baron five hundred dollars to help him get to Valley Forge. President Laurens wrote to tell Washington that "this illustrious Stranger" had fully satisfied the Witherspoon committee and all of Congress, and that he "expects to be of use in planning Encampments &c. and promoting the discipline of the Army."[29] Before he had even laid eyes on the army, the Baron de Steuben had earned the trust and support of nearly every political leader at the heart of the rebellion. Now it was up to him to prove to Washington that he could fulfill that promise.

CHAPTER 4

A Man Profound in the Science of War

[FEBRUARY—MARCH 1778]

Your army is the growth of a century, mine of a day.

STEUBEN TO THE BARON DE GAUDY, CA. 1787[1]

THOMAS CONWAY was angry. Bitter and defeated, but mostly just angry.

It was late April 1778, and the fiery Irish-born general had sat down at his desk in his Fishkill headquarters to pour out his frustrations in a letter to his old mentor and ally Horatio Gates. Conway's military career in America was drawing to a premature close, and it all seemed so unfair.

After building up an enviable reputation as a high-ranking officer in the French army, Conway had been ushered along to Congress by Silas Deane. Since then he had commanded a brigade in Washington's army with distinction. At Brandywine, his brigade held steadfast when all around it the rest of the army fell apart, and it proved its worth once again at Germantown. His superior, Maj. Gen. John Sullivan, proclaimed it the best-disciplined brigade in the entire army, bar none, and Conway the most knowledgeable officer. His star was in the ascendant; and now, only six months later, his name was vilified in Congress and at Washington's headquarters. So where, and how, had everything gone so wrong?

True, he had made a few impolitic remarks about General Washington's shortcomings, but then, so many other prominent men were saying the exact same things. Sam Adams, Benjamin Rush, Thomas Mifflin, Horatio Gates—the list of men who found Washington wanting in ability read like a who's who of American military and political leaders. All had pointed out the incontrovertible fact: that the amateur Washington was losing battles while Gates had captured an entire British army intact. Conway's only mistake was in getting caught—that, and losing his temper when Washington confronted him about it. "We know but the *great Frederick* in Europe and the *great Washington* in this continent," he had written Washington, vicious sarcasm practically dripping from his quill. "I certainly was never so rash as to pretend to such a prodigious height."

The very idea that mediocre Washington was his superior, and that there were men who would stifle any attempt to point out his faults, sickened him. Like his friend Charles Lee, he found it inexplicable that Americans "might fancy and call themselves republicans," but "they always have a god of the day, whose infallibility is not to be disputed: to him all the people must bow down and sing Hosannas."[2] At least there were still some men of character in Congress, men who recognized that Conway would be ideal for the task of instilling discipline in the ramshackle Continental Army. The Board of War had gladly given him the newly created position of inspector general, with the rank of major general, over Washington's shrill objections.

But when Conway went to Valley Forge in December to take up his new duties, the vindictive Washington gave him the cold shoulder, ignoring or shooting down all of his proposals for reform. Conway could not do his job, thanks to Washington's implacable hostility and the undisguised contempt of the general's attack dogs, young sycophants like Lafayette and Alexander Hamilton. Conway was shut out. He had no choice but to leave Valley Forge without having accomplished anything. Everything had gone downhill from there. Washington, his lackeys at headquarters, and his self-righteous defenders in

Congress had silenced Conway's friends. Conway had served his adopted country to the best of his ability and yet now found himself, through no fault of his own, a pariah. Worst of all, he had been replaced—not in title, but in function, and that was the greatest insult.

Less than two months after Conway departed Valley Forge, Washington found a replacement for him. This Baron de Steuben—a man whom everyone saluted as "lieutenant general under Frederick of Prussia," though for the life of him Conway could not recall ever having heard of such a man in Europe—had been entrusted with the task of training and organizing Washington's army. This Prussian upstart was doing what Conway was supposed to be doing. And all the while, the gullible Americans were bowing and scraping to him as if he were some omniscient military savior sent from Heaven.

Here was Conway, consigned to a remote village on the Hudson, commanding guard details and watching over supplies like a common clerk, while the unknown Prussian got all the credit for what Conway *would* have been doing if Washington had been more professional. "I am told that Baron Steuben is now in possession of the same place to which I was appointed," Conway complained to Gates.

> I Do not pretend to be superior to Baron Steuben as to Genius or merit but having been peculiarly employ'd in training troops to all field manouvres, having much more practice than he has, speaking the Language, I can venture to say that I would have effected in one Month or six Weeks, what he will not be able to accomplish in six Months.[3]

With that said, Conway asked to be given a better assignment or else be allowed to resign his commission and return to France. Congress accepted his resignation six days later.

———

CONWAY'S GRIEVANCES had a great deal of substance. As he was officially inspector general until his resignation, he *should* have been the man stomping through the snow, cursing Washington's "model company" as he put them through their paces on the parade ground. It should have been him, but it wasn't, and the usurper Steuben would be the man who would enter Revolutionary legend as the "Drillmaster of Valley Forge."

If Steuben's main achievement was teaching drill to disspirited American soldiers, then any European officer could have filled his shoes. Lafayette said as much when he insulted Conway, not so subtly, in January 1778: "[I] do not believe . . . that the departement of maneuvers, administration of [regiments] &c &c is a very difficult thing. Every man who is not stupid and has been six month[s] in a french garrison must be pretty far advanced in that so easy knowledge but certainly no body can deny that kind of merit to Mr de connway in a very high degree." Nor did the Baron ever claim that he alone was capable of doing what he did at Valley Forge. "I willingly allow that the few things I have hitherto shewn, are (tho Essential) so simple that each Major could perhaps have introduced them," he admitted to Henry Laurens. "However, notwithstanding the number of Foreign Officers of Merit here long before my arrival I found the business left for me."[4] Steuben became drillmaster by default; it was a job that he neither wanted nor asked for.

Anybody with a rudimentary military background *could* have taught the Continental infantry how to march and maneuver. But to say that anybody could have accomplished what Steuben did at Valley Forge— and beyond—is to misunderstand the Baron's method and purpose. His success owed in equal parts to his expertise, his ability to understand the men he taught, and the force of his personality. He understood the character of American citizen-soldiers better than most American officers did, and he adjusted his teaching methods accordingly. Through a combination of charm, intimidation, and calculated theatrics, he bent the jaded Continentals to his will while earning their respect and affection. And all this he did in the space of less than three months.

———◦⬦◦———

S TEUBEN, with Duponceau and Ponthière in tow, left for Valley Forge on February 19. Their spirits buoyed by the warm reception at York, they moved fast on fresh horses, covering the ninety miles to camp in five days. Unburdened by the worries he had carried from Boston on his thick shoulders, Steuben was lighthearted, even a little cocky. He was a celebrity now, though he scarcely understood why.

The citizens of Lancaster, one of many German-populated towns on the road to Valley Forge, saluted their countryman Steuben with a grand ball held in his honor. It was the Baron's first carefree evening in a very long time, and he enjoyed it thoroughly, flirting and dancing with the local German women with the energy of a much younger man. William North, a young infantry captain who first set eyes upon his future master at Lancaster that evening, was astonished by the Baron's skill as a dancer, at his "graceful entry and manner in a ball-room."[5]

Compared with this, the welcome that Steuben found in Valley Forge was somewhat less cordial.

When later describing his first encounter with George Washington to Chancellor Frank, Steuben typically embroidered the particulars a bit, probably because the actual meeting was such a letdown. As the Baron recounted it, when he and his party drew close to the encampment on February 24, 1778, Washington and his aides rode out to meet them. The American general made quite a show of hospitality, providing his esteemed guests with an immaculately dressed honor guard on horseback to accompany them into camp.[6]

Washington did indeed ride out to greet Steuben. In reality, though, the commanding general was not very effusive; he did not bow to Steuben as Congress did, he did not treat him as a long-lost brother as Gates had. After a perfunctory exchange of translated pleasantries, the tall Virginian and the stocky German rode side by side along the dirt road that led to the new bridge over the partly frozen Schuylkill and thence into the encampment, their staff members trailing quietly behind them.

Steuben didn't know it, but the general was actually quite pleased to see his new guest, and had been looking forward to this meeting from the day he received the Prussian's gracious letter from Portsmouth, five weeks earlier. He just didn't let it show, and not only because of his customary dignified reserve. The Baron had, inadvertently, chosen a very bad month to come to Valley Forge, in many ways the worst month in Washington's career to date. The commanding general had much on his mind. Washington's primary concern was the health of the army, which had been suffering from want and neglect for several weeks now. Congress had shown little interest in addressing the supply issues that had sapped the army's strength, but in February the heavens themselves seemed to turn against the troops, too. Heavy snow, followed by rain, followed by severe cold and ice—these made transportation all but impossible, impeding the already minimal flow of food, clothing, and firewood into the camp. The lack of horses made the situation even worse; hundreds of horses would die as a result of lack of fodder. The Continentals were fast becoming, in the words of one sympathetic congressional delegate, "the skeleton of an army," half-naked and underfed.[7]

Then there were the political machinations against the commander. With the aid of Henry Laurens, his most powerful ally in Congress, Washington had just recently begun to uncover truly disturbing evidence of the plot to remove him from command. Thomas Conway's enmity was beyond doubt, but now there was written proof that clearly implicated Gates, Mifflin, and Rush. Their complicity was no longer a matter of merely criticizing Washington's leadership. Gates had recently taken up residence in York, as president of the Board of War, where he could work more closely with the true Whigs who favored him. He, Mifflin, and Conway persuaded Congress to dispatch a committee to Valley Forge—the Committee in Camp—to investigate the condition of the army and, it was hoped, to reveal Washington's incompetence and embarrass the general. They had tried to win over the Marquis de Lafayette to their side by offering him command over a harebrained, poorly planned expedition to conquer Canada, something as unlikely to yield positive results now as it had been in 1775. So far, Washington had fought back against his enemies, displaying a degree of political savvy that none of them had anticipated, but at the day of Steuben's arrival the plot had not yet been dissolved.[8]

But the general-in-chief also had good reason to be circumspect regarding Steuben. As familiar as he was with what transpired in York, he must have known that the Baron and Horatio Gates had become quite chummy there. Although Steuben had studiously avoided lodging in Gates's spacious house, Gates had pushed his hospitality upon him anyway: in the thirteen days the foreigners had sojourned in York, Gates had Steuben and his party over for dinner no fewer than six times. Steuben, in fact, had even managed to charm Gates's highly unpopular wife, Elizabeth, an unpleasant woman whom even one of Gates's closest friends characterized as "a Medusa who governs with a rod of scorpions."[9] Gates was still a dangerous enemy, the linchpin of the plot against Washington as well as its nominal head. For all Washington knew, the Baron could well be involved somehow in the plot. Therefore, until the general knew Steuben better, it would not make sense to embrace this newcomer too closely.

———

STEUBEN DID NOT DWELL on the cool reception outside Valley Forge, for soon the camp itself came into view. At this distance it was an invigorating sight for an old soldier who had been away from army life too long. Nearly ten thousand soldiers, plus a good number of women and other noncombatants, bustled about a city of nearly one thousand log huts occupying more than two thousand acres of land. Valley Forge was then the third largest city in America, and one of the best defended. The Schuylkill and the Valley Creek secured its northern and western flanks, and earthen fortifications protected the rest, with much of the army's artillery sited upon a central plateau, ready to sweep all of the approaches if necessary.

Valley Forge may have been hell on earth for the enlisted men and the junior officers, as Steuben would soon discover, but it was not all that unpleasant for the army's generals. Certainly it was much cozier than Steuben had been led to believe. In York, Henry Laurens had warned him that even General Washington "lives himself in a Hut, that is a little temporary Cabin such as are inhabited by the poorest Boors." The Baron was therefore delighted to find that the general actually maintained his headquarters at the modest stone farmhouse of Isaac Potts, near the confluence of the Schuylkill and Valley Creek, at the northwest corner of the encampment. Better yet, Steuben was immediately ushered into warm and comfortable quarters of his own, a house until recently occupied by the Baron de Kalb.[10]

The Baron made himself right at home. He was a soldier again, thank God, surrounded by all the familiar features of a winter cantonment: the sound of shouted commands and ringing axes, the smell of dense smoke, the kind that came from burning green wood, the constant activity of men performing fatigue duties. He knew no one here, apart from the immediate circle of his staff, but his was not the type of personality to be deterred by unfamiliarity, and he was never socially isolated.

As Steuben was preparing to leave York, Henry Laurens had suggested to him that he seek out his son, Lt. Col. John Laurens. Twenty-three-year-old Colonel Laurens, an aide on Washington's staff, had much in common with the older Baron: he was an avid student of the art of war; he embraced the progressive political and social thought of the Enlightenment; and he spoke the Baron's language, and not just in

Henry Laurens. President of the Continental Congress when Steuben first came to the United States in 1777–78. He and the Baron became fast friends, and Laurens was one of Steuben's most vocal supporters, but the two men fell out in a dispute over pay in 1779. *(Library of Congress)*

John Laurens, by Charles Willson Peale, from a miniature after Charles Willson Peale, ca. 1784. The young and idealistic aide-de-camp to Washington befriended Steuben as soon as the Baron reached Valley Forge. *(Independence National Historical Park)*

terms of ideals. "The Baron has learned that you speak French," Henry jokingly informed John, "& that you are not, une Mauvais Garçon."[11]

The president had judged right. John Laurens fell in love with the Baron on sight. So, too, did Laurens's best friend and fellow aide, Lt. Col. Alexander Hamilton. And the Prussian was equally smitten with them. Here were two impressionable young men who understood his speech and who hung on his every word as he regaled them with tales of bloody battles decided by massive cavalry charges and the point of the bayonet, of warrior-kings and glittering courts. He could converse with them on topics ranging from infantry tactics to the works of Seneca, Cervantes, and Voltaire. He represented a touch of Enlightenment sophistication—something for which the young Laurens and Hamilton were starved—in the rough-hewn society of the camp, and they in turn helped him forget his homesickness. Steuben could relax in their presence. He regarded the two aides as his intellectual and social equals, and felt completely at home joking informally with them and being on the receiving end of their good-natured barbs. The bonds forged between Steuben, Laurens, and Hamilton would last to the end of their days—though for Laurens, sadly, that day was not far off.

Their friendship had practical advantages, too. Washington trusted Laurens and Hamilton implicitly; their advocacy on Steuben's behalf helped to speed the general's acceptance of the Prussian. And through his father, Laurens served as the Baron's foremost ally in Congress. The elder Laurens had already been impressed by "this illustrious Stranger" while dining with him at York; now he received regular reports about

Alexander Hamilton, by Charles Willson Peale, from life, c. 1790–1795. Another aide to Washington, and John Laurens's best friend, Hamilton never swerved in his loyalty to Steuben, and after the war he led the fight to secure adequate compensation for the Baron's services. *(Independence National Historical Park)*

Pierre Étienne Duponceau. This portrait shows Duponceau at around the age of seventy, when he had already established himself as a successful Philadelphia lawyer and a distinguished scholar of linguistics. But at age seventeen, he was Steuben's translator and personal secretary. *(The American Philosophical Society, Philadelphia)*

Steuben's progress at Valley Forge, reports that overflowed with praise and wide-eyed admiration. "I have since had several long Conversations with the Baron Stuben," young Laurens wrote his father shortly after the Baron's arrival. "[He] appears to me a man profound in the Science of War and well disposed to render his best services to the United States."[12]

Only a couple of days passed before General Washington took advantage of those services. He had been studying Steuben intently, and not from a distance, for Steuben was a guest at his dinner table no fewer than ten times in his first fourteen evenings in camp.[13] To get a sense of what Steuben could do, Washington gave the Baron unlimited access to the camp, allowing him to poke and prod and give his professional opinion on the operations of the army. Steuben leaped into the role with gusto. Over the next couple of weeks, he spent hours each day riding through camp, observing the men at drill and at work, taking note of problems and drafting solutions. As he took stock of the army, he showered the commanding general with memoranda on a wide variety of topics: how to build an effective corps of light infantry, how to maneuver large bodies of troops more efficiently than the Continentals could, how to improve security in the camp, and how to fine-tune the camp's fortifications.

His counsel was invariably blunt. After making an inspection tour of the camp's defenses, the Baron presented Washington with a dour assessment: there were tremendous gaps in the outer entrenchments; many of the redoubts were unfinished or poorly situated; General Sullivan's bridge over the Schuylkill was indefensible. Washington was not the least offended by the criticism. He craved this kind of straightforward advice, and his meetings with Steuben over dinner grew into regular professional consultations on the health of the army.[14]

Still, Washington kept his thoughts to himself. To Henry Laurens he remarked only that the Baron "appears to be much of a Gentleman, and as far as I have had an opportunity of judging, a man of military knowledge and acquainted with the World." Washington's coolness fretted the Congress's president. "I am anxious to know whether [Steuben] will find amusement & employment in your Camp & whether he is likely to be a valuable addition to the Main Army," he wrote in concern to his son in early March. "It is remarkable that your General has kept such a profound silence on the Officer's name although I have had occasion to announce it to His Excellency in three several letters."[15]

Laurens needn't have worried. Washington's reserve did not signal a lack of interest in the Baron. The problem was finding a suitable channel for Steuben's abilities. There were so many deficiencies in the Continental Army that cried out for redress, all of which could use the trained eye of a professional soldier. The most pressing crises lay within the departments of the quartermaster general and commissary general, that part of the army administration charged with the procurement and distribution of supplies. The quartermaster general's department was rife with mismanagement and blatant corruption, largely the fault of Washington's nemesis Thomas Mifflin. A small, overworked staff, coupled with intolerable working conditions and little political support—both the fault of the Whig ideologues in Congress—had hobbled the Commissary. These twin failings lay behind nearly all of the army's miseries at Valley Forge.

James Lovell, Sam Adams's whiggish friend from Massachusetts, thought Steuben the perfect choice to serve as quartermaster general. Lovell's motivation was undoubtedly political; like his allies in Congress, he vehemently opposed both of the men whom Washington had nominated to replace the incompetent Mifflin—Philip Schuyler and Nathanael Greene, both just too close to Washington. Steuben was popular in Congress, however, and perhaps the Whigs thought they could control him. And hadn't Steuben served as a quartermaster in the Prussian army, the very model of efficiency? Indeed he had, but of course the duties were not the same, and Lovell—like most Americans—was unaware of the difference. Yet there were legitimate objections to Lovell's proposal, upon which both pro- and anti-Washington partisans could agree. Since a quartermaster's duties were as much civil as military, purchasing supplies and finding contractors, an uninitiated foreigner like Steuben would be hard pressed to comprehend the difficulties of working with American civilians. Moreover, as the Baron was still a "stranger," it would not be fitting to trust him with funds and accounts worth tens of thousands of dollars.

Washington was inclined to agree, and he had his heart set on Greene anyway. So, too, did his aides, for although they worshipped the Baron, they did not think that this would be the best use for his abilities. "[He] seems perfectly aware of the disadvantages under which our army has laboured from short inlistments and frequent changes," John Laurens wrote to his father at the end of February. So why not, John Laurens asked, make him inspector general?[16]

The inspector general was the most vital staff officer in an eighteenth-century army. He wore many hats. First, it was the inspector's duty to keep the army properly trained and well drilled. Second, an inspector was supposed to ensure that his army maintained its discipline on the march and in camp: encampments had to be laid out in a certain regulated way, for the sake of efficiency and cleanliness; guard details had to be posted according to a strict regimen. Third, the inspector acted as the enforcing arm of the supply officers. Someone had to make sure that the men were adequately clothed and fed, and that they kept up a soldierly appearance. An attentive inspector would spot deficiencies promptly so that the quartermaster could issue replacements as needed. Finally, he acted as a kind of truant officer, keeping an accurate record of regimental strengths and holding commanders accountable for the whereabouts of their men.

Ever since the battles for Philadelphia in the autumn of 1777, the need for such an officer was widely acknowledged. Complaints about irregularities in the army's conduct and about the unnecessary wastage of valuable military supplies came to Washington's desk in a veritable flood. The officers who had foreign military experience, being most attuned to the importance of following proper and standardized procedure, pointed out the army's failings incessantly. The Continentals lacked the necessary discipline on the drill field, in camp, and therefore also in battle. Officers and men were too familiar with one another, breeding insubordination. "I must confess to you, Sir, it is painfull to me, to see the Commander in chief['s] orders Slighted or ill-obeyed in many essential parts," the Baron de Kalb noted.[17]

Supply presented the thorniest problems. Continental property was not accounted for. "The spoil and waste of tents, arms, ammunition, accoutrements and camp equipage" was ruinous.[18] Men whose enlistments had expired frequently took their muskets and equipment—all of it government property—home with them, while new recruits rarely had sufficient stocks of the same items.

And this was only the tip of the iceberg. The entire army was in an organizational shambles. It was to be expected that regiments were not even close to full strength; what was truly frustrating, though, was the fact that the sizes of individual regiments were so inconsistent. When an entire brigade was no bigger than a single regiment in another brigade, when one regiment consisted of five or six companies while another contained more than a dozen, it was almost impossible for the high command to estimate the strength of the army as a whole, let alone make intelligent plans for the coming campaign. Company and regimental officers were often completely ignorant of the whereabouts of their men.

Within Congress there existed a "mania for reform," but nothing was actually done until November 1777, when the Board of War appointed Thomas Conway as the army's first inspector general. That appointment was actually a political move, an attempt to discredit Washington—and as it turned out, a futile gesture. Washington was predisposed to disregard anything Conway had to suggest.

Steuben filled a critical need at a critical time. His poor command of the language might be a temporary hindrance, but he had the requisite knowledge and experience. And he had another vital quality: a practical appreciation of the American character, remarkable for a man who had been in the country for so brief a time. "He seems to understand what our Soldiers are capable of," John Laurens observed approvingly. He knew, in other words, that Americans were not Europeans. They were citizens, not subjects; if he were to achieve anything with them, he would have to take a different approach than he would if dealing with Prussian serfs. "[He] is not so starch a Systematist as to be averse from adapting established forms to stubborn Circumstances. He will not give us the perfect instructions absolutely speaking, but the best which we are in condition to receive."[19]

With or without Steuben, the army had to be reorganized *now*. Within a few short weeks the snows would thaw, the roads would dry, and the spring campaign would be upon them. "We want some kind of general Tutoring in this way so much," John Laurens told his father, "that as obnoxious as Conway is to most of the Army, rather than take the Field without the advantages that might be derived from a judicious exercise of his office, I would wish every motive of dissatisfaction respecting him for the present to be suppressed."[20] The aide had hit upon the single obstacle to putting the Baron in charge: there already was an inspector general.

Yet over the next few weeks, the Baron made such a name for himself that all reservations about substituting him for the volatile Conway quickly evaporated. His broad grasp of military affairs could have made him appear intimidating, a condescending know-it-all, if he had had a different temperament; but when combined with his openhearted friendliness, his literary wit, and his simple desire just to be liked, his knowledge was well received by nearly everyone he met. He won over the army command just as he had the factionalized Congress. "The Baron Stüben has had the fortune to please uncommonly for a Stranger, at first Sight," John Laurens wrote, proud of his new friend and mentor. "All the Gen¹ Officers who have seen him are prepossessed in his favor and conceive highly of his Abilities."[21]

The congressional Committee in Camp also sought him out for his advice. Their leader, Francis Dana, consulted with Steuben on Washington's proposal to enlist Native Americans as an organized corps of light infantry, and at his request, the Baron gave Dana a detailed lesson on the use of "irregular" forces in European warfare—something Steuben knew a great deal about firsthand. Dana was enthralled by the Baron's analysis of the Austrian Grenzer, light infantry recruited in the border regions of Croatia, whom Steuben described as "a kind of White Indian."[22]

But Steuben was not content with merely being accepted by his new comrades. He had to immerse himself in the social scene at camp, too, which was surprisingly vibrant. Officers of all grades made the best of their unpleasant circumstances, hosting dinner parties and "carousals" in the evenings, and the presence of so many generals' wives in the camp lent the whole an air of almost surreal gaiety amid the army's sufferings.

The Baron fit right in. Like most of the European-born officers, he became a regular guest at the table of Caty Greene, the vivacious spouse of Maj. Gen. Nathanael Greene. Mrs. Greene, an incurable flirt who was fluent in French, took an immediate shine to Steuben. So, too, did Martha Washington and Kitty Alexander, the daughter of Maj. Gen. William Alexander, Lord Stirling. Men and women alike tended to find Steuben charming, but women in particular found his manner especially endearing. Several years later, when visiting with the prominent Livingston family of New York, the Baron was introduced to a young lady friend of the Livingstons. "I am very happy," Steuben purred, "in the honor of being presented to you, Mademoiselle, though I see it is at an infinite risk. I have, from my youth, been cautioned to guard myself against mischief, but I had no idea that her attractions were so powerful."[23]

In their first month at Valley Forge, the Baron and Duponceau attended a dinner engagement or party almost every night. Only rarely did Steuben stay in his quarters for an evening "at home" with his staff. When he did, it was not often a quiet evening. The Baron delighted in throwing his own parties for his American hosts. By pooling his rations with those of his staff and trading the surplus for little luxuries, he could present a relatively well-stocked table for his officer guests. He was anxious to make sure that junior officers were welcome, too. "Poor fellows," he once remarked, "they have field officers' stomachs, without their pay or rations."[24]

At the request of his aides, the Baron hosted a party exclusively for their lower-ranking friends. He insisted, though, that "none should be admitted that had on a whole pair of breeches," making light of the shortages that affected the junior officers as they did the enlisted men. His *Sansculottes*, he called them, "those without breeches"—the same name that would later be applied to radical republicans in the French Revolution—and never was there "such a set of ragged, and at the same time merry fellows" at Valley Forge. Duponceau led the group in singing a few raucous American songs he had learned, while the captains and lieutenants—including Lord Stirling's aide-de-camp, the future President James Monroe—indulged in the feast put together by Carl Vogel: "tough beefsteak and potatoes, with hickory nuts for our dessert." Over this rough fare, and several rounds of a flaming high-proof concoction dubbed "Salamanders," the Baron quickly earned a reputation as a bacchanalian lord of mirth. It was not the kind of behavior that the Continentals expected out of a Prussian nobleman, and they liked it. Only a couple of weeks into his stay, Steuben had already made himself a legend.[25]

THE BARON SENSED that he was accepted, that although he may not have made himself indispensable yet, he was seen as having the potential for it. For, less than a week after he rode into Valley Forge for the first time, he intentionally let it slip that he was not precisely the man everyone thought he was.

Thus far, he had told every American leader he met that he had no interest in rank or pay, and had made a great show of refusing even the humble rank of captain. He said the very same thing to Washington in their first interview. But by the end of February, he said something much different to John Laurens, with no attempt at secrecy: "The Baron proposes to take the rank of Major General with the pay, rations, &c." This was no trifling ambition. "Major general" was the highest rank the Continental Army had to give; only Washington ranked higher. Such an appointment would put Steuben, who had been at Valley Forge for a matter of days, and in the United States for less than three months, on the same level as leaders who had been with the army from the very beginning of the war. He did not ask for a field command—not *yet*—"as he is not acquainted with our lang[uage] and the genious of the people," but that very sentiment implied that he intended to command troops in the field once he had established himself.[26]

He didn't stop there, but continued to compromise the packaging that had been so carefully designed for him by his backers in Paris. On March 9, he revealed—again to John Laurens—that he had never been a "lieutenant-general in Prussian service." In Prussia, he said, he had never risen above the rank of colonel. It was another lie, just one of lesser magnitude. His generalship came not from Prussia but from Baden—another lie. Three days later, maybe forgetting the details of his latest untruth, he informed Henry Laurens that his commission came instead from the ineffectual army of the Holy Roman Empire, the *Reichsarmee*. There he had been a general commanding the "Circle of Swabia," one of the ten administrative districts into which the Empire was divided.* This, too, was an unvarnished fabrication.[27]

Steuben was far too crafty to let something slip in an unguarded moment. His declarations were no accident—he *wanted* Washington and Congress to know. It was a form of professional damage control. A lieutenant general under Frederick the Great would have been a very high profile commander. Americans might be too parochial to know the names of Frederick's chief generals, but not so the many foreign officers—Prussians as well as French—who served in the Continental

---

* This claim, like Steuben's claim to baronial status, has sometimes been misinterpreted. For centuries, the Empire was divided into ten Circles (*Reichskreise*), each of which contained several—sometimes dozens of—German territorial states. In addition to adjudicating local disputes among the member princes, the Circles provided contingents of troops for the (usually ineffectual) Imperial Army (*Reichsarmee*) when called upon by the Emperor to do so. The Swabian Circle (*der schwäbische Kreis*) was one of the more active districts in this regard. All Circles had a military commander (*Kreisoberst*, or "Circle Colonel"), but the Swabian Circle also frequently designated a Circle General or Circle Field Marshal (*Kreisgeneral* or *Kreisfeldmarschall*). This, however, was a very high profile position, being held at one time by one of the most celebrated soldiers of the early eighteenth century, Margrave Ludwig Wilhelm of Baden, better known as *Türkenlouis*. By claiming that he had been general in the Circle, Steuben was making a potentially big mistake: any of the more experienced Europeans in the Continental Army, such as Conway, the Baron de Kalb, or the Baron d'Arendt, would surely have heard of Steuben had he held such a post.

Army. It was only a matter of time before Steuben's fictitious past would be discovered and denounced. By tweaking the details of his story, Steuben instantly gave himself a lower profile . . . and a past that would be much harder to debunk than the one that Deane, Franklin, and Beaumarchais had invented for him. By "outing" himself, chalking up his "error" to misunderstanding or miscommunication, he avoided the scandal that might have ensued had he been uncloaked by a hostile rival—like Thomas Conway.

Regardless of the details, either General Washington or President Laurens could have ejected Steuben then and there. The Baron had admitted, baldly and without apology, that he had been dishonest with both men and with Congress. He *did* desire rank and pay after all, and his credentials had been falsified. Yet neither Washington nor Laurens so much as batted an eye over the revelation—for they had already decided that Steuben's worth more than made up for his self-serving dishonesty.

<hr />

DURING HIS FIRST THREE WEEKS at Valley Forge, Steuben was everywhere. He poked his aquiline nose into the leaky, mud-chinked log huts that served as barracks, talking briefly with individual soldiers, asking about their health, their rations, their officers, and all the minutiae of life in camp.

Staff officers rarely concerned themselves with such matters; almost never did they deign to listen to the men in the ranks. But the Baron did—to him, raised in the Prussian service, this was what good officers were supposed to do—and the men took notice of his genuine interest in their welfare. What really caught their attention, what brought them out of the near stupor into which hunger, boredom, and despair had driven them, was the Prussian's appearance. They emerged from their huts to watch him pass, usually on horseback and always dressed in his dark blue regimental coat and cloak, carefully bedecked with the Star of Fidelity, a barrel-chested man riding tall in his saddle. He did have a sword, but more often he carried a straight, silver-headed swagger stick—called an *Exerzierstock* in German—which was all the fashion among Prussian officers. Azor would follow him, as would Duponceau and sometimes John Laurens or Alex Hamilton, translating Steuben's blunt but kindly interrogations into English.

In a different century, he might have appeared comically pompous, but here he inspired dumbstruck wonder. "Never before, or since, have I had such an impression of the ancient fabled God of War as when I looked on the baron," wrote Ashbel Green, a sixteen-year-old private who would later serve as president of the College of New Jersey and chaplain to Congress. "He seemed to me a perfect personification of Mars. The trappings of his horse, the enormous holsters of his pistols, his large size, and his strikingly martial aspect, all seemed to favor the idea."[28]

And Steuben found the men fascinating, too. He loved the attention he got from them. Most of all, he admired the resilience of the ordinary Continental soldiers. They lived in unbearable conditions and were terribly disorganized, nearly bereft of food or clothing, sometimes all but forgotten by absentee officers. Few had serviceable blankets, many were without shoes or breeches, with little more than a linen hunting frock and underdrawers to stand between their nakedness and the elements. Their rations looked bad enough on paper, but despite the Herculean efforts of the commissaries, they rarely lived up to the prescribed minimal standard. The men frequently went for days at a time without the smallest piece of salt meat or dried fish, subsisting mostly on "fire-cakes" made from flour and water. It was not an unusual sight to see groups of men boiling shoes and leather accoutrements in order to make them digestible.

The men huddled for warmth around their scattered campfires, listless eyes sunk deep in gaunt faces, staring up at Steuben as he passed by. They did not often have the energy or inclination to show him the deference to which he was accustomed, but this did not offend him. These soldiers seemed to have been abandoned by their country, and although their numbers had dwindled alarmingly, the fact that there were any men at all astounded him. As he later told one of his aides, "no European army could have been kept together under such dreadful deprivations."[29]

STEUBEN HAD ALREADY FORMED a fairly accurate impression of the army, its organizational and procedural flaws and the nature of its men, when Washington gave him his first solid assignment: the Baron was to take over the training of the army.

Perhaps Lafayette was correct, that drill could be taught by any officer, but that still trivializes the task that lay ahead of the Baron de Steuben in early March 1778. He would not have to train a single regiment but, rather, scores of them simultaneously. If new recruits rendezvoused with the army in the springtime, as everyone hoped they would, then they would have to be fed into the training regimen while the process of retraining the old hands was still going on. Steuben would have to do this without the authority of a legitimate rank, and without even a decent command of the English language. And he would have no more than three months in which to accomplish this minor miracle.

A European army to fight a European war, but in America—that was what Washington wanted. Though most of the army's leaders agreed with him, there were naysayers, too, men who thought that the best chance for winning independence was to fight a "war of posts," a guerrilla war. American soldiers, as free men unaccustomed to deference, would never be fully capable of emulating their European counterparts. They were better suited to fighting an irregular war of raids and ambushes, avoiding outright confrontations with superior forces. They would never allow themselves to be led dumbly to the slaughter, like the poor Redcoats at Bunker Hill in 1775. Instead, by fighting a war of posts, eventually the Continentals would convince the British crown that crushing the revolt was not worth the investment in blood and treasure. And it would be infinitely less expensive for the Americans to rely on improvised militia levies than on a standing army. One did not need an army of automatons to fight King George's slaves.

But there was much to recommend Washington's more conventional approach. A successful war of posts required patience and stamina, qualities that the Americans generally had not exhibited. The British, moreover, were no strangers to irregular warfare. In the French and Indian War, and against the Jacobite rebels in the Scottish Highlands, they had learned a great deal about counterinsurgency tactics. If the Americans were to defeat the British, if they wanted to earn the respect of the great powers of Europe, they would have to fight the war in both ways—as a war of posts and as a conventional war.

This meant that the Continental Army would have to learn the intricacies of linear warfare, and learn them well. And this, in turn, entailed drill and lots of it. Drill was an essential ingredient in linear warfare. To the casual observer, drill may not appear to be anything more than a series of stylized movements performed in unison by a group of soldiers, a practice that has about as much a place on the modern battlefield as horses and flintlock muskets. Yet even today, drill exercises remain an important component of basic military training—and in part for the same reasons that made it so fundamental in eighteenth-century warfare. Drill instills discipline. Constant practice of repetitive motions and movements turn men into unthinking cogs in a larger military machine. It breaks down individuality, replacing the inclination to think with the instinct to obey.

In Steuben's day, this kind of discipline was vital because there was no room in linear tactics for soldiers who thought for themselves, at least not in the line infantry. Thought was a tactical liability, for thought and emotion could induce panic in stressful situations. Once an individual soldier perceived that he was in great peril—that a hostile battalion was marching toward him, bayonets levelled at chest height, or was about to fire a volley in his direction—he would likely seek cover or, even worse, flee. If he had a loaded musket in his hand, he might be tempted to fire it, even without being ordered to do so.

Such instincts had to be suppressed, for they were dangerous. Once panic set in, it would become infectious, and under fire, a company, a regiment, or even a larger unit would easily succumb to a herd mentality that could push reason and physical courage to the side. Once a single soldier fired off his musket without being ordered to, then "fire discipline" was compromised: the entire unit was likely to join in, and the effect of restrained volley fire at close range was lost. Once a single soldier decided that he should seek safety in flight, then others would flee, too. Even if his comrades did not decide to turn and run, their cohesion could be shattered. When an entire regiment or brigade lost the will to stand fast and fight, it became easy pickings for a determined assault, especially a headlong rush of enemy cavalry with sabres drawn.

Visceral reactions to the stresses of combat were difficult enough to suppress when casualties were light. The noise and smoke of the battlefield were sufficient to panic raw troops. But when men began to fall, when the screams of the wounded and the dying filled the air, then all bets were off. Soft lead musket balls, travelling at subsonic speeds, could cause ghastly wounds, especially at the short ranges characteristic of eighteenth-century battles. Artillery casualties were worse yet; the damage caused by solid shot—ordinary cast-iron cannonballs—to flesh and bone, even at long range, was unspeakable. A man who witnessed a comrade or filemate mangled by solid shot or torn to pieces by grapeshot or canister, or who saw the entire rank in front of him practically melt into the ground after a point-blank volley of musketry, would have to be very tough indeed not to run away in sheer terror.[30]

Drill did not inoculate soldiers against the horrors of the battlefield. But it helped. Troops who had been exercised on the parade ground, day in and day out, for months at a time, were more likely to respond to their officers' commands in the heat of battle without thinking about the awful carnage all around them.

What made drill especially important for armies of the period was the intricacy of linear tactics, and two elements in particular: firepower and movement. Soldiers trained to load and fire at the same rapid rate would be much more efficient than those who were not trained as a group. They would also be more likely to fire by volley when required to do so, and could better restrain themselves from the instinct to shoot until given the command by their officers.

Discipline of movement was even more essential than fire discipline. The mere act of forming an army in line-of-battle involved a complex series of motions: first it would have to be moved to the desired deployment point in a marching column; then the individual subunits, the battalions or regiments, would have to be deployed in long lines, two or three ranks deep, facing the enemy; and finally those subunits would have to be placed alongside each other, flank meeting flank, to form a full line of battle. The process could take hours to perform. In a large but untrained force, it could well prove impossible. And that was only for initial deployment. If it became necessary to change the disposition of forces in the midst of battle to meet unanticipated threats—for example, to shift or turn a flank in order to meet an enveloping movement by the enemy—then drill made all the difference between victory and defeat. Only an army in which the men did precisely as they were told without hesitation could execute such actions.

The Continental Army in 1778 was not unfamiliar with drill. It had, in fact, experienced quite a great deal of it. The problem was that there was no uniform "system," no standard to which all the army could be held. The absence of uniformity was a curse that pervaded almost every aspect of life in the Continental Army. Choice of a drill manual was left to the regimental commanders themselves. Without an accepted standard, colonels used whatever resources they had at hand. Frequently they relied on the current British military manual, the *Regulations* of 1764; others turned to drill manuals published in the colonies before the war for the use of local militia outfits. "Each Colo[nel] Exercised his Reg[imen]t according to his own Ideas, or those of any Military Author that might have fallen into his hands," Steuben complained.[31] The differences were enough to cause some confusion when units operated together in larger formations.

Nor was drill evenly practiced or enforced. Some commanders were sticklers for drill—Anthony Wayne, for example; others were all but indifferent. Commissioned officers rarely participated in the training of their men, but—following British practice—left that task to their sergeants, something Steuben found unconscionable. With so little direction from above, very few soldiers in the army had experienced drill in larger formations. Regimental drill was unusual, and drill in entire brigades or divisions all but unknown in the Continental Army.

Such was the army—if army it could be called—that was thrust upon the Baron de Steuben for training in mid-March 1778. The Baron had not drilled so much as a single company in nearly twenty years. Then he had had the advantages of time, support, an established procedure, youth . . . and insignificance. As a mere line officer, one among many hundreds, he had to worry only about pleasing his regimental commander. But this was an entire army. Much hinged on his performance, and all eyes were on him.

CHAPTER 5

On the Parade-Ground
at Valley Forge

[MARCH—APRIL 1778]

[Steuben] is now Teaching the Most Simple Parts of
the Exercise such as Positition and Marching of a
Soldier in a Manner Quite different from that, they
Have been heretofore used to, In my Oppinion More
agreable to the Dictates of Reason & Common Sence
than any Mode I have before seen.

HENRY BEEKMAN LIVINGSTON TO ROBERT R. LIVINGSTON,
MARCH 25, 1778[1]

ON THURSDAY, March 19, the Baron de Steuben resumed the military career he had left behind some
fifteen years before.

It was mid-morning, and he had already been awake for
hours. He had been at his desk, working by candlelight long
after sunset, and had roused himself again at 3:00 A.M. after
very little sleep. The early start on the day afforded him the
chance to put himself together. He was very particular about
his appearance, and this was an especially important day. After
his manservant Vogel dressed and powdered his long graying
hair, braiding it into a tight queue as he had worn while a young
lieutenant at Breslau, he still had time to put on his uniform
and fuss over the details. He lit his pipe, tried to enjoy a cup of

coffee—a precious luxury in the camp, but one the Baron found very difficult to live without—and reviewed the notes he had written the night before. Donning his heavy woolen cloak, he went out into the cold gray light of the winter morning, saddled and mounted his horse, and rode northeast to meet the men waiting for him on the Grand Parade.

The men, hardened veterans of Washington's previous campaigns, were drawn up in line of battle, two ranks deep, on the frozen, packed earth of the Parade. They craned their necks to catch a glimpse of the portly German as his horse cantered toward them. Many of them had seen him as he made his rounds of the camp, not entirely sure as to who he was or what he wanted from them. Perhaps now they would find out.

The Baron, for his part, was apprehensive—and with good reason. Today he could not rely on wit and charm. It was not that he was unprepared. He had been readying himself for the better part of a week—no, that was not quite right; he had been awaiting this moment for most of his adult life. He was an introspective man; he knew that a great deal rode on today's events, that his new life in the New World, his chance to resurrect his failed career, would begin as soon as he set foot on the Grand Parade.

Precisely one week ago, General Washington had informed Steuben that he would be acting as inspector general, but in an unofficial capacity. Congress could not give him the rank he desired, nor could Washington nominate him for it. The commander in chief still would not risk alienating his American-born generals. He could not afford to be the author of more rancor, not when the wounds opened by the plot against him were yet raw. And although humbled, Thomas Conway remained an obstacle, for he was still inspector general by congressional decree. There was no way that Steuben, with or without Washington's blessing, could usurp that position without bruising a few egos in the process. There was nothing, however, to prevent Washington from using Steuben as an outside consultant of sorts.

Steuben had already been acting in this capacity for several weeks, but so far he had only been offering advice. Now he would be expected to put his ideas into action. The army needed *so* much repair, more than one man could possibly do in such a short period of time. The Baron focused on the army's organizational flaws: the uneven sizes of the regiments and brigades, the almost criminal neglect of guard duty, problems that not only made the proper administration of the army a nightmare but that actually impeded its performance in the field and compromised its safety in camp. Solving the first problem would be a simple matter of reorganizing and consolidating the army's regiments so that every one of them maintained an equal and reasonable size, but the regimental commanders would have none of it. "Everyone of them would command his own Reg[imen]t, tho' he could have no more than 40 men under Arms," Steuben complained.[2] What he could do, and what Washington wanted him to do, was to attend to the "discipline" of the troops, retraining them in accordance with a "universal system."

Although woefully understrength—its numbers pared back drastically by desertion and disease—the army at Valley Forge was large enough that training the entire force by late spring would be well nigh impossible for the Baron and his small band of assistants. So he suggested an eminently practical shortcut: he would train a single company of handpicked veterans, who would learn the basics of drill and maneuver directly under his tutelage. Once he felt satisfied with their progress, he would turn them loose on the rest of the army, sending them back to their respective brigades, where they would function as drill instructors. Steuben would teach teachers.

It was not a novel concept. Conway had suggested the same thing several months before. But the general-in-chief had not been inclined to accept anything Conway had to offer. The idea meant much more coming from Steuben. On March 17, Washington ordered the formation of a "model company," one hundred strong, to be drawn from each brigade in the army. They were to be assigned temporarily to Washington's headquarters guard of fifty Virginians, and were to assemble on the Grand Parade at guard mount on Thursday morning, there to await the Baron's instructions.[3]

Together, on the Grand Parade, the model company and the Baron would attempt to settle a question that had vexed the Cause since the beginning of the war three years before: Was it possible to turn a collection of farmers, landless laborers, tradesmen, and Irish and German immigrants into an *army*, one capable of taking on the Redcoats? Britain did not have the greatest or most modern army in Europe, but it was still infinitely better, man for man and battalion for battalion, than anything the Americans had been able to put in the field. Could the Americans effect the transformation, and in time?

Steuben and his pupils were going to try.

His assistants trailing behind him, the Baron drew up in front of the assembled company, halted, and proceeded to dismount. Those watching could not help but notice a curious juxtaposition. The immaculately dressed, well-fed, and bejewelled German nobleman looked very much as one would expect of a Prussian soldier: his hat of fine black beaver, a bicorn blocked in the French style, sitting atop queued and powdered hair; dark blue cloak; knee-high riding boots wrapped impossibly tight around his calves. Standing before the company—a little soft, perhaps, in the midriff, but still at attention without being rigid, his *Exerzierstock* gripped in his right hand—he appeared to be the very embodiment of Old World society, of aristocracy and privilege, the very same values the men were fighting against. He beamed confidence and optimism. And opposite him, the men, representing nearly every state in the union, dressed in a kaleidoscopic array of tattered clothing, hats and coats of every description, with some wearing blankets in lieu of overcoats. They were gaunt, maybe even a bit jaded, and had the look of men who had traveled far and seen much—heartbreak and hardship both.

Steuben did not take much time to reflect on the sight. With Ponthière and the newest member of his staff, Jean-Baptiste Ternant, standing deferentially behind him, the stumpy Prussian with the stern manner and kindly face pulled out the sheaf of notes he had scrawled the night before and went straight to work. Duponceau, Hamilton, and Laurens were close at hand to aid in translation.

The Baron started, appropriately enough, at the beginning, treating the model company as if it consisted of raw recruits—not from condescension, but from necessity, as the men had been trained in so many different ways. "The only part which retained a shadow of Uniformity," Steuben observed with some annoyance, "was the least Essential of all, the Manual Exercise, as it was nearly an Imitation of that Established in the English Army." First things first—how to march. "The most Essential part which is the March & Manœuvring step," the Baron reported, "was as varied as the Colour of our Uniforms."[4] That would have to change, and fast. It mattered little if the men could handle their muskets in unison—that was what Steuben meant by the term "Manual Exercise," the manual of arms—if they could not even keep step with one another.

On Steuben's order, the oversize company stacked their muskets and re-formed, unarmed and in a single rank. At one hundred and

Von Steuben Instructing Troops at Valley Forge, by Edwin Austin Abbey (1852–1911). Abbey's imagining of the Baron drilling the "model company" in March 1778 is probably not too far off the mark, although Steuben spent most of his time with the model company teaching marching and maneuvers, and very little on the use of the musket (the "Manual Exercise"). *(Brian Hunt & Pennsylvania Capitol Preservation Committee)*

fifty men, it was too large a body to be taught anything as a group, so the Baron first selected a twenty-man squad. He gave his instructions verbally to the squad as the rest of the men looked on, reading laboriously from the notes he had written with the help of his aides. First he explained the "Position of the Soldier," the eighteenth-century version of "Attention": the soldier was to stand straight, feet slightly apart and spread at the toes, forming a loose *V;* his shoulders back, chest forward; with his head cocked slightly to the right so the left eye formed a straight line with the buttons of the waistcoat—for those soldiers fortunate enough to possess such a garment.

Then he demonstrated that stance himself so that each man could see him clearly and imitate him exactly. He walked down the line from flank to flank, checking each man's position, not hesitating to point out deficiencies, his big hands roughly pushing men into the correct posture as if he were arranging scenery on a stage. His ministrations were gruff and never tender, but even when playing the role of drill sergeant he could not hide his essential affability. He complimented those who got it right; he joked and swore, effortlessly, at those who did not. The men found it difficult to suppress the occasional chuckle. Steuben did not discourage them from finding humor in the lesson, and sometimes laughed with them.

Next he taught the men how to dress their ranks, to turn their heads and cast their eyes to the left or right, each soldier aligning himself on his neighbor so that the ranks became perfectly straight. And then the marching step: the key ingredient to well-ordered infantry tactics, which in the Baron's estimation was the most obvious shortcoming of the Continentals. Driven on by his barked commands, the men learned to move forward at a uniform gait and at a consistent pace, the "common step" of seventy-five paces per minute, each step covering precisely twenty-eight inches.* Step, step, step, step . . . each man's left heel touching the ground at the same moment as that of his

---

*The length of the uniform marching step was later changed to twenty-four inches, after critics pointed out that the twenty-eight-inch step was proving to be awkward for the men.

fellows on either side of him, and along the same imaginary line drawn upon the ground, so that the line of men maintained a straight front as it moved forward. The speed of marching was entirely new to the soldiers, who were accustomed to the standard British pace of sixty steps per minute. As one observer noted approvingly, "Slow Time is a Medium between what was in our service slow and Quick Time[;] Quick Time is about as Quick as a Common Country Dance."[5]

Finally, the men were taught how to face 90 degrees to the right, 90 degrees to the left, and to face to the rear, which must *always* be done by spinning 180 degrees clockwise on both heels. And that was it. It was all over in about an hour.

In mid-afternoon the model company fell in again for another lesson. After reviewing the morning's lesson as a single body, the men broke once again into squads to practice wheeling. In performing a wheel, the entire line would march forward in a giant arc, swinging like a gate upon a pivot fixed at either the right or left flank of the squad. As simple as it sounds, of all the basic maneuvers it was by far the most difficult to master, for unless the soldiers kept their intervals and their pace, the line would collapse into an inchoate muddle of confused men before it even described a quarter of a circle.

And collapse it often did, despite the best efforts of the men. Sometimes they simply misunderstood the Baron's fractured English, or just did not recognize a shouted command. Frustrated by his failure to communicate and his assistants' inability to help, Steuben would become wroth with himself when basic movements went awry. At such moments his complexion darkened visibly, and he began to sputter. He vented his exasperation in streams of shouted invective and profanity, directed at no one in particular. To a civilian, these outbursts would have appeared inappropriate and maybe frightening, but the men of the model company—like soldiers everywhere—were discriminating connoisseurs of foul language. They approved heartily.

With dinnertime, the day's work on the drill field came to an end. The model company broke ranks and returned to their fires to cook what few scraps their messmates had been able to scrounge, and to tell their less fortunate comrades of the day's excitement. Pervasive boredom was almost as much a hardship as hunger; the school on the Grand Parade, driven by the eccentric but no longer mysterious Baron, was the stuff of great storytelling.

And so it went for the next four or five days. The process had the semblance of order and careful planning. No one beyond the Baron's little circle knew that he was making it up as he went along. Each evening when he retired to his quarters, he took a quick dinner before returning to his desk and working out the lesson for the next day in his hastily scribbled, inelegant French, which he then gave to Duponceau for translation and revision. After several hours working by candlelight, he turned in, only to rise again at three o'clock in the morning to do it all over again—to dress, drink his coffee, and smoke his pipe, to study the day's lesson and practice the words in English.[6]

Then, promptly at nine o'clock, just as on the first day of training, he and his staff galloped through the snow to the Grand Parade. "There was no waiting for a tardy aide-de-camp, and those who followed wished they had not slept," one of his assistants recalled. "Nor was there need of chiding. When duty was neglected or military etiquette infringed, the Baron's look was quite sufficient."[7]

The instruction of the model company followed the same pattern each day: the review of old lessons, the separation into squads, the explanation of the new lesson for the day. Steuben's assistants would give personalized instruction to each of the squads. The Baron, in the meantime, flitted about from one squad to the next, fussing, fuming, correcting, praising. When he was satisfied that the men had been coached enough, the company reassembled and performed the new lessons again, together. And thus the instruction proceeded each morning and each afternoon. Soon the men were marching in two ranks, and making use of the faster marching pace, the "quick step" of 120 paces per minute.

The members of the model company weren't the only ones who learned from the exercises. From the very first day of instruction, the drill sessions on the Parade attracted quite a crowd of spectators. Men and officers turned out in force each day, lining the perimeter of the

Parade to watch with a mixture of amusement and awe as the Baron put the company through its paces. The men found welcome diversion in what transpired there, in the occasional comic blunders of the company, in the frantic energy of the excitable German, who acted in a manner that none of them had ever seen in an officer before. Mostly, though, what they witnessed was the complete transformation of the model company. After three or four days on the Parade, the company was able to march, wheel, and change front with a precision and speed not yet seen in Continental troops.

Steuben was aware that he and his students had become the center of attention, but he did not shrink from it. On the contrary. He drew strength and self-assurance from the admiration his men attracted, from the newfound confidence that animated their faces and buoyed their undernourished spirits as they performed increasingly complicated maneuvers to the cheers of the crowd. And the Baron, always the showman—one might say exhibitionist—gloried in the laughter that accompanied his extraordinary fits of anger when something went wrong. Pretty soon he was playing to the amusement of the crowd, intentionally exaggerating his anger in order to make the drill sessions true spectacles. He stomped and he cursed, shaking a fist or gesticulating violently with a huge finger as he called for the wrath of the gods to rain down upon his clumsier men.

His cursing was a blend of French and German obscenities, linked together by a few words of English. It was virtually unintelligible to anyone save him, but he took care to punctuate his shouted profanity with his favorite English oath, the only one he knew: "Goddam!" So long as he kept his calm, he might ask one of his bilingual assistants to translate his curses for the benefit of the men, though they really needed no translation. Sometimes he was so transported by the ferocity of his over-dramatized wrath that he sputtered until he ran out of oaths. "My dear Duponceau," he would then call out to his translator, "come and swear for me in English, these fellows won't do what I bid them."[8]

Certainly many of the Baron's apoplectic fits were genuine, but just as many were feigned, acted for the benefit of the company and the crowd of onlookers. It amused the men, but they never found Steuben to be clownish or ridiculous. His tantrums bonded him to the men; they humanized him. He would always insist on appropriate military decorum—not allowing private soldiers to address him unless asked to do so, for in his mind it was necessary to keep some distance between those who led and those who were led. But at the same time he wanted the men to know that he was a soldier, too, that he shared their privations and their coarser instincts.

This kind of behavior came naturally to Steuben. He liked to be liked; he enjoyed working a crowd. It was also calculated, reflecting a deeper understanding of the soldiers under his command than one might expect from a foreigner who had been in America for all of four months. True, soldiers were soldiers, whether in Valley Forge or in the Breslau garrison, but there was a difference between these Americans and the Prussians he had led in his youth. Prussian soldiers, and European soldiers generally, were peasants, bred to deference. They obeyed their officers in part because they feared the consequences of disobedience, but also because they were accustomed to obeying those who ranked above them in the social hierarchy. They did not expect any kind of interaction with their officers.

But Americans, Steuben found, were not like this at all. Over the generations, they had shed much of that ingrained deference to established authority. They did not respect officers just because they were officers. Steuben's experience on the Grand Parade confirmed his initial assessment of the Continentals. On occasion, the men of the model company were not content merely to do what they had been told to do; they wanted know *why* they should do it. "The genius of this nation," Steuben wrote to an old comrade in Prussia after the war, "is not to be compared . . . with that of the Prussians, Austrians, or French. You say to your soldier, 'Do this,' and he does it; but I am obliged to say, 'This is the reason why you ought to do that,' and *then* he does it."[9]

Taken to extremes, this kind of attitude, Steuben knew, could be dangerous. Commanders could not lead effectively if their men were too familiar with them. But since this aspect of the American character could not be entirely suppressed, the Baron learned to work around it. Indeed, he made it a virtue, and an integral part of his training regimen. When composing his lessons for the model company, he could have relied entirely on an established military manual, picking it as the standard for the army. He could have translated the official Prussian regulations into English, for he knew these by heart. But he did neither. He created his own system, based on his experience, but one stripped of every nonessential movement, every element that did not have a practical purpose. There was no sense, with time in such short supply, in teaching the men things that they would never use and didn't need to know.

Whatever Steuben did, it was working. General Washington already wagered that it would. On March 19, the very day the model company began its training, he took the first tentative steps toward the creation of a functioning inspector general's office—without inviting or even making a single reference to Thomas Conway. The general announced the imminent appointment of an inspector general, and asked brigade commanders to nominate suitable officers as "brigade inspectors," who would serve as Steuben's assistants in each brigade staff. Three days later, obviously impressed by the progress Steuben had made with the model company, Washington prohibited all brigade commanders from conducting drill on their own until the "new Regulations"—for such he was already calling Steuben's embryonic, still-evolving system—were put in place and distributed in writing. This was a serious step, for in writing this order, Washington was limiting the command authority of his generals. In time it would cause him some grief.[10]

———

THE RETRAINING of the entire army at Valley Forge began in earnest on March 24, 1778. Washington's order of March 22 had ruffled some feathers among the colonels and the brigadiers, but not enough to make him back down. He had already seen enough of the "happy Effects" of the Baron's handiwork to know that he had made the right decision, and the painful awareness that the army was in a race against time compelled him to throw the full weight of his support behind the quirky Prussian. Horatio Gates, whom Steuben had been politic enough to keep apprised of his progress, said the same thing: ". . . few Armies want Discipline more than Ours. . . . Our Time is short, and we have much, too much to do; therefore, we should only attempt to do that which is most for our present Benefit."[11]

Early on the morning of the twenty-fourth, Washington gave the order: "At nine oclock precisely all the Brigades will begin their exercise, each regiment on its own parade, and the Inspector Genl will attend the exercise."[12]

General Washington was now referring to Steuben publicly as "Inspector General," a great compliment and a mark of high favor, to be sure, but an onerous burden as well. Steuben was no longer a mere volunteer, drilling a single company of men. He was now responsible for training all of the Continental infantry at Valley Forge. Washington's order put him temporarily above all other officers in the army, making him answerable to Washington alone.

The pressure to perform would be great; the grueling physical pace would be even worse. Steuben would have to supervise the training of thousands of men, riding from brigade to brigade, observing each regiment at drill, taking notes, pointing out recurring problems. And he would have to extend his "system"—which was not fully worked out yet—from the level of the company to that of regiments and brigades.

Fortunately, he would not be entirely on his own. He had the core of his staff—Duponceau, Ponthière, Francy, and Des Epiniers—and two valuable new additions, picked up by the Baron at Valley Forge as he scouted the army for untapped talent. The first of these was Lt. Col. François-Louis Teissèdre de Fleury, a brilliant twenty-nine-year-old engineer. Fleury, who had entered the Continental service early in 1777, had previously served as a staff officer in the French army; when Steuben and Duponceau made his acquaintance at York in February

1778, the Baron knew instantly that Fleury's administrative experience would come in handy.

The second newcomer was twenty-three-year-old Benjamin Walker, a British-born captain in the 2nd New York Regiment. Walker was a rare bird, an American line officer who was fluent in French. He introduced himself to Steuben one day during the training of the model company. A complicated maneuver had gone completely awry, and neither Steuben nor one of his aides was able to come up with the proper commands to restore order to the company. Walker emerged from the crowd of laughing spectators. Doffing his hat and bowing ceremoniously, he addressed the Baron in perfect French. Could His Excellency make use of his services? Steuben gratefully accepted, so moved and relieved that he embraced Walker as if he had known him for years. Soon Walker was detached from his infantry company to serve as Steuben's personal aide-de-camp. He would become one of the very few lifelong friends Steuben made in the army.[13]

Washington saw to it that Steuben had an adequate bureaucracy of his own. He picked four promising field officers—Col. William Davies of Virginia, Col. Francis Barber of New Jersey, Col. John Brooks of Massachusetts, and the Frenchman Ternant—to act as "sub-inspectors." The sub-inspectors would be Steuben's immediate subordinates, supervising divisions and larger bodies of troops, intermediaries between the Baron and the brigade inspectors.[14]

On March 28, as an additional mark of esteem and trust, Washington made Steuben's appointment official—or at least as official as he could:

> Baron Steuben, a Lieutenant General in Foreign Service and a Gentleman of great military Experience having obligingly undertaken to exercise the office of Inspector General in this Army, The Commander in Chief 'til the pleasure of Congress shall be known desires he may be respected and obeyed as such. . . . The Importance of establishing a Uniform System of

useful Manœuvres and regularity of discipline must be obvious,
the Deficiency of our Army in these Respects must be equally
so; the time we shall probably have to introduce the necessary
Reformation is short. . . .[15]

Steuben hardly needed to be reminded of the urgency of the task.
As soon as Washington directed him to take over the training of the
entire army, the Baron sat down to sketch out a detailed instructional
plan—a syllabus—for the coming weeks.

According to this syllabus, each new lesson would be conveyed by
the Baron to the sub-inspectors and the brigade inspectors, who in turn
would teach a selected twenty-man squad from each brigade. Every
captain commanding an infantry company would follow suit, training
his company one squad at a time, until the entire army was schooled in
the basics. Then drill in larger formations would commence. No officer
was exempt from participating in the drills. They would have to work
as hard as the men, if not harder, and they would have to learn exactly
as the men did: every afternoon, the brigade inspectors would assemble
all majors, captains, and most lieutenants, drilling them on the day's
lesson as if they were privates themselves. It must have been endlessly
entertaining for the men, watching their proud leaders bumbling about
the parade ground, muskets in hand, with the Baron stopping by occasionally to yell and curse at them when they failed to execute the lessons
correctly. But in the Prussian army most officers started off in the very
same way, and Steuben knew no better system of training.

In the meantime, each installment of the training regimen was
transmitted in writing as well. There was no time to draw up a complete set of regulations, edit them, and have them printed; that would
have to wait for a more relaxed season. Instead, the brigade inspectors
would report to Steuben's headquarters to make a handwritten copy of
each new lesson, bring it to his assigned brigade, and allow each regimental adjutant and clerk to copy the instructions verbatim into the
regimental orderly books. Clerks, the human Xerox machines of the
day, must have despised the system.[16]

The lessons followed an unusual and innovative pattern. Customarily, new recruits were first taught the very basics of the marching step, and were then instructed in the Manual Exercise, the series of postures and movements that taught each soldier how to manipulate his musket: how to load and fire, how to fix and unfix the bayonet; how to shoulder, order, ground, and salute with his "firelock," or musket. Each movement was taught "by the motions," broken down into small components so that the men could perform everything in unison and at the same pace. Once these motions were taught, soldiers were then exercised in squads and larger formations, with battalion/regimental, brigade, and division maneuvers coming last.

Steuben turned this order on its head. The Manual Exercise, he reasoned, was the least important component of training. The ability to maneuver in large units was far more essential. So although he composed a very brief, very simple Manual Exercise for the training program, he spent little time on this, and pushed the men right along from marching in squads to marching in battalions and brigades. Other concepts, such as the Manual Exercise and the use of the bayonet, would be taught along the way, but the emphasis was almost entirely on precision marching. This approach, while unconventional by European (and American) standards, was pragmatic. Most American officers thought so, too. The colonel of a New York regiment described it to a friend:

> He is now Teaching the Most Simple Parts of the Exercise such as Positition [sic] and Marching of a Soldier in a Manner Quite different from that, they Have been heretofore used to, In my Oppinion [sic] More agreable [sic] to the Dictates of Reason & Common Sence [sic] than any Mode I have before seen.[17]

Even stodgy, conservative Gates approved wholeheartedly. "Considering the few Moments that is left us for this necessary Work," he told Steuben, "I should rather recommend the Discipline of the Leggs, than the Firelocks, or the Hands; the preservation of Order at all

Times is essentially necessary. It leads to Victory, it Secures a Retreat, it saves a Country."[18]

The pace of the instruction was ambitious, almost ridiculously so, by contemporary European standards. In the first days of the training regimen, the men learned to march in the "direct step"—that is, straight ahead—in both "common time" and "quick time." They learned the "oblique step"—while facing straight ahead, each soldier would step out with the left foot ahead and to the left, bringing the right foot alongside it, so that the entire line remained straight but moved diagonally to the left at roughly a forty-five-degree angle. At the Baron's insistence, the marching was done without the accompaniment of field music, namely the fifes and drums that usually beat out the cadence, and initially the soldiers were not allowed to march with their muskets. They would also have to march in absolute silence: "they must not stir their hands, blow their noses, or much less talk."[19]

By the second week of April, only three weeks into the program, entire regiments were drilling together, executing such maneuvers as "forming column of platoons" by wheeling (see Figure 1) and deploying a column of platoons into line of battle. Here the marching practice paid off, for although these maneuvers seem simple on paper, they required each unit and subunit to maintain precise intervals, and each man to march at precisely the same rate and length of stride. By the end of April, Steuben hoped, the entire army would be maneuvering in large units, and would be able to stage "Sham Battles" with artillery and cavalry.

Steuben, and, more important, the troops themselves, did not disappoint. Their progress was astounding. The Baron had taught drill to many kinds of men before—ordinary Prussian infantry, the unruly volunteers of the Free Battalions, the more patriotic native Prussian conscripts who filled Frederick's ranks at the end of the Seven Years' War—but he had experienced nothing like this. He was his own harshest critic, but even he was impressed with what he and his pupils had accomplished. "My Enterprize Succeeded better than I had dared to expect," he reported to Congress later that year, "and I had the Satisfaction, in a

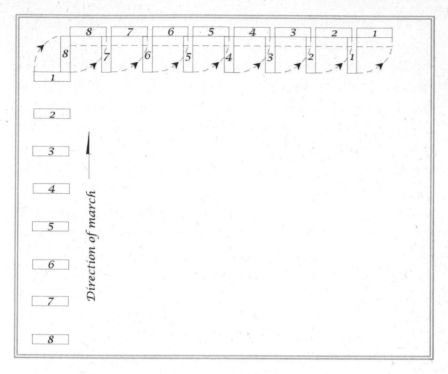

Infantry battalion of eight platoons, deploying from column
to line of battle, wheeling by platoons

month's time, to see not only a regular Step introduced in the Army, but I also made maneuvers with ten and twelve Battalions with as much precision as the Evolution of a Single Company."[20]

THE MEN COMPLAINED about the intensity of the training program—"it was a continual drill," recalled Pvt. Joseph Plumb Martin of the 8th Connecticut Regiment when reflecting on his life at Valley Forge—but only halfheartedly, as soldiers tend to complain about anything and everything.[21] Though fast-paced, the program was not physically draining. Steuben insisted that no soldier should have to exercise more than two hours each day. Any more than that, he argued, would fatigue the men and ultimately prove counterproductive.

The Baron, however, held himself to a much more demanding schedule. It was no easy thing for a man his age—at forty-seven he was hardly young—but he kept up. Through the remainder of March and all of April, and for some time to come, he continued to work late and rise very early. When he wasn't conferring with his subordinates or other officers, he observed the drills and stepped in where necessary to make a point. Few soldiers were accustomed to the sight of an officer, much less one of the Baron's dignity and elevated reputation, grabbing a musket to perform the manual of arms, taking the time to adjust the gear of a private soldier, or marching along with an awkward squad as if he were a common sergeant. He just couldn't restrain himself from getting involved.

Those closest to him were astonished by the way in which he drove himself, and found it difficult to match his seemingly inexhaustible store of energy. "The Baron discovers the greatest zeal, and an activity which is hardly to be expected at his years," John Laurens wrote in wonder to his father. "He is exerting himself like a Lieutenant anxious for promotion."[22]

There was a purpose to his exertions that went beyond his ambition to accomplish his task by sheer force of will. He wanted to set an example for the Continental officers, hoping that they would eventually discard the "pernicious English habit" of leaving the responsibility of drill to their NCOs. His American colleagues took note of this. "The Officers in general seem to entertain a high opinion of him, and he sets them an excellent example in descending to the functions of a drill-Serjeant," John Laurens wrote. Alexander Scammell, colonel of the 3rd New Hampshire Regiment and Washington's adjutant general, could not find enough compliments to pay to the drillmaster:

> The Baron Steuben sets us a truly noble example. He has undertaken the Discipline of the army & shows himself to be a perfect Master of it, not only in the grand manieuvres, but in every Minutia. To see a Gentleman dignified with a Lt Genls Commission from the great prussian Monarch, condescend

with a grace peculiar to himself, to take under his direction a Squad of ten or twelve men in Capacity of a Drill Serjt, & induce the Officers & men to admire him and improve exceeding fast under his Instructions.[23]

Steuben considered this lesson—that the officers should, as in the Prussian army, take responsibility for their men—one of the most important that he could impart. A couple of years later, when he witnessed a regimental colonel tutoring a single raw recruit in the manual of arms, he exclaimed to one of his aides, "Do you see there, sir, your Colonel instructing that recruit? I thank God for that!"[24]

———

THE REACTION TO STEUBEN'S REFORMS, from officers and men alike, was almost universally positive. They understood the practical value of what they were learning under the Baron's firm hand, but most important they amazed themselves. That was one of the benefits of intensive training in drill, one that Steuben understood fully: drill instills pride. Though many in the army had been veterans of several campaigns, the Baron's schooling made them feel like *soldiers*, like men who now stood a chance of defeating the Redcoats on even terms. The transformation in morale was nothing short of miraculous. "Discipline flourishes and daily improves under the indefatigable Efforts of Baron Steuben—who is much esteem'd by us," wrote Alexander Scammell to Timothy Pickering, member of the Board of War.[25]

And esteemed by General Washington, too. He did not shower Steuben with praise—that was not his style—but his support was unstinting. Now that the Baron had proven his worth, now that he had been accepted, the general could risk giving him some reward for his efforts. The chance to do so seemed to drop from the sky at the most opportune time, as if by divine intervention. At the end of April, Congress accepted Thomas Conway's petulant offer of resignation. The post of inspector general was officially vacant as a result, and Washington did not hesitate. On the very same day, he took pen in hand to inform Congress that he wished that the Baron should replace Conway. "He appears to me to have an accurate knowledge of every part of military discipline and arrangements," the general expanded, "and to be a man of sense and judgment." And since Steuben had once held high rank in Europe, it would be inappropriate for Congress to offer him anything less than the rank of major general.[26]

Major generalship—the very rank for which Steuben had hoped. The promotion would totally change his relationship to the army, to Washington, to Congress; it would put him on the same level as Washington's highest-ranking subordinates, make him answerable only to Washington himself, and provide him with a substantial salary. Congress did not waste a moment, but voted unanimously to give him the appointment and the commission five days later. Slyly, Washington kept the good news to himself. He had plans to make the announcement with just a bit of ceremony.

Some sort of ceremony was definitely in order. On May 1, word reached Valley Forge of the most welcome development of the year, and perhaps of the entire war. After months of careful negotiation by the commissioners in Paris, King Louix XVI had finally signed a military alliance with the United States. Within months, presumably, French troops, warships, muskets, and gold would pour into North America. The achievement of independence was no longer in doubt.

Washington was as elated as anyone, and he decided to celebrate the occasion with an official day of thanksgiving at Valley Forge. What better way to celebrate a military partnership than to show off the army's new abilities? It would demonstrate to the French that the United States took its end of the bargain seriously. And it would be deeply satisfying to Washington personally. He could reassure his allies in Congress that their confidence in him had not been misplaced, and prove to his detractors that they had gravely underestimated him.

Hence the Grand Review of May 6, 1778. Washington left the choreography of the Review to Steuben, who pounced upon the assignment as if he were starved for work. In just a couple of days, he worked out all of the intricate details, writing instructions for each brigade and regiment,

even drawing diagrams. Everything had to be laid out well in advance so
that there would be no room for embarrassing errors.

The Review went off without a hitch on that crisp May morning.
The boom of a cannon echoing over the encampment signalled the
end of an open-air church service and the beginning of the maneuvers
that Steuben had devised for the occasion. The entire army marched
by files onto the Grand Parade, and though their uniforms were di-
shevelled, they moved like soldiers, silent and perfectly in cadence, to
the music of the fifes and drums. They formed two parallel lines of
battle, each two ranks deep, and after three salvos of thirteen cannon
each rang out from the artillery park, the infantry gave its salute to
France and the Alliance. It did so with an elaborate display, called a
feu de joie. The first two men—one in the front rank, one in the
rear—on the far right flank of the first line raised their muskets and
fired into the air, followed immediately by the next two men on their
left. The coordinated, rolling fire continued in this fashion, two muskets booming at a time from right to left along the first line, then
commencing on the second line from left to right, and beginning all
over again with the first line. The process was repeated three times.
Not a man fired out of turn.[27]

It was a spectacle rarely seen even in the best-trained European
armies. The onlookers applauded in awestruck approval as the smoke
billowing from the muzzles of ten thousand muskets obscured the
neatly aligned ranks from their view. John Laurens could hardly contain his excitement:

> The order with which the whole was conducted, the beautiful
> effect of the running fire which was executed to perfection, the
> martial appearance of the Troops, gave sensible pleasure to
> every one present. . . . The plan as formed by Baron von Steu-
> ben succeeded in every particular, which is in a great measure
> to be attributed to his unwearied attention and to the visible
> progress which the troops have already made under his disci-
> pline. . . . Triumph beamed in every countenance.[28]

When it was all over, the men broke ranks, returning to their huts to take a well-deserved break and enjoy the gill of rum that Washington had ordered for each of them as a reward for their performance. The generals retired to a "cold collation" with their commander in chief and their wives. Warm handshakes and self-congratulatory smiles all around, toasts to Washington, the king of France, and the Alliance, "with as much sincerity as that of the British King used to be in former times." "I thought I should be devoured," Duponceau later reminisced, "by the caresses which the American officers lavished upon me as one of their new allies."[29] Washington waited for just this moment to spring the surprise on his "dear Baron": that he was a volunteer aide no longer, but one of Washington's generals, and inspector general on top of that.

It was a great day, for the Cause, for the army, and for Steuben. Though the Baron's greatest contributions to the American army were yet to come, it was on the whole the most satisfying moment of his life. The forcibly retired infantry captain who so feared dying as an unknown, a mediocrity, was now a major general and the object of sincere accolades. After just about a month of hard work, the army bore his personal imprint more than that of any other man. The army was, of course, a creation of the American people, of the individual states, and of Washington himself, but its metamorphosis was his, its current shape and form were his.

Yet all the while, as Major General de Steuben swelled with pride at his creation and basked in the heartfelt congratulations of his fellow generals, a nagging question flitted unseen through his mind, a question that had not left him since General Washington first raised it only a couple of weeks before: Was the army ready for battle? Did the staged performance on the Grand Parade signal that the army was any better prepared to meet the Redcoats than it had been at Brandywine?

In Philadelphia the British were stirring from their long and comfortable slumber, and Washington was determined to make use of his army while the men were still animated by their newfound confidence.

CHAPTER 6

Jealousies and Hindrances

[MAY—JUNE 1778]

Some perhaps will inquire, Who is that Man who
meddles with our Discipline? On what authority does
he introduce such or such Thing? In such a Case, I'll
have nothing to answer. I'll leave the care of my
Vindication to Congress.

STEUBEN TO HENRY LAURENS,
APRIL 2, 1778[1]

THE SUN ROSE EARLY IN MID-MAY, and although there
had been some heavy rains in the previous days, the
morning of May 20, 1778, dawned clear and cool. It
was already light when the men first stirred and roused themselves for roll call, breakfast, and the plethora of fatigue duties
that had to be performed each and every morning. The drill
would commence in midmorning, for neither Washington nor
Steuben was about to allow for any slacking, even after the
army's stellar performance two weeks before at the Grand
Review.

The morning began much as any other, yet there was something different about the mood in camp today. The atmosphere
was somehow electric; there was a tangible feeling of apprehen-
sion, even as the men went about cleaning their muskets, shav-
ing, mending torn clothing. All of them knew that only

yesterday the Marquis de Lafayette had left camp with nearly a fifth of the army to scout the countryside to the east of the cantonment. There had been no word from him since.

At around eight o'clock, a cannon-shot thundered from the artillery park, then another, then another.

The series of cannon blasts was an alarm: Valley Forge was in danger. There was neither need nor time for explanation. The men sprang into action, ceasing their chores. Stumbling out of their fetid, smoky huts, they grabbed their muskets and accoutrements as they rushed to join their companies in line. They were not panicked, for they knew by training and habit where they had to go and what they had to do. Within fifteen minutes, the entire army was arranged in line of battle, ready to form columns and march at a moment's notice.

The army remained on high alert for hours. Rumors whispered through the ranks soon acquainted the men with the broad outlines of the situation: Lafayette's detachment was in trouble, and therefore it was likely that a British force was on its way to punish Valley Forge itself. It was near nightfall when the army was allowed to relax its vigilance. But the excitement did not end there, for dispatch riders had come with reassuring news from Lafayette himself. On that very day, Lafayette and his Continentals had met the British in combat, and they had not done badly.

T HE INTRICACIES of the feu de joie showed that the army was more battle-ready than it had ever been. Perhaps the display was a frivolity, but its successful execution required that the Continental Line be capable of all sorts of complicated evolutions—deploying from marching column into line of battle, forming columns again, delivering crisp, perfectly timed volleys of musketry—all of which had their place on the eighteenth-century battlefield.[2]

Still, impressive though it may have been to those who witnessed it, the feu de joie did not in itself signify that the Continentals were ready to go toe-to-toe with the Redcoats. It did indeed require martial skills, but the event was nonetheless an act of stylized ceremony; it bore no resemblance to combat. No one had fired back at the Continentals. There were no mangled, broken men or panicked horses, no musketry or cannon-shot to tear jagged holes in the neatly aligned ranks of soldiers, no waves of gleaming and levelled bayonets, no agonized screams, no blood. A great number of the men at the Grand Review had lived through the battles around New York in 1776 and Philadelphia in 1777, and they knew what battle was like. The feu de joie was not battle.

But battle was not far off, because Washington was eager for action. In mid-April, he had asked his generals to give their opinions on three proposed operational plans: Should the army try to force the British from Philadelphia, or launch a surprise attack on New York? Or should it forego offensive operations altogether and remain at Valley Forge to hone its skills further? The generals split almost evenly over the three options. Though at that point not yet a general, Steuben joined with Lafayette in urging caution. The army should maintain a defensive posture where it was, continue with rigorous training, and not intentionally court danger. After some thought, Washington decided that the foreigners were probably right, for the time being.[3]

But Washington could not leave the subject alone for very long. Less than three weeks later, only two days after the Grand Review, he summoned all of his generals to his headquarters for a council of war. The question he posed was the same—attack Philadelphia, New York, or not at all? There was little support for an immediate offensive, but all agreed, even the wary Europeans, that preparations should be made for offensive operations in the not-too-distant future.

The generals were beginning to echo the enthusiasm and impatience of their commander in chief, for the condition of the army had much improved since mid-April. Thanks to the dedication and competence of Nathanael Greene and Jeremiah Wadsworth, the new quartermaster and commissary generals, respectively, steady supplies of clothing and food were finally making their way into Valley Forge. The return of fair weather lightened the overall mood and reduced the virulence of the afflictions—such as dysentery and scabies—plaguing the soldiers. Army-wide inoculations significantly curtailed the incidence of smallpox, the scourge of eighteenth-century armies. And two months of constant drill built muscle and sinew as much as it did confidence. The army was spoiling for a fight.

The situation in Philadelphia was changing, too. Intelligence received from spies in the hostage capital reported two important developments. First, the anticipated change of command was about to take place. Sir Henry Clinton was on his way to Philadelphia to supplant the hedonistic Sir William Howe, and would arrive there on May 8—the very day of Washington's latest council of war. Soon Sir William would be on his way back to England. Second, rumor had it that Clinton would likely evacuate the city within a few weeks. The French alliance troubled him, for if the French managed to gain naval superiority off Chesapeake Bay, then Philadelphia would be very vulnerable. New York City would be much more secure.[4]

In light of these developments, and bolstered by the cautious optimism of his generals, Washington made the decision to allow a small force to probe the British defenses to the north and west of Philadelphia. Lafayette, eager to prove himself, offered to command the expedition, and Washington accepted.

On the morning of May 19, 1778, Lafayette's detachment marched out of Valley Forge and toward Philadelphia. The force was substantial: more than two thousand soldiers of the Continental Line, a battery of five cannon, approximately six hundred Pennsylvania militia, forty-seven warriors of the Oneida nation, and a handful of French Canadians who had accompanied the Oneidas from the north. Lafayette had recruited the Oneidas earlier that spring, as he was preparing to lead the abortive invasion of Canada that Congress had pushed upon him. They had arrived at Valley Forge six days before Lafayette's departure, and their appearance caused quite a stir among the Continentals. Most of the men there had never seen an Indian before.[5]

Lafayette's motley corps marched about halfway to Philadelphia that day, crossing the Schuylkill at Swede's Ford, then proceeding along the Swede's Ford Road leading to the southeast along the course of the Schuylkill. After a march of just under fifteen miles, Lafayette halted his force at the tiny hamlet of Barren Hill. It seemed a good and secure location for a night's rest. Barren Hill, as its name implied, was a treeless plateau overlooking the Schuylkill to the west, dense forest to the north, and cultivated fields to the south. Nearby was a cross-roads, where one easterly road—called the Ridge Road—led directly to Philadelphia.

Lafayette deployed his men in a defensive posture facing to the southeast, his right flank anchored on the bluffs of the Schuylkill, his left flank hanging, exposed, in the air. "We . . . placed our guards, sent off our scouting parties, and waited for—I know not what," recalled seventeen-year-old private Joseph Plumb Martin. To the militia and the Canadians fell the duty of guarding the roads that converged at Barren Hill. The rest of the Continentals relaxed. Private Martin and a couple of Oneida warriors amused themselves by stirring up an enormous quantity of bats that had taken refuge in the eaves of an old house.[6]

The men were blissfully unaware that the British knew precisely where the Americans were. They had walked straight into a trap.

Clinton and Howe had received word of Lafayette's expedition almost as soon as it began. The marquis had presented them with an opportunity that simply could not be missed. His force was travelling through open country, within striking distance of Philadelphia but distant enough from Valley Forge that he could not be reinforced quickly. The Schuylkill, swollen and treacherous from the spring rains, would make a rapid retreat to the Forge difficult. And the British had no reason to expect that the Continentals would be any more formidable than they had been in the previous campaign. Howe ordered that preparations should be made to receive Lafayette as a distinguished guest—there was no doubt that he would be taken prisoner.

During the night of the nineteenth and the early morning hours of the twentieth, the British set their trap. Three full divisions, at least ten thousand British and German troops, marched out of Philadelphia to confront Lafayette's force, which was outnumbered by more than four to one.

As the British approached Barren Hill, the three divisions separated and took up their positions. The first, under the command of Gen. Charles Grant, moved northward up the Swede's Ford Road, cutting off Lafayette's line of retreat back to Valley Forge. Gen. Charles Grey's column marched eastward toward Lafayette's exposed left flank, while the main body, under the joint command of Clinton and Howe, pushed up the Ridge Road and directly toward the American front and right. This latter force would keep Lafayette from retreating downstream to the next nearest ford, Levering's. The Schuylkill prevented a direct retreat to the west. Lafayette was being enveloped.

The marquis was completely oblivious to his impending doom. The Pennsylvania militia, which was supposed to guard the northern passage to Swede's Ford, left inexplicably in the night, and hence Lafayette was rendered blind in that direction. It was not until just after dawn on the morning of the twentieth that Lafayette learned anything of the British presence. A miller who lived near the Swede's Ford Road rushed to Lafayette's camp to report the proximity of Grant's column. Around the same time, American pickets to the south along the Ridge Road encountered a body of British light dragoons, the lead elements of the Howe-Clinton column. The pickets—Oneida warriors, the Canadians, and portions of Col. Dan Morgan's legendary rifle regiment—engaged the British in a brisk firefight, driving the dragoons back before retiring toward the American main body.

It was just about too late for Lafayette to do anything but stand and take his chances, slim as they were. The men did not have to be apprised of the situation; word spread quickly through the ranks. Private Martin recounted, "Just at dawn of the day the officers' waiters came, almost breathless, after the horses. Upon inquiring for the cause of the unusual hurry, we were told that the British were advancing upon us in our rear. How they could get there was to us a mystery, but they *were* there."[7]

With the British almost upon him, Lafayette's first instinct was to prepare for the inevitable onslaught. Since the most immediate danger came from Grey's column, on Lafayette's exposed left flank, the marquis wisely decided to "refuse" the flank, extending his line to the left and bending it back at a right angle so as to face Grey's oncoming Redcoats. The angle of the American left was now anchored around a small Lutheran church and cemetery, fortified by a chest-high stone wall that afforded the Continentals there a modicum of protection. The Americans steeled themselves for the British attack. "I began to think I should soon have some better sport than killing bats," Private Martin mused.

Although Lafayette did not know the exact strength of the enemy moving rapidly toward him, he knew that he was woefully outmatched. He *must* escape—but how?

There was one option left open to him. A short distance upstream, between Barren Hill and Swede's Ford, there was yet another crossing: Matson's Ford. It was not an ideal place to cross. The Schuylkill was deeper there than it was at Swede's or Levering's, so there was no guarantee the army could get across. And Grant's Redcoats, blocking the road to Swede's, were closer to Matson's Ford than Lafayette was. If Lafayette set out for Matson's and the British detected the movement in time, Grant could beat the Americans there. The British could cut off their line of retreat or, worse, pour musket fire into the backs of the fleeing Continentals as they foundered in the turbulent waters.

Lafayette took the chance. With Morgan's riflemen and the Oneidas screening them, the Continentals changed formation from line of battle to marching column in the blink of an eye. This was the kind of maneuver that previously would have wasted much valuable time, but these men were not the Continentals of 1776 or 1777. Grant, thinking that the Americans intended to drive him from Swede's Ford Road, maintained a defensive posture and did not move until it was too late. The Continentals waded uncertainly into Matson's Ford—with Lafayette plunging his horse impulsively into the water ahead of his men—while the Oneidas delayed the British cavalry threatening the American rear guard. Even then, escape was not a sure thing. The river was deep and the current strong at Matson's. The men had to link arms as they pushed into the roiling chest-deep water—some men lost their muskets, but not a man drowned.[8]

Lafayette had made his escape. Clinton and Howe gave up the chase and withdrew to Philadelphia, while the Americans rested for the night on the west bank of the Schuylkill, returning to Valley Forge the next day.

The "battle" of Barren Hill had been a close scrape and a near disaster. "It was a very Luckey afair on our side, that we Did not Loose our whole Detachment," noted Henry Dearborn, lieutenant colonel of the 3rd New Hampshire Regiment.[9] Lafayette could count himself very lucky indeed, having lost only six Canadians during the initial clash with the dragoons on the Ridge Road. It could have gone much, much worse. The entire force could have been taken captive. The loss of one fifth of Washington's army would have wrecked American morale and negated any chance Washington might have had for a successful offensive in the summer. Washington, Steuben, and Greene had done much to boost the spirits of the army over the winter months; Barren Hill could have undone their handiwork in a matter of hours.

Lafayette credited his "victory" to his own quick thinking. In public, Henry Laurens and George Washington encouraged that notion, praising Lafayette's consummate skill as a tactician. Privately, Washington expressed some doubts as to Lafayette's readiness to handle an independent command. Lafayette had been careless to have been ensnared so readily. But it would not do to express such sentiments openly. Reprimanding the marquis would serve no purpose other than to dampen morale, cast Washington's leadership in a bad light, and embarrass America's French allies.

Among Washington's generals there were accolades, too, but the praise went not so much to Lafayette as to the men themselves. Lafayette's corps had escaped because the men had kept their cool, responding quickly and smartly to the orders given them. Barren Hill, if it can be called a battle at all, was a soldier's battle.

And that was the lesson of Barren Hill, the significance of which was far greater than the anticlimatic encounter's minimal strategic importance: that American soldiers, properly trained, could maneuver with disciplined precision and order as well as most European armies.

The Continental Army could not have performed so well, in similar circumstances, before April 1778, before a down-on-his luck Prussian nobleman taught them the basics of modern tactics. That transformation had been Steuben's doing, and his contemporaries gave him full credit. To the clergyman William Gordon, who had befriended the Baron in Boston, "The orderly manner in which the Americans retreated on this occasion . . . is to be ascribed to the improvement made in their discipline owing greatly to the Baron De Steuben." Henry Laurens was just as impressed by the response of the main army at Valley Forge to the alarm on the morning of May 20: "To the honour of Major General Baron Stüben, the whole Army in fifteen minutes were under Arms formed & ready to March."[10]

———

STEUBEN DID NOT RECORD HIS THOUGHTS on the Barren Hill episode. It was not the kind of operation he would have approved if it had been his place to do so. He knew better than anyone the extent of the army's battle-readiness, and the perils of sending an expeditionary force under an inexperienced commander deep into enemy territory. In allowing the operation to go forward, Washington had gone against his better judgement. Eager to test his reformed army, the commander in chief was willing to take dangerous risks.

Steuben knew what this implied for rebel strategy: Washington was not going to sit quietly in Valley Forge and wait for the British to attack him. He intended to take the field that spring and move directly against the enemy. If the army were to be ready for a campaign of that sort in the summer of 1778, then the Baron had much more work to do.

The task that now faced Steuben was much less daunting than the one he had taken upon himself in late March. He was no longer a stranger; he had a smoothly functioning staff and a formidable hierarchy of sub-inspectors and brigade inspectors, and the army was already well versed in the basics. There still existed a huge disparity in the sizes of individual regiments, but that could not be fixed overnight, and the Baron would just have to work around it, as he had done so far. What he could do was focus his attention on grand maneuvers, putting the largest units possible—usually entire divisions—through the paces of complicated maneuvers. Barren Hill had shown just how important this could be.

Practice maneuvers for larger units had actually commenced before the Grand Review, but they were held more frequently afterward, and even more so after Barren Hill. These were taxing all-day affairs from which no soldier or officer was excused. The division and brigade commanders took them very seriously, viewing poor performance at drill as a stain upon their honor. Steuben did not command these maneuvers per se—the major generals and brigadiers were qualified to do that by now—but he supervised them in person, and he set out in detail the specific movements that each brigade and division was to perform.

The division maneuvers were designed to teach rapidity and precision in movements that would most likely be used in battle. One example should suffice. On May 16, 1778, Steuben scheduled a drill session for the four brigades led by Generals Learned, Paterson, Muhlenberg, and Weedon. First, the men had to be organized into units that were roughly equal in size. Steuben was uncomfortable with the organizational structure of American military units, so he temporarily—just for purposes of drill—would reconfigure the regiments in the Prussian manner. In the American service, the regiment was the basic tactical unit; it usually consisted of a half dozen to a dozen companies. In the Prussian service, the battalion was the basic unit of infantry. Two or more battalions made up a regiment, with the latter acting more as an administrative unit. Each battalion was then divided into four or five companies, and each company into two platoons. As Steuben would point out time and again, it didn't matter what terminology was used, so long as all units of the same type were close to one another in size.

Prior to instruction, Steuben would line up all the men in each brigade, and he and his assistants would then count them off and reapportion them, making battalions of around four to five hundred men. These battalions were then subdivided into eight platoons of roughly fifty men each, plus officers. There was a distinct advantage to this system. The men learned to work with different officers and different comrades, a process of homogenization that made for a more efficient army.[11]

Then the maneuvers could begin. This took up most of the daylight hours. The four brigades, organized as two divisions, formed two divisional lines of battle, each two ranks deep. They practiced forming "columns of platoons." If the order was given to form column of platoons to the right, each platoon would wheel ninety degrees clockwise, pivoting on the rightmost man in the platoon. Now each division would be formed up in a deep, narrow column, its width being equal to the battle-line width of one platoon, twenty to twenty-five men across (forty to fifty men formed in two ranks), with the platoons following closely upon one another in succession. Such a column could move forward much more rapidly, and was much more maneuverable, than a division in line of battle. When the order was given to form into line, the column would halt and the platoons would wheel ninety degrees counterclockwise on a left-hand pivot, placing the platoons back into their original positions in the line. This was practiced in the opposite direction (i.e., to the left) as well. Then the same maneuver was executed again, but this time in "column of divisions"—the term "division" here meaning a group of two platoons. Finally, this maneuver was combined with firing drills. When a column of divisions wheeled back into line of battle, each division would unleash a volley of musketry as soon as it resumed its position in the grand line of battle. In this way, an entire brigade or larger unit could be moved rapidly and directly into a firefight in column, wheel into line of battle, and begin to pour a rolling fire into an oncoming enemy in a matter of seconds.

Further exercises included the practice of "moving fire," something for which the Prussian army was renowned. "Firing by platoons in retreat": as the battalions did an about-face and marched away from the enemy, individual platoons would take turns covering the retreat by halting, performing an about-face, firing a volley into their pursuers, doing another about-face, and marching at the quick-step to resume their place in the line of the retreating battalion. A similar maneuver involved volley fire by platoons while the line of battle was advancing toward the enemy.

These movements sound hopelessly complicated to modern ears. They *were* complicated, which is why they required constant practice. But they also made the difference between an army that could attack, retreat, and change formation quickly, and an army that found it an almost insurmountable challenge just to form up for battle. It was this marriage of fluidity, rapid motion, and constant firepower that had set the Prussian army apart from its foes and allies.

The accolades poured in unsolicited. A Pennsylvania militia officer watching one of the divisional drills of May 1778 wrote in astonishment to a friend that the Continentals he saw were "as well disciplined as any of the british troops can be, they performed several manovres [*sic*] with great exactness & dispatch, under the direction of Baron Stuben, and . . . I am informed that our whole army are in as good order as them 15 regiments."[12]

In Congress, too, admiration for Steuben's work in May and June was nearly universal. William Henry Drayton, friend of Henry Laurens and new congressional delegate from South Carolina, congratulated the Baron. Because of the "rapid advance of our young Soldiers in the art military under your auspices," he wrote, "you are my Dear Baron, intitled to the thanks of every American."[13] Richard Peters told his fellow Board of War member Timothy Pickering that he

> continued to be pleased with the Appearance of every thing [at Valley Forge]. Discipline seems to be growing apace & America will be under lasting Obligations to the Baron Steuben as the Father of it. He is much respected by the Officers & beloved by the Soldiers who themselves seem to be convinced of the Propriety & Necessity of his Regulations. I am astonished at the Progress he has made with the Troops.[14]

S TEUBEN HIMSELF was not quite so satisfied with his progress. As he reported, with evident dissatisfaction, to Congress at the end of May:

> The little time, the situation of the Army & in part every Circumstance has prevented me from getting more forward. I have hitherto Confined myself to an uniform formation of the Troops . . . an easy March, & a few Evolutions to give the Officers some Idea how to conduct their Troops. We have not in fact yet taught the Soldiers the Elementary Principles nor have I even instructed them in the Manual Excercise indeed the Discipline as yet is but just touched upon. . . . In all these I was obliged to submit to Circumstances which . . . has hinder'd me from proceeding further.[15]

He did not elaborate much upon these "Circumstances" in writing, but those closest to him knew exactly what he meant: Steuben had begun to make enemies. They were not the same as Washington's, not precisely. The Baron's popularity in Congress was universal, and cut across party lines. Washington liked and admired him, as did most of the major generals. To them, he was frank, erudite, witty, and warm; but to others he was tactless, abrasive, imperious, and power-hungry.

To some of the brigadiers, he was a foreign parvenu, and that was enough in itself.

Thomas Conway was one of those enemies—naturally, since Steuben had replaced him. The former inspector general still had powerful adherents at Valley Forge who shared his sentiments. One of these former allies stood out—in rank, reputation, and influence—above all others: Maj. Gen. Charles Lee.[16]

Lee, the senior-most of Washington's major generals, was not present at Valley Forge when Steuben arrived in February. In December 1776, before the crossing of the Delaware and the Christmas miracle at Trenton, Lee had been captured by a British cavalry patrol as he sat in a tavern at Basking Ridge, New Jersey, still dressed in his nightgown.

Steuben was probably the most experienced officer in Continental service, measured by the richness of his experience in the Seven Years' War, but Lee had the longest service record. A Briton by birth, and a soldier by profession from the age of twelve, he had served for nearly thirty years in the British and Polish armies. Few, if any, of his fellow officers in America could match him in military learning. None knew so much as he did about the inner workings of the British army, whose recent crop of leaders—Howe, Clinton, Charles Cornwallis, Thomas Gage—he could count among his friends. Lee considered himself to be the foremost American authority on the art of war in Europe, and he was not far off the mark in thinking so highly of himself.

Later events would cast Lee in a most unflattering light; no American officer, save Benedict Arnold, has been so vilified as he. To some of his detractors, he was little better than a traitor; even his defenders acknowledged that while in British captivity he had given Clinton advice on how best to fight the American rebels. He did not intend to betray his adopted country, but rather hoped for a compromise peace between Britain and her former colonies, a peace that he himself would broker. In his defense, though, it should be pointed out that Lee considered himself an American. He had spent much of his British service in the colonies during the French and Indian War, marrying the daughter of a Seneca chieftain, and returned after the end of his British career in 1773 to settle down in Virginia. Like Washington, he became a gentleman-planter and a patriot, speaking out against British misrule and openly espousing the cause of independence.

But the similarities with Washington ended there. Washington had the outward appearance and the inner character of a great leader. Lee, by contrast, cut a poor figure. Short, thin, and perpetually stooped in stature, with a large hawkish nose jutting prominently from his pinched face, he was known—even among his friends—as a coarse and vulgar man. There was no doubting his intelligence, but that intelligence was tempered by neither modesty nor tact. In the words of one acquaintance, he was "a good scholar and soldier . . . full of fire and passion, but little good manners: a great sloven, wretchedly profane, and a great admirer of dogs."[17]

Lee's greatest public sin, apart from his uncouth manner and his preference for low-born women, was that he despised Washington. To Lee, the general-in-chief knew little about tactics and less about the art of command. He *knew* that he was Washington's better in these regards, and his vanity and envy overcame his better judgement. He could not hide his contempt for Washington, nor did he try to, and for that reason alone he made a poor subordinate. As the functioning second-in-command of the army, a man upon whom Washington should have been able to rely, Lee proved instead to be churlish and uncooperative, obeying Washington's orders at his own pace and only when it suited him.

Yet there was no getting rid of him. None of the other major generals dared challenge the man, for he had an indefinable mystique that lent great authority to his opinions. Other men seemed to defer to him, whether they liked him or not. Washington valued Lee's experience and wisdom, and tried his best to work with him, but over time it became more and more difficult to do so. Washington did not like Lee, but he respected him, probably more than Lee deserved.

There was more to their mutual dislike than a clash of egos. Washington and Lee had two very different strategic philosophies.

Washington aspired to lead an army built on the European model, while Lee subscribed to the Whiggish idea that freedom-loving, virtuous Americans were much better equipped to fight an irregular "war of posts" than they were to meet the Redcoats head on. Any attempt, therefore, to fashion the Continentals into a professional army would be misguided and fruitless. "It is in vain for Congress to withstand british Troops in the Field," Lee proclaimed to Elias Boudinot, Continental commissioner for prisoners. Washington only underscored his own egotism by claiming otherwise.

After more than a year in British hands, Lee was exchanged on April 21, 1778, and was honored with a reception at Valley Forge two days later. He spent the next month in York, hobnobbing with his friends in Congress, and returned to the army on the very day of the scrap at Barren Hill. Washington was not pleased to see him come back. Lee was not pleased with what he found upon his return.

The army he found at Valley Forge was much different than the one he had left in December 1776. *That* army had been on the verge of dissolution, low in morale and with so many enlistments due to expire at year's end. It vindicated Lee's ideas on the conduct of the war. *This* army was a reasonable facsimile of a professional European army, at least in bearing, and it contradicted Lee's beliefs regarding Americans and war. Unable to concede that he might have been wrong, Lee instead steadfastly refused to admit that anything had changed. As he remarked to Boudinot, the army at Valley Forge "was in worse shape than I had expected," and Washington was still "not fit to command a sergeant's guard."

It was only natural that Lee's disapproval would extend to the Baron de Steuben. Steuben had superceded Lee as the army's resident expert on military affairs, and had displaced Lee's ally Conway as inspector general. He was a newcomer, too, and close to Washington. Steuben encouraged Washington's irrational belief that American soldiers could be made the equal of their British foes.

And as if to rub salt into a raw wound, Steuben made no attempt to conceal his low opinion of the British military. To Steuben, the British army was second-rate at best, a haven for mediocre talent, its officers unimaginative, ignorant, and negligent of their men. Steuben's prejudices reflected the common sentiment of military men in continental Europe, but as Lee thought the British army to be without parallel in the modern world, Steuben's ideas rubbed him the wrong way.

Lee adamantly refused even to acknowledge that Steuben existed. He preferred to undermine the Baron indirectly, by instigating dissatisfaction with the new inspector general within the officer corps. Alex Hamilton knew this firsthand. "You have no doubt heard while you were with the army," he reported to his friend Boudinot, "of the obstacles thrown in [Steuben's] way by many of the General officers, excited to it by Lee and Mifflin I believe, in the execution of the Inspectorship."[18] It was not sheer coincidence that most of the subsequent complaints about Steuben came from officers in Lee's command.

The substance of those complaints came down to one thing: the Baron de Steuben wielded too much authority over his fellow generals. Some of the measures the Baron had adopted during the training program, though they were necessary and had Washington's full approval, irritated a few of the brigade commanders. Steuben had prohibited the use of any drill but his own or the introduction of any maneuvers that he had not approved, and he temporarily suspended the right of the colonels and brigadiers to exercise their men except when under the supervision of brigade inspectors. He had even dared to lecture the field officers on the need to be patient and kind with their men. The men "are not to be used ill, Either by abusive Words, or otherwise but their faults are to be pointed out with patience," Steuben had ordered. "There will be no other punishment for the soldier who is inattentive to Instruction but to make him Exercise for a whole hour after the others have done."[19] Who was he, a stranger without rank, to tell honest and long-serving American officers how to treat their men?

Even worse, by restructuring the regiments into temporary battalions, Steuben had temporarily deprived some officers of their commands. This would not do.

Steuben's most vocal critic, Brig. Gen. James Mitchell Varnum of Rhode Island, was a brigade commander under Lee. He would be Lee's mouthpiece. Precisely one day before the Grand Review, Varnum raised his concerns about Steuben with Washington in a long, rambling grievance. "I have observed for some Time since," he wrote, "the progressive Encroachment of a newfangled Power, which, if not checked, may prove destructive to this Army. I mean the Office of Inspector."

The Baron, as the head of this "newfangled Power," threatened the integrity and harmony of the army in several ways, Varnum argued. First, he and his assistants were given unlimited access to sensitive information, including precise strength reports from each brigade. Only the commander in chief should be privy to these statistics. Certainly they should not be entrusted to ordinary staff officers, and never to a foreigner. With Loyalists and spies everywhere, it would be all too easy for these strength reports to be leaked to the enemy. When, therefore, Steuben directed the brigade inspectors to collect current reports of all men fit for duty two days before the Grand Review, Varnum was "filled . . . with Horror."

But security, Varnum claimed, was a lesser issue. What really troubled him was what he saw as the unreasonable reach of the Baron's authority. "If the Baron, by his Aids, & Inspectors can manage my Brigade without my Orders, his Power is directly in Opposition to your Excellency's, and there are two commanders in Chief at the same Time." That this power could be granted to a foreigner made it that much more galling. Varnum portrayed Steuben as knowledgeable but condescending to the native-born officers. He was "too much prejudiced against the American Officers from an ignorance of their Abilities . . . [and] may have extended his Authority farther than he otherwise would."

This was largely what Varnum's grievances boiled down to: Steuben was a foreign know-it-all. "I am sensible," he concluded, "that great Politeness and Respect are due to the Foreign Officers; But our complaisance should never subjugate our Reason." For so many of the foreign officers didn't have the talents they claimed to, or even "Qualities worth Emulation." "The world will laugh at us," Varnum concluded, "when they view the List of Appointments and Promotions in their favor."[20]

———

THERE WAS SOMETHING to be said for these criticisms. Trustworthy though Steuben may have been, Varnum's concern about sensitive information was a valid and understandable one. So, too, is there a grain of truth to the complaint about the scope of the Baron's authority. While the training was in full swing, Steuben's power over the troops was indeed second only to Washington's.

On the other hand, Varnum's complaints—which were by no means voiced only by the Rhode Island brigadier—reflected social, political, and cultural differences between him and Steuben. Although the Continental Army was striving for professionalism, there was something very egalitarian about the officer corps. Continental officers, as a group, were loath to give up their authority, even if only temporarily, not even when the reasons were solid ones. They were very sensitive about their "rights," even when the protection of those rights stood in the way of progress.

The Baron, however, came from an army in which neither officers nor men pretended to have rights, and from a society in which competency and efficiency were prized commodities. From his perspective, the good of the service was the goal; it came before the feelings of individual officers. Training the army in such a short time required the concentration of all the necessary powers into the hands of the most qualified leaders. Good officers would understand this; others would just have to come to terms with it.

Steuben could not comprehend how anyone could raise objections to his actions as inspector general, especially when all orders concerning training had been issued through Washington's headquarters and not his. The results spoke for themselves.

Hence resistance to his methods troubled him. Innumerable petty objections absorbed much of his time and energy. In early June 1778, for example, he directed the brigade inspectors to find out how many soldiers each brigade furnished daily for guard duty, so that he could work out a rotation schedule that drew guards equitably from each regiment. He also asked for the names of all field officers, so that regimental drills could be scheduled at General Washington's pleasure. One of his brigade inspectors immediately ran into problems with these harmless requests. The major of his assigned brigade refused to provide him with the information desired: he was under strict orders, he said, not to provide "returns"—reports of unit strengths—to anyone.

In the face of such unyielding obstinacy, there was little the Baron could do. Territorial squabbles between him and the Varnums of the army kept him from doing his job. As John Laurens pointed out sadly to his father a few days later, "some Jealousies against [Steuben] have occasioned him great trouble, and interrupted his progress in the Military instruction."[21]

Steuben's response to this kind of resistance revealed that he did not fully understand the politics of the army, or the kind of pressures Washington had to deal with on a day-to-day basis. If individual officers were going to protest the extent of his authority, and if those protests kept him from doing what Washington had ordered him to do, then in his mind there was only one possible solution: to expand his authority even farther.

It did not help that Congress had not yet decided exactly what the inspector general was supposed to do, or how far he could go in doing it. There was more to being inspector general than just teaching drill, but Congress had not yet bothered to stipulate what those responsibilities might entail, or even where the inspector general fit within the chain of command.

So, late in May, Steuben began work on a proposal for the organization of the inspector general's office, to be submitted to the Board of War for its approval. His early draft proposals reflected his frustration with the "obstacles thrown in his way." Some of his ideas were clearly excessive. One, for example, gave the inspector general total authority over all "matters of discipline and military police"; without exception, any officer or enlisted man who did not obey the orders of the inspector or his assistants would be subject to immediate court-martial.[22]

The Board of War did not raise any significant objection to the tone or scope of Steuben's proposed regulations. The Board, after all, was happy with the Baron. He had accomplished what Washington's generals had not been able to, and as Steuben had made no demands on them, financial or otherwise, they were inclined to give him whatever he wanted.

But the Board, prudently, decided to sound out Washington, and Washington did what he did best: to keep peace within the army. Washington knew Steuben's worth, and did not feel threatened by the Baron in any way, but he recognized the rancor that would result if Steuben's ideas were implemented. So, instead of trying to negotiate with Congress and the Baron, the general-in-chief took the matter into his own hands.

In orders dated June 15, 1778, Washington made his own provisions for the conduct of the inspector general and presented them to the army. The purpose of the inspector general's office, he declared, was to institute "a System of Rules & Regulations for the exercise of the Troops in the Manual & Manœuvres," to establish some order in guard duty and the "internal Police of Camps and Garrisons." These "Rules & Regulations," however, would first have to be approved by the commander in chief, and then they would be issued as orders by Washington himself—not by Steuben. From now on, generals and field officers would take charge of drilling their respective commands, although a representative of the inspector's office would attend to assist them and to ensure that the regulations were indeed being followed.

It was a brilliant order, demonstrating the very qualities that made Washington such a great leader. He reduced Steuben to the position of a mere staff officer, who could not act independently of the commander in chief, thereby negating any complaint about the inspector's excessive authority. At the same time, he made the generals and the field officers responsible for seeing to it that the new regulations were enforced and the new drill put into practice. If Steuben's regulations were not followed to the letter, then the generals and the regimental commanders would have to answer to Washington, not to the Baron. Finally, Washington's order married Steuben's authority to his own. Since every measure the inspector introduced would have to go through general headquarters, the inspector spoke for Washington. At one stroke, Washington silenced those critics who thought the inspector's power excessive, and yet augmented that same power so that it was unquestionable.[23]

Steuben did not object outright to the order. On the surface, he seemed to be pleased with it. "It gives me great Satisfaction," he wrote to Washington, "to see that Your Excellency has taken such a wise Step . . . as to engage the General Officers and the Field Officers . . . to take Command of the Troops in our daily Exercise." He meant this sincerely; he wanted the officers to take charge of drill. But the rest of his letter fairly reeked with sarcasm. He had taken charge of drill, he told Washington—clearly tongue in cheek—because he had hoped to "save [the officers] the trouble of descending to those Toilsome & fastidious details which we chearfully [sic] encountered from the beginning for the good of the Service." He concluded the letter with a request for leave, so he could see friends in York.[24]

Washington praised the Baron for his flexibility—"the army has derived every advantage from the institution under you, that could be expected in so short a time"—but underneath the passivity of Steuben's response the commanding general detected something that was not quite right. And he worried about the request to travel to York. Steuben claimed that he only wanted to visit friends. Washington didn't buy it. He feared that Steuben planned to meet with his supporters in

Congress, with the intention of amending Washington's order and cajoling the Board of War into fashioning an "inspectorate" that suited his aspirations.[25]

This Washington could not tolerate, even if he had stood behind the Baron during the reforms in March and April. Steuben could not be allowed to compromise the carefully managed harmony in the high command. He would have to be headed off.

Before Steuben left for York, Washington gave him confidential letters to be handed to Henry Laurens and the young New York delegate William Duer. To Laurens, Washington merely hinted at his suspicions, while taking care to add that the Baron had been of great service. With Duer, the general was brutally candid . . . and secretive, for the letter was written in Alex Hamilton's hand and bore the aide's signature as well. But the words were clearly Washington's: "It will not be amiss to be on your guard," he warned Duer. "The baron is a gentleman for whom I have a particular esteem. . . . But I am apprehensive, with all his good qualities, a fondness for power and importance, natural to every man, may lead him to wish for more extensive prerogatives in his department than it will be for the good of the service to grant."

When Washington had first made Steuben the acting inspector general, he related to Duer, he had allowed him a great deal of latitude, necessary for accomplishing so much in so short a period of time. He had to curtail these powers earlier than he had anticipated because some officers had reacted badly. "The novelty of the office excited questions about its boundaries; the extent of its operations alarmed the officers of every rank for their own rights." Their "jealousies and discontents" had grown so heated, Washington feared, that the success of Steuben's reforms might be "overturned." Hopefully the general orders of June 15 would set everything right, but Duer would still have to keep an eye on the touchy Prussian:

There is one thing which the baron has much at heart, which, in good policy, he can by no means be indulged in: it is the power of enforcing that part of the discipline which we understand by subordination, or an obedience to orders. This power can only be properly lodged in the commander in chief and would inflame the whole army if put in other hands.

Washington was very close to being entirely correct. What motivated Steuben was not so much a hunger for power for its own sake, but a desire for accomplishment and efficiency that pushed him to be overzealous. His style of leadership, which owed to his Prussian upbringing, was geared solely toward results, and did not take the personalities and feelings of other officers into account. In the Continental Army such considerations were paramount. Washington understood this, but Steuben did not.[26]

For the moment, though, Steuben's sometimes autocratic manner was a moot point. The British were on the move, and the long sojourn at Valley Forge was coming to an end.

CHAPTER 7

Trial by Combat

[JUNE 1778]

All of my undertakings here have met with the most
fortunate progress.

STEUBEN TO DANIEL MARIANUS FRANK,
JULY 4, 1779[1]

STEUBEN WAS PREPARING for his trip to York when the
news came: the British were leaving Philadelphia.

The Baron's mind was occupied with other matters,
things that concerned him personally and professionally. Then
came the intelligence about the evacuation, passed along on the
morning of June 17 to Washington's headquarters by a Philadelphia washerwoman who laundered the uniforms of high-
ranking British officers. Sir Henry Clinton's army was going to
give up its foothold in eastern Pennsylvania and retreat, possibly to New York City. That very morning, the advance elements of the British army were already in the process of crossing
the Delaware into New Jersey.

Washington had anxiously anticipated this development—he
had, in fact, been planning for it from early spring. He had already sent portions of William Maxwell's New Jersey Brigade to
reinforce Jersey militia across the Delaware, to monitor any move
the British might make, but this force was not strong enough to

do anything more than harass Clinton's troops—if they actually retreated in that direction. Washington would not have to do anything, really, for by crossing the Delaware, Clinton showed that he was not interested in marching on Valley Forge. But if the American commander wanted to take a chance and try to destroy part or all of Clinton's army before it could reach the safety of New York, he would have to act *now*.

Gut instinct told Washington to *attack*, that here was an opportunity not to be missed, but where it came to strategy Washington led by consensus. He wanted to hear what his generals had to say. On the evening of the seventeenth, Washington assembled all of his major generals—Charles Lee, Nathanael Greene, Benedict Arnold, Lord Stirling, the Marquis de Lafayette, and Steuben—and most of his brigadiers at his Valley Forge headquarters, the Isaac Potts house. The general-in-chief laid out what he knew of Clinton's movements, gave his frank assessment of the condition of the Continental Army, and asked his generals to present their views on the strategic options. Should the army remain at Valley Forge and wait for another opportunity? Should Washington send a detachment to reinforce the brigade in New Jersey? Or should he hazard it all and send the entire army from Valley Forge to attack the British directly as they made their painfully slow exit from Philadelphia?

Their responses could not have pleased him much. Two of his brigadiers—including, predictably, the pugnacious Anthony Wayne—favored a "general engagement," an outright attack; Nathanael Greene supported this view, as did Lafayette, albeit with some reservations. But the rest, the majority, counselled caution. Charles Lee stated outright that the Americans were not ready for an open battle with the British, and probably never would be.

Steuben was also circumspect. Clinton, he feared, might be trying to lure Washington into a trap. The British had done so at Barren Hill, less than a month before. Now the stakes were much higher. Washington should follow the retreat carefully, sending a substantial body of troops to cover the fords of the Delaware above Trenton and to observe Clinton's movements. If Clinton's objective was indeed New

York, the Baron suggested, then Washington would be certain of it and could bring up the main army if circumstances warranted it.[2]

So the army would watch and wait. With no pressing business other than his desire to meet with the Board of War, Steuben rode out from Valley Forge for York the very next morning.

The Baron was still on the road to York—mounted, presumably, on one of the two "fine horses" given to him by Congress three weeks before—when a courier from headquarters caught up with him. He brought new orders from Washington: Steuben must return to camp immediately. The British had completely evacuated Philadelphia and had crossed into New Jersey; Washington, in response, was sending nearly his entire army—some thirteen thousand men—in pursuit. Cutting his trip short, Steuben wheeled about and spurred his horse back to the Forge.

When he reached camp later that day, the entire army was on the move. Washington had hoped so keenly for a chase that he had already written Lee's marching orders three weeks before, and now altered them slightly to accord to present circumstances. Lee's advance guard of three brigades had left at 3:00 P.M., followed by Wayne's division at five o'clock. The main body, under Lafayette and the Baron de Kalb, would march out at four o'clock the next morning, and Lord Stirling's rear guard would wait until the morning of the twenty-first. The army headed not to Philadelphia, but rather to the north and east: to Coryell's Ferry on the Delaware, just west of Princeton. If Clinton hoped to make it safely to New York, no matter by which route, he would have to cut north. By moving east, the Continentals could catch up to the British without any forced marches or Herculean efforts.

The chase was on.

Washington had a significant advantage. Because he had reacted so quickly, the British had only a shadow of a head start. The American line of march was no longer than the one Clinton would have to follow, and the Americans travelled much lighter. And once the British entered New Jersey, they encountered resistance. Maxwell's New Jersey Continentals, supplemented by the Jersey militia under Philemon

Dickinson, harassed Clinton's scarlet-clad columns practically from the moment the British set foot on the east bank of the Delaware at Cooper's Ferry. The Jerseymen did not risk an open battle, but instead hurriedly destroyed bridges immediately in front of Clinton's army, stopping occasionally to fire on the passing Redcoats from barns, mills, and farmhouses along the route. They were no more than an annoyance to Clinton, but that was their intention: the Jersey troops forced Clinton to deploy skirmishers on his flanks, while the entire army had to pause for burned and shattered bridges to be rebuilt.

And then there was the heat, the unforgiving, unrelenting heat. Those who recorded their recollections of the New Jersey campaign of 1778—British, German, or American—noted this above all other miseries. There were a few severe downpours over the next nine days, which transformed the dirt roads into nearly impassible quagmires, but during the day the brutal heat always returned. Temperatures soared well into the nineties. Both sides suffered, but the British appear to have gotten the worst of it. Dehydrated, exhausted men dropped in frighteningly large numbers, felled by heatstroke. Johann Ewald, a captain in the Hessian light infantry (*Jäger*) corps, noted that "no water was to be found on the entire march."[3]

There was something more behind the sluggishness of Clinton's retreat than the vicissitudes of a harsh summer. Clinton's cumbersome baggage train—some fifteen thousand wagons carrying the personal belongings of the officers, spare camp equipage, and all the comforts of home taken from Philadelphia—slowed the army, as did the unusually large number of noncombatants that followed in the army's wake. Alongside the British columns walked some one thousand civilians, including more than seven hundred women and children. This was hardly out of character for European armies, which often resembled travelling cities, and the British army was one of the worst offenders in this regard.

And Clinton was not in any particular hurry. He did not savor the idea of a clash with Washington, but neither did he shrink from it. The British had a significant advantage over the Americans in sheer numbers: roughly twenty thousand troops of all types, as opposed to thirteen thousand Continentals, exclusive of militia. With such an advantage, neither Clinton nor his officers harbored any real concern that they might be "burgoyn'd"—that is, trapped, cut off, and forced into a humiliating surrender, the fate of "Gentleman Johnny" Burgoyne's army at Saratoga the previous year. The British took their time, in other words, because they had no fear.

Washington could not help but be encouraged by the slow progress of the British retreat. His army was relatively unimpeded by baggage or civilians, while Maxwell and Dickinson provided him with detailed intelligence as they shadowed Clinton's every move. Although Clinton had more and better-trained troops than Washington did, the British force was strung out haphazardly in a thin column several miles in length. If the Continentals moved quickly enough, they just might be able to draw near to Clinton, isolate his rear guard, and defeat him in detail.

Even moving at a modest pace—Washington, fearing heavy casualties from the heat, did not want to push his army too hard—the Continentals caught up with Clinton within a few short days. By the afternoon of Monday, June 22, the entire American army had reached the Delaware at Coryell's Ferry; it crossed the river that night, and by the morning of the twenty-third, was encamped at Hopewell, New Jersey. There Washington's sources informed him of Clinton's position: after a march of only thirty miles in six days, the head of the British column had just then halted at Crosswicks, New Jersey, a mere seventeen miles south-southeast of Hopewell. The Continentals were within striking distance of the British. With a momentous decision ahead of him, Washington bivouacked his men at Hopewell to rest as he pondered his next move.[4]

S TEUBEN HAD just caught up with the army when it made camp at Hopewell.

After his abortive trip to York, the Baron had returned to Valley Forge to confer with Washington. As he did not have a command in the line, he was free to serve Washington in other ways. So instead of following the army to Coryell's, he and his staff rode immediately for Philadelphia. There they could observe British movements from the rear, in the event that Clinton doubled back and tried to maneuver around behind the Continentals.

Steuben spent the next four days in Philadelphia impatiently awaiting a summons from Washington. He did his best to enjoy himself, taking up residence on New Street in the city's German quarter and flirting with the local girls there in his native tongue; he "fancied himself again in his native country," Duponceau recalled years later. But despite the parties and the gaiety, the city was a depressing sight—Duponceau thought that the British had left it "filthy"—and though Benedict Arnold soon arrived with a regiment of Continentals to restore order, Philadelphia citizens with Patriot sympathies could not be restrained from punishing those who had collaborated with the British during the occupation. On the twenty-third, the Baron left the city in a hurry, arriving at Washington's camp that evening.

The army was preparing for battle when Steuben rode through the picket line and into the camp at Hopewell. The men were cleaning their muskets and assembling paper cartridges; they were also thinning out their few possessions, for Washington had decreed that they must march light, with no unnecessary baggage, not even tents. After nearly seven months in winter quarters, and with their enemy fleeing before them, they were eager for battle. Their commander in chief, however, had not yet settled on a specific course of action.

On the morning of June 24, a council of war convened at Washington's headquarters. After briefing the generals on the strength and position of the British forces, Washington proposed a deliberate movement against Clinton with the intention of forcing a battle. Charles Lee responded first. It might be acceptable, he contended, to reinforce Maxwell and Dickinson as they played havoc on Clinton's flanks, but to do anything more than that would be to risk destruction. Any outright attack would be suicidal. Even if the Continentals equalled the British in numbers, they would never equal them in discipline. Challenging the British to battle would be tantamount to "building them a golden bridge," freely giving them an easy victory to no good purpose. Instead, Lee proposed, the main army should march to the Hudson Highlands, there to await the arrival of the promised French expeditionary force. The French, being professionals, would at least have a fighting chance against the British.

Lee spoke from experience, and many of his juniors deferred to him even if they did not like him personally. Steuben was one of these men. Lafayette, Greene, and Wayne, however, could not abide Lee's caution, not when such an unprecedented opportunity presented itself. At no point in the war thus far had the British made themselves so vulnerable. It would be "disgraceful and humiliating to allow the enemy to cross the Jerseys in tranquility," Lafayette countered. Wayne suggested that a strong force—around twenty-five hundred men—be sent forward to goad the British into a counterattack.

Washington proposed a compromise: that a strong advance guard of fifteen hundred Continentals be sent to reinforce the Jersey troops and militia already nipping at Clinton's flanks, while the main army followed closely behind to monitor the situation. Like most compromises, it fully satisfied no one. Lee, Lafayette, and Greene agreed to it, albeit for very different reasons; Wayne truculently refused to sign his name to the proposal. Washington himself was not happy with his own compromise, but it was better than doing nothing, and he was not one to overrule the advice of the majority except in the most extraordinary circumstances.

Within hours the situation would change completely. After the council adjourned, Lafayette conferred privately with five of his colleagues, including Wayne, Greene, and Steuben. Together they began to incline toward Wayne's position. Wayne and Greene wrote individually to Washington to protest the compromise. Lafayette wrote on behalf of Steuben and the French engineer Louis Duportail, who begged the marquis to explain to Washington "how sorry, how distressed they are to see that we were going to loose [*sic*] an occasion which may be reputed as one of the finest ever offered."[5]

Washington did not wait to summon another council. He had already begun to act, rather liberally, on the compromise plan: before the day was out, he had sent more than two thousand Continentals, including six hundred of Dan Morgan's Virginia riflemen, to reinforce the Jersey troops currently hounding the British. Emboldened by the protests of his more aggressive generals, Washington dispatched another one thousand Continentals the following morning. The American advance guard now numbered nearly five thousand men. Charles Lee, as the senior-most major general, by right deserved to command the force, but as he evinced no interest in what he saw as a doomed enterprise, Washington gave the command to Lafayette. This was no simple reconnaissance. Washington intended to start a fight.

S TEUBEN'S BLOOD WAS UP. Doubtless he would have liked to accompany Lafayette to the front, just to be in the thick of the action, but he had not yet come to the point in his career where he *expected* such an honor. The Baron was still anxious to prove himself; he wanted to be indispensable.

Washington did have use for a man of Steuben's talents. Although he had many scouts, many eyes and ears, watching the British at every turn, none of them had the Baron's experience in European warfare. Steuben would finally get the chance to do what he had been trained to do, so many years ago, in Frederick the Great's royal suite: to collect and analyze intelligence so that his commander could employ his army as the situation warranted.

If Washington were to launch an attack, one vital question needed to be answered: What route would Clinton take to New York City? There were two obvious options. Either he could travel due north from his current position, through Cranbury and thence to the Amboys, approaching New York by land; or, alternatively, he could take a more easterly route, to Sandy Hook, where naval transports could ferry his troops to Staten Island. New York was not far away; if Clinton really pushed his troops along, and if Washington miscalculated the route,

Map of the northern theater of the war, 1778–80

the British could evade the Continentals altogether and seek safety in the hilly country of northern New Jersey.

Sometime in the evening of the twenty-fourth, before Lafayette had departed, Steuben—accompanied by Duponceau, Ben Walker, and a small cavalry escort—slipped out of the camp at Hopewell to find the British army.

He did not have to travel very far, for the British column had barely inched along since its arrival at Crosswicks two days before. Clinton's two divisions had separated, with Cornwallis's rear guard halting at Allentown on the night of the twenty-fourth, and Hessian general Wilhelm von Knyphausen's division taking its rest at Imlaystown, just under four miles to the east. Riding all night, Steuben and his party reached the outskirts of Allentown by dawn on the twenty-fifth. From here he reconnoitered both British divisions. At eight o'clock that morning, Knyphausen's division broke camp and marched north along the road that led north to Freehold. This would seem to indicate that Clinton's destination was Sandy Hook and not the Amboys. Cornwallis's division at Allentown, however, had not yet moved, and this was critical. Allentown was at a crossroads, where the road that ran from Crosswicks forked. The right fork went east-northeast through Freehold and toward Sandy Hook; the left fork, due north through Hightstown and Cranbury and to the Amboys.

The Baron rode north, skirting the British, but by noon on the twenty-fifth he still did not know where Cornwallis was headed, or if Cornwallis had moved at all. Three hours later, Steuben had reached Hightstown, nearly eight miles north-northeast of Allentown, where he received the word: Cornwallis's division was on the march, and had taken the right fork toward Monmouth Courthouse and Freehold. Clinton was bound for Sandy Hook.

Steuben understood the urgency of the situation. Washington, of course, would have to be alerted, but first the commanders of the advance guard must be apprised of Clinton's movements. With Ben Walker at his side, translating his French into passable English, Steuben dictated a terse note to Brig. Gen. Charles Scott, who commanded a portion of Lafayette's corps. Scott, a profane Virginian who would later serve as governor of Kentucky, had led his command of 1,440 light troops through Princeton and toward Allentown the previous day, and was anxiously awaiting further word from Steuben. The Baron offered his advice: "I therefore submit to your Judgement whether it would not be best to advance your Corps as far as this place [Hightstown]."[6]

The waiting and uncertainty were over, at least for the time being. Lafayette could follow Clinton more closely, and Washington could move the main body to Lafayette's support. That night the various elements of the advance guard rendezvoused at Hightstown, and on the morning of the twenty-sixth they marched by different paths toward Englishtown. Washington brought the eight thousand men of the main army to Cranbury to await further developments.

Clinton paid little heed to Washington's troop dispositions. He was well aware that he was being followed: the Jersey militia continued to dog him, and Steuben himself had moved so close to Clinton's forces "as to fire a Pistol at their Horsemen whilst feeding their Horses." But the British columns moved at a languorous pace, probably more because of the brutal heat than for any other reason. On the morning of the twenty-sixth, Knyphausen's division had reached the town of Freehold, while the rear guard under Cornwallis had halted at Monmouth Courthouse. And there they stayed. Just after noon on June 27, Steuben rode to a hill less than two miles from Monmouth, from which vantage point he could observe Cornwallis clearly with his spyglass. He reported to Washington in some bewilderment that the British "have some tents pitched & their Horses are at Pasture & [they have] not the least appearance of moving."[7]

Washington had already made up his mind to attack. He waited only on the most fortuitous moment to do so: when the head of Knyphausen's column set off again toward Sandy Hook, but before Cornwallis's division broke camp. An attack at this point would catch Lord Cornwallis at his most vulnerable, when the rest of Clinton's army would be slowest to react to an attack from the rear. If Washington acted quickly and decisively, Cornwallis could be defeated, or at least heavily mauled, before Knyphausen came to his relief. Yet the Americans needed all the time the British could spare them, for Washington faced an unforeseen problem: a last-minute change of command.

The problem was in large part Washington's own doing. He had entrusted the entire advance guard, and therefore the honor of leading the assault, to Lafayette. Maybe the marquis was not Washington's most brilliant lieutenant, but he was the most eager, and in this situation zeal and daring were more important attributes than tactical proficiency. Charles Lee had disdained to take part in Washington's plan, but once it was obvious that Washington intended to go through with it, Lee changed his mind. He was not about to let the young Frenchman take the honor that should have been his by right, not if there was any chance of gaining glory by it.

Washington, unfortunately, acceded to Lee's demand. It may be that his sense of propriety overrode his visceral instincts; perhaps he still hoped that he might win Lee over with such a gesture. For all of Lee's insubordination and personal contempt, Washington never really snubbed him, and at Valley Forge he had welcomed Lee back from captivity as he would a prodigal son. It would prove to be a grave error.

Transferring the forward command from Lafayette to Lee was Washington's first fatal mistake. Giving Lee carte blanche to arrange the details of the actual attack was his second, and it came very close to costing him the battle that ensued.

Clinton's army had not moved since its arrival at Monmouth Courthouse on June 26. Knyphausen's division had encamped just east of the village, along the road to Middletown and Sandy Hook; Cornwallis's troops settled down on the high ground west of Monmouth. The troops needed a rest. Despite a recent heavy rain, water was in short supply, with the locals having sabotaged their wells before fleeing the area. Dehydrated soldiers could be pushed only so far before collapsing in such hot weather. The heat, as well as the swarms of biting insects that followed the army, sapped British morale, which was already sagging because the Redcoats were retreating before an inferior enemy.

There were tactical considerations to keep in mind, too. Clinton had an inkling that Washington would force a confrontation, and that in itself was good reason to hold still for a while. If he could entice Washington into a frontal assault there, on the high ground outside Monmouth, then the rebels would be at a terrible disadvantage.

Washington, however, did not oblige him yet. On Saturday afternoon, June 27, Washington rode to Englishtown to confer with Lee. In the presence of Lee's staff, the commander in chief gave Lee his orders: he was to attack the British rear guard in the morning, as soon as he knew that Clinton was on the move. Washington was no more specific than this, leaving the operational details to Lee's discretion. It was an unwise decision on Washington's part, but although Lee had never been a dutiful subordinate, Washington had no reason to doubt his competence or physical courage.

The change of command was a mistake nonetheless. Whether from complacency or willful insubordination, Lee did next to nothing to prepare for the next day's action. He had not bothered to conduct his own reconnaissance of the enemy's positions since taking command on Saturday morning; he sent a handful of militia forward to scout the area that evening, but only after Washington had ordered him to do so. And when he met with his officers late Saturday afternoon, Lee told them only to have their troops ready to move by five o'clock the next morning. Lee's men were not prepared for battle because Lee had not prepared them.

B Y SUNDAY MORNING, Steuben was spent. He had been in the saddle for more than three full days with hardly a moment's rest. The urgency of his errands and the excitement of impending battle invigorated him. But at nearly forty-eight years of age, he was not a young man, and he had his limits. He had been riding through unfamiliar country, often at night, without even the blessing of a luminous moon to help guide his way. Late on Saturday night, the increasingly threatening skies opened up, a torrential downpour pelting his face and soaking his heavy woolen uniform as he blindly groped his way around the British lines. The mission was as dangerous as it was uncomfortable. There was no telling when he might run afoul of a British outpost or a cavalry patrol; without a significant escort to protect him, the danger of death or capture was very real. Still, the Baron kept at his task into the early morning hours of the twenty-eighth. Aching and weary to the bone, he rode around both British divisions, scanning their bivouacs for any sign of movement that might be revealed by the patchy and desultory light of the campfires.

In the early morning hours, his vigilance paid off. At around three o'clock on Sunday, the men of Knyphausen's division emerged from their improvised brush shelters—like Washington's men, they were travelling without tents—extinguished their fires, and formed up for the last leg of the march to Middletown. Within an hour they were on the road north, with their baggage train following immediately behind. Clinton's army was in motion; the moment Washington was waiting for had finally arrived.

Dawn came early that morning, at about half past four, yet it was still quite dark when Steuben sought out Philemon Dickinson to pass him the welcome news. Soon Dickinson's militia, who also had been watching the British closely, was exchanging fire with elements of Cornwallis's cavalry before being driven off. The word spread to both Lee and Washington. Washington was elated with the development, and quickly roused his own men so that he could hurry to support Lee.

What happened over the next few hours defies simple reconstruction. Of all the major engagements of the Revolution, Monmouth remains the most imperfectly understood. Because most of the detailed American accounts were entered as testimony in an acrimonious court-martial after the battle, it is difficult for the historian to separate impartial eyewitness accounts from the special pleading that one would expect to find in legal proceedings. Steuben himself wrote a detailed description of the battle several years after the fact, but he was prone to exaggeration when recounting his American exploits for his European friends; hence much of his narrative is demonstrably wrong, and all of it is highly suspect. Fortunately, there is enough common ground in the plethora of after-action reports to allow us to see the broad outlines of the battle of Monmouth, as well as Steuben's personal role in the action.[8]

That role was greater than the Baron could possibly have foreseen. He must have been giddy with anticipation as the sun rose that Sunday morning. Soldiering was what he loved above all things, and he had not been in battle since he was in his early thirties. Steuben felt like a young man again, and like a young man, he was a tad careless in his exhilaration. As he continued to reconnoiter the British positions, he and John Laurens rode so close to the British lines that Steuben was immediately spotted, recognized . . . and pursued. The British generals were aware of his presence, and Knyphausen had issued orders that every effort should be made to capture the distinguished Baron unharmed. Two dragoons broke from the British lines and charged straight for him. He paused only long enough to draw both of his enormous horse pistols from the holsters lashed to his saddle and fire each of them at his pursuers; then he turned his horse about and galloped to safety, so fast that his cocked hat flew off his head during his retreat.[9]

Shortly after his escape from the dragoons, Steuben worked his way toward Englishtown, where Lee had encamped that night. Lee had not ignored the intelligence related by Steuben and Dickinson, but his failure to prepare his subordinates adequately for that day showed plainly as the sun ascended in the sky. Sometime between three and four o'clock, having received the news of Clinton's march, Lee ordered Brig. Gen. William Grayson to lead two brigades down the road from Englishtown to Monmouth Courthouse, a march of around six miles. Poor planning delayed the movement, for Grayson knew nothing of the local countryside and had to find a guide at the last minute. He did not get going until nearly six o'clock.

The rest of the advance guard was not ready to march until eight. They were little better prepared than Grayson. Lee had recalled Grayson before the latter could make contact with the enemy, and in his place sent Anthony Wayne with two small regiments. These two regiments fared only a little better than Grayson. The terrain over which they had to march was not conducive to rapid, large-scale troop movements. The fields and orchards that lay on either side of the Englishtown Road between the Tennent (Freehold) Meetinghouse and Monmouth Courthouse were broken up by a series of morasses and deep ravines. They were not impassable but made it very difficult to maintain order and cohesion in an advancing line of battle. To make matters worse, one of Wayne's units, Jackson's Additional Regiment, had not been supplied with musket cartridges and had to round up ammunition en route. Wayne's two regiments would therefore take the field in a piecemeal fashion. Both of these problems—difficult terrain and poor ammunition supply—could have been obviated if Charles Lee had been attentive to his duties.

When Steuben came upon the bulk of Lee's forces on the English-town Road, they were still a good distance from Monmouth. Corn-wallis's division had already broken camp and moved north along the Middletown Road. To the Baron, it seemed like a good opportunity had been thrown away by virtue of Lee's tardiness. "Having seen that the enemy was marching, and doubting of our being able to overtake them, having seen nothing in my way but some militia which followed at some distance," he later testified, Steuben became convinced that there would be no battle that day. Disappointed and exhausted, his last reserves of energy expended, he continued on to Englishtown to make his report to Washington. The commander in chief was not yet there, so Steuben, on the verge of collapse, sought out lodgings in the village, claimed a room for himself, and flopped down to sleep without re-moving his clothes. The time was roughly nine o'clock.

He awoke after a nap of no more than an hour and a half.

It could be that the sound of distant gunfire roused him from his slumber, or maybe it was the tramping feet of Washington's eight thousand troops as they approached Englishtown. Whatever the reason, Steuben jerked awake, bolted from his temporary quarters, mounted, and rode eastward down the Englishtown Road, hoping once more to find Washington. No sooner had he left Englishtown than he distinctly heard the muffled boom of distant cannon-fire. A battle was definitely in the offing, and the Baron urged his horse to a faster gait.[10]

Around the time he passed the Tennent Meetinghouse, Steuben saw the first signs of defeat: first, some of Dickinson's militia who had been driven back awhile before, and then the Continentals. The militia-men, predictably, were slightly unnerved—who wouldn't be, after being ridden down by British cavalry?—but the Continentals, streaming to the rear in growing numbers, were not. They still had their muskets and leather accoutrements, a sign that they had not scampered in fear, and they did not have the look of defeated soldiers. The men looked bewildered; their officers appeared angry. Some of them openly cursed Charles Lee for ordering a general retreat.

Alarmed by what he saw, Steuben continued to ride toward the sound of the fighting. He caught a glimpse of Washington, and nudged his horse in his direction; but before he could get within speaking distance of his commander, he saw from a distance what had become of Lee's division. The entire advance guard was withdrawing, some units faster than others, moving in his direction parallel to the Englishtown Road. Around fifteen hundred British troops, mostly infantry, were on their heels. Lee's Continentals were, Steuben later recalled, "retreating in great disorder," their cohesion disrupted by the ravines and swampy morasses that made retreat in line almost impossible. Just like the men he encountered on the road, though, Lee's troops were not scampering for their lives as they had so many times in the past. Their training at Valley Forge had at least proven useful in helping the troops maintain their composure under stress.

Steuben did not know all of the details, and would not until the smoke had long since cleared from the boggy fields that spread along the Englishtown Road. He could, however, discern the obvious: Lee's attack had failed, and miserably.

After the uneventful advance of Grayson's two brigades and Wayne's tiny force, Wayne had taken control of the forward elements while the rest of Lee's corps moved up along the road that led from the Tennent Meetinghouse to Monmouth. Wayne pushed eastward across the plain near the courthouse. Along the way, he encountered nothing more than a handful of British cavalry, which he brushed aside without much effort. A much larger British force, however, was forming a line along the Middletown Road north of Monmouth. Wayne liked a good fight. Impetuously, he advanced on the British position with only one small regiment, which stood alone to face a counterattack by British cavalry. Thanks to what one historian has called their "Steuben-instilled instinct," this regiment—William Butler's Pennsylvanians—held firm, repulsing the British horse with crisp volleys of musketry delivered at point-blank range. Wayne halted his advance until the rest of Lee's troops could catch up with him.

Lee saw what he thought might be a golden opportunity to cut off and envelop the rearmost elements of Cornwallis's division, which he estimated at no more than 1,500 to 2,000 men. This prospect, however, quickly vanished, for soon a growing body of British infantry began to move south toward him on the Middletown Road. Clinton was not retreating; quite the opposite: he was turning to fight with the bulk of his forces. Hastily, Lee attempted to shore up his line to receive the inevitable onslaught, with Lafayette's command moving to protect the right flank and Charles Scott's troops bolstering the center. Lee's intentions were sound, but they failed in the execution: there was not enough room in which to maneuver, and Lee had neglected to inform his subordinates just what it was he planned to do. Lafayette's troops never reached the right flank, leaving a gap in the American line that Cornwallis quickly exploited. The right flank began to crumble. This left Scott's troops, now on the American right, exposed, and Scott saw no other option than to withdraw to the southwest.

Scott's withdrawal proved to be the undoing of the entire enterprise. The American left began to fall apart as well, and within minutes word passed through the ranks that Lee had ordered a general retreat. The American line of retreat, which crossed the forbidding East Ravine and led through a soggy quagmire known as the East Morass, rendered an orderly withdrawal impossible. If Cornwallis moved quickly enough, his troops could envelop and destroy Lee's command before Washington's main army could come to its rescue.

The commander in chief was doing everything in his power to push his troops to Lee's support, but not because he suspected that anything was wrong. He had set his force in motion from Manalapan as soon as he had received Steuben's report much earlier that morning, and to speed the army's progress he had ordered the men to discard their blankets and knapsacks. The only word he had received from Lee was encouraging. Alex Hamilton had met Washington along the way to inform him that Lee was advancing against Cornwallis. Washington was only two miles away from Monmouth Courthouse when he spotted the first signs of trouble: stragglers, first in pairs and small clusters, then eventually in whole companies, officers as well as enlisted men. By the time he reached the bridge that crossed the West Ravine, Washington could discern that entire battalions and brigades were turning away from the action and heading back toward Englishtown.

For a man who was ordinarily so collected, even stoic, George Washington had a ferocious temper, which only rarely showed itself in public. He had erupted in a wrath of legendary proportions during the battle at Kips Bay nearly two years before. His temper burst forth again as he rode into the midst of Lee's retreating troops at Monmouth. It may have been a relief to see that the troops who were now streaming away from the fighting were neither unnerved nor frightened, only confused, but that very fact made Lee's withdrawal inexplicable to Washington. He was angry because he was disappointed, because after months of waiting for this very moment, he was witnessing everything for which he had worked so hard unravelling before his very eyes. The men who were marching to the rear all seemed to agree that they were retreating not because they were defeated but because General Lee had ordered it. Their officers were inclined to agree that the sudden withdrawal had been unnecessary. When one of Washington's aides confronted Col. Matthias Ogden, commander of the 1st New Jersey Regiment, about the reason for the retreat, the flustered Ogden replied, "By God! They are flying from a shadow!"[11]

Despite Washington's visibly foul mood, his presence breathed new life into Lee's broken command. His timing was perfect. The Redcoats were close now, and since it would take time to bring up and deploy the main body, it would be necessary to re-form at least part of the advance guard and hold off the British advance until a new defensive line could be formed. And it was imperative that the retreat be checked immediately so that the malaise of Lee's men did not spread through the rest of the army like a contagion.

The regiments in Washington's immediate presence, mostly from Maxwell's New Jersey Brigade, rallied first, and without much difficulty. Their training did not fail them, and Washington's talent for inspiration came through. As the Jerseymen formed a new line of battle, he rode before them and addressed them directly. "Gen Washington on that occasion asked the troops if they could fight and . . . they answered him with three cheers."[12] The retreat slowly abated. On the American right, where the pursuit was the hottest, Anthony Wayne's little brigade of Pennsylvanians only grudgingly gave ground, finally halting and holding firm at a well-placed hedgerow.

So far, Lee was nowhere to be found, but as the troops rallied around Washington, he finally emerged—slouched in his saddle, head low, utterly defeated. For more than two centuries, Lee has remained the whipping boy for Monmouth, and the notion persists that he alone stood between the might-have-beens and the actual outcome of the battle. Yet Lee was not a villain. He stood to gain nothing from a failed attack, and once he launched his attack on Cornwallis he was fully committed to it. His principal sins were his failures to prepare adequately or to communicate effectively with his subordinates.

Washington, however, was not acquainted with the finer points; all he knew was that his army was on the verge of being routed, and that Lee was immediately responsible. His face twisted and reddened with anger, Washington confronted Lee directly. Precisely what transpired between the two generals at the West Morass has become a hotly debated issue. Several officers—not all of whom were actually present—insisted that Washington was so enraged that he swore in public, a remarkable thing: Lafayette said that Washington called Lee a "damned poltroon"; Charles Scott recalled that his commander "swore on that day till the leaves shook on the trees . . . he swore like an angel from Heaven." All those within earshot of the meeting agreed, however, that Lee was confused and uncharacteristically inarticulate, stammering, "Sir, sir," when Washington asked him the reason for the retreat. Lee, who appeared highly embarrassed to those present, then responded that contradictory intelligence, and disobedience of his orders, was responsible for the failure.

Lee was a beaten man, probably realizing that his military career was over. He retired to Englishtown, where he would wait out the rest of the battle that he had begun, leaving Washington and his other generals to save the army as best they could.

R EGRETTABLY, Steuben did not see the confrontation. As a discerning connoisseur of profanity, one wonders what he would have thought of Washington's deportment on that occasion. Instead, the Baron arrived near the West Morass just before Washington and Lee exchanged words, and went straight to work.

The inspector general had no troops to command, but his appearance was nearly as much a relief to Washington as if he had brought a fresh brigade with him. Washington did not lack troops. True, Lee's men were disorganized, but they were not racing from the field, nor were they yet physically drained. They needed only inspiration and direction to form a serviceable defensive line, and Washington could not be everywhere at once. As a familiar figure whose presence might comfort Lee's dejected soldiers, Steuben was a godsend.

The Baron had no trouble finding Washington—it would be hard to miss such an angry giant mounted on a fine white charger—but he did not yet approach his general for instructions. He knew by instinct and long experience what needed to be done. He spotted Henry Knox, Washington's rotund artillery chief, and after consulting with him, helped to form and position a battery of light artillery on the American right flank. Then he rode north, straight into the thick of the retreating troops on the left flank, where the disarray was the greatest—passing, incidentally, a silent and humbled Charles Lee, now on his way to the rear after Washington's tongue-lashing—and exhorted the men in his broken English to stand and fight. After restoring a modicum of order in this sector of the field, Steuben rode to find

Washington, who curtly ordered the Baron to go west, rally those of Lee's troops who had already left the field, and reform them in the vicinity of Englishtown.

While the improvised American line held off the British counterattack, Steuben hurried west to Englishtown, accompanied by Ben Walker and Ternant. Here he found, once again, Charles Lee, who had been stunned into near passivity by the events of the past few hours. This time Lee addressed Steuben directly, asking the Prussian what he was about. When Steuben replied that he was under orders to rally Lee's troops, Lee responded pitifully that he was glad to see Steuben had taken on the duty, for he himself was "tired out."

Steuben did not tarry by Lee. In Englishtown he found much of Scott's command and portions of Maxwell's New Jersey Brigade. Once again, the weeks spent in training at Valley Forge proved their value. Even though the soldiers at Englishtown were completely without organization, an inchoate mass of men from several different regiments, Steuben managed to reform them into platoons, companies, and battalions in a matter of minutes. He marched them, in a perfectly formed line of battle, to take a defensive posture on the Weamacock Creek, east of Englishtown. With that duty completed, Steuben left the reformed troops to the care of their officers and spurred his horse back to the battle itself.

By now the battle was fully developed—a confusing, swirling affair, compounded by the horrid din of what was later described as the heaviest cannonade of the entire war. "The dust and smoke . . . sometimes so shut out the view," an American officer noted, "that one could form no idea of what was going on." Monmouth was not one fight, but several; in separate actions all along the American line, Clinton and Cornwallis attempted to break through the center while enveloping both flanks. But the Continentals held, even when assailed by Clinton's elite—the 42nd Regiment of Foot (the famous "Black Watch"), a full brigade of grenadiers, and a battalion from the Guards brigade—coolly pouring volley after volley into the relentless waves of scarlet, without breaking or even flinching.

Steuben kept to a frenetic pace, positioning reinforcements from the main body, feeding brigades into the fight as they arrived on the field. It was now midafternoon, the temperature was soaring well into the nineties, and Clinton was having second thoughts about his counterattack. The best veteran regiments in his army had proven unable to smash through the American line in repeated bayonet charges, and he had lost a good number of men, and several of his field officers, to the heat and the withering volleys of musketry.

William Woodford's Virginia Brigade, part of Nathanael Greene's force holding the right flank, took control of a rise known as Comb's Hill. Soon an artillery battery appeared on Comb's, unlimbered, and pounded the British left, while Lord Stirling's division made similar progress on the American left. Unable to push the Continentals any further, Clinton prudently decided to disengage. The same broken terrain that had hampered Lee's retreat that morning also disrupted the British withdrawal, and Washington pounced on the chance to strike back as the Redcoats lost their cohesion. New Hampshire and Virginia troops under Col. Joseph Cilley lunged forward in a spirited counterattack on the British center, engaging the British in a sharp firefight at an orchard south of the Englishtown Road. Finally, Washington ordered simultaneous attacks on both flanks, but the sun set before they could be set in motion.

Dusk also denied Steuben his part in the glory of the final assault. At about 5:30 P.M., half an hour after the artillery on both sides had ceased their mutual exchange of fire, Washington sent for the Baron. The enemy was retreating "in confusion," Washington related; Steuben must move up at once, bringing some infantry along to support the counterattack. Jumping at the chance to get back in the fray, Steuben took command of three brigades (then under Brig. Gen. John Paterson of Massachusetts), which he had just placed in a defensive position east of Englishtown. Here he encountered the dejected Lee, who tried to stop him, challenging the veracity of the intelligence that the Baron had received from Washington. The British, Lee told Steuben, could not *possibly* be withdrawing "in confusion"; there was no chance that the Continentals could have repulsed a determined attack by the enemy he so revered. Steuben ignored him, and hurried Paterson's troops down the road to Monmouth. The British had fallen back, however, before Steuben's detachment could make their grand entrance.[13]

Thus ended the Battle of Monmouth. The performance of his army in the wake of Lee's defeat gave Washington hope that he could seek a rematch early the next morning, but Clinton could see no good reason to stay in the vicinity. The entire British army silently crept away to the north shortly after midnight, and did not halt until it reached Middletown the next evening. American scouts discovered the empty British camps early on the morning of June 29. Instead of pursuing the British—which would have been sheer folly, given the exhausted condition of the Continentals—Washington led most of the army north toward the Hudson Valley, while Maxwell and Dan Morgan watched the British march to Sandy Hook from a safe distance.

M ONMOUTH WAS THE LAST GREAT BATTLE of the war in the northern states. Though, chronologically speaking, the war was not yet half over—the conflict had lasted for just over three years so far, and nearly another five would pass before the peace—it was the last time Washington would lead an army in an open fight against a British army. The clash was not especially costly, with fewer than four hundred total casualties on each side; neither could it be considered decisive. Clinton's army still reached New York in one piece, and Washington's army was barely bloodied. Monmouth does not stand comparison with earlier battles such as Trenton or Saratoga, for it neither boosted nor strengthened American morale in a significant way, nor did it weaken British resolve to crush the rebellion. Tactically, the battle was a draw, though both Washington and Clinton claimed it as a great victory.

Monmouth did, however, reveal significant flaws within the Continental Army, particularly problems of leadership and command.

Charles Lee would bear the brunt of the blame for the fact that, at Monmouth, the Continentals had missed the chance to destroy an entire British field army. Lee was an easy target, and made himself an easy scapegoat by arguing with Washington after the battle and demanding a court-martial to clear his name and redeem his honor. He did not realize until it was too late that attacking Washington was a poor political move, for virtually the entire officer corps rallied behind their commander in chief, and would gang up on Lee in the court-martial that followed. Junior generals who previously had quaked in Lee's shadow now found the courage to condemn him.

If there is any blame to be assigned for a "missed opportunity" at Monmouth, then Washington must surely share in it, and possibly claim a greater share than Lee. His decision to transfer forward command to Lee stands out as his greatest mistake—not because Lee would bungle the opening attack, but rather because a leader closer to Washington's heart, like Lafayette, would *perhaps* have cooperated more effectively with his sub-commanders. But Washington, unlike Lee, redeemed himself by rallying the army and turning the day to his advantage.

Monmouth was not a turning point in the war. It was, however, a turning point in the history of the Continental Army. Even with an uncertain chain of command and lackluster leadership, the rebels had performed magnificently. At Bunker Hill, Trenton, Princeton, and even Germantown, they had displayed great fortitude and bravery, but at Monmouth they showed *discipline* for the first time. Despite a disappointing early phase, namely Lee's opening attack, the rebels had rallied once Washington arrived on the scene, and they did so quickly because they had never really panicked in the first place. The Continentals held firm as musket balls and solid shot slammed into their ranks, as fabled regiments like the Highlanders of the Black Watch advanced on their lines with bayonets levelled. They held their ground through all of these things, mounted a furious counterattack, and drove the Redcoats from the field. The British had retreated, not they.

Alex Hamilton, never one to give undue credit to his own army, assessed the performance of the Continentals with uncharacteristic enthusiasm:

> The behaviour of the officers and men in general was such as could not easily be surpassed. Our troops, after the first impulse from mismanagement, behaved with more spirit & moved with greater order than the British troops. You know my way of thinking about our army, and that I am not apt to flatter it. I assure you I never was pleased with them before this day.[14]

Like Barren Hill, but on an infinitely grander scale, Monmouth was a soldier's battle, in which any success the rebels could claim owed mostly to the qualities of the rank and file, not to brilliant leadership. And that, in turn, must be partly credited to Steuben. If anything proved the worth of the training program at Valley Forge, it was the performance of the Continentals at Monmouth.

Americans *could* stand and fight in the conventional European manner, and could do so as well as their British counterparts. They no longer panicked at the glint of sunlight off burnished bayonets. Hamilton noted the change in the army's conduct. He had watched in awe as Steuben, who had just arrived on the battlefield, rallied Lee's Jerseymen and marched them in perfect order to take their place in the line. They had suffered a great shock that morning, and now they were advancing under heavy musketry, moving as calmly and precisely as if they were on parade. Until that moment, Hamilton later told Ben Walker, he had never fully understood the concept of military discipline.[15]

The battle was a high point in Steuben's life, too, one that in many ways he would never surpass. His name was linked inextricably to the rebirth of the army, a rebirth that had taken place in the snows of Valley Forge. If Valley Forge and Monmouth had been his sole contributions to the Continental Army, that would have been legacy enough. But the battle brought his talents to light in other ways, too. His pre-battle reconnaissance, his actions in re-forming the army at the West Morass and Englishtown—these reassured the Baron that his tutelage under Frederick and Prince Henry had not been for naught, that he understood the art of war and of leadership.

Curiously, though, the performance of the army that bore his indelible personal stamp was not Steuben's main point of pride. It wasn't that he didn't take pleasure in the achievement of the men, *his* men, with whom he had bonded so deeply during the crash course in military discipline that winter. He did, but he was also immensely proud of himself. His reconnaissance before the battle, which he had conducted with the boundless energy of a much younger (and trimmer) man, had provided Washington with vital intelligence. And, most important, he had led troops under fire.

That was what he desired above all things, the ambition he had carried with him from boyhood. At heart he was a soldier and not an administrator. There was nothing he wanted more than the pulsing thrill of battle. He had been denied that visceral joy for nearly two decades. Monmouth brought it all back to him, enlivening his memories of that bloody day outside Prague in 1757 when he had first drawn his sword to lead his blue-clad company through the maelstrom of fire and smoke and toward the waiting Austrians.

Monmouth vindicated Steuben as an organizer; it proved him as a battlefield commander, and he had the profound satisfaction of watching his creation *work*. When he wrote about the battle to his friends in Europe, he characteristically exaggerated his role. His inflated account was full of blatant falsehoods: he had, he claimed, commanded an entire wing of Washington's army and had all but defeated Clinton single-handedly. "I was fortunate enough," he wrote to Chancellor Frank, "to decide the day to our advantage . . . every soldier wished that he was under my command." Even his counterfactual boasting revealed his heart's loftiest aspirations.[16]

The Baron was on his way to great deeds, great responsibility, and greater glory—of this he was convinced. And why not? Six months ago he was just another European émigré in search of a job; four months ago he was a gentleman volunteer without rank or assignment. Now he was a general, with a track record of administrative success and command skills proven on the field. Surely Washington could see that. Surely a real field command would be his, and soon.

This was the unfortunate legacy of Monmouth for the Baron de Steuben: it sent his hopes soaring skyward. He felt that he deserved a field command, although he had never asked for one and one had never been promised to him. Over the following year, this conviction would try his patience—and that of Washington and Congress—and test the depth of his devotion to the Cause he claimed to have adopted as his own.

CHAPTER 8

The Blue Book

[JULY 1778—APRIL 1779]

I know very well that whatever be one's Circumstances,
the best is to put on a cheerful face, or as the French
term it*: faire bonne mine à mauvais jeu.*

STEUBEN TO HENRY LAURENS,
OCTOBER 1, 1778[1]

STEUBEN'S PRIMARY DUTY to the army was as inspector
general. He had not been able to attend to that duty
since the opening of the campaign in mid-June, and it
was not probable that he would be able to resume his work for
some time. It was too late for the Continentals to ambush Clinton again, but the army would have to position itself in such a
way as to keep the British bottled up in New York. And there
was another piece of army business that Washington could not
allow to fall by the wayside, even though taking care of it could
delay the march north.

That piece of business was Charles Lee. Lee's performance
may not have been anywhere near as negligent as his many enemies liked to imagine it, but he had been insubordinate in the
past, and while Washington had tolerated these earlier incidents with saintlike patience, he could not afford to do so any
longer. Lee must be made an example of.

So Charles Lee would stand before a court-martial. The

trial was a perfunctory affair. Lee didn't stand a chance. His fellow generals stood shoulder to shoulder with Washington, providing the court with reams of damning testimony. If Lee had shown even a modicum of contrition, he might have escaped with little more than a verbal dressing-down and a bruised ego. But he remained unrepentant to the end. As late as October, he proudly proclaimed to Henry Laurens that "I am myself inflexibly persuaded, that I am not only guiltless, but that the success of the 28th of June ought principally, in justice, to be ascribed to me." The court did not agree; it found Lee guilty and sentenced him to a one-year suspension from command.[2]

Lee's removal from the service, though it deprived Washington of a genuinely capable general, was a great boon to the army, for it helped to restore harmony to the high command. Steuben also benefitted, for Lee and his sympathizers had been foremost among those who had caused problems for the Baron at Valley Forge. At the moment, however, the court-martial was a tremendous inconvenience. Washington wanted to move the army north to join forces with Horatio Gates, so that the Continentals would be prepared to cooperate with the French when Admiral D'Estaing's fleet arrived. The Comte D'Estaing was expected to appear off the southern New England coast any day now; time was of the essence. But because all of the army's major generals and many of its brigadiers were involved in the court-martial, no commanders were available to lead the troops from the New Brunswick area to the Hudson Valley.

Washington did the best he could with what he had at hand. He could most readily spare the foreign generals. So he split the army into two large wings, giving one to Baron de Kalb and the other to the Baron de Steuben. Steuben officially took command of his three brigades on July 2. Four days later, his wing left New Brunswick for White Plains.[3]

———

FOR STEUBEN, the march was a great adventure, and his spirits soared. He knew that there was little possibility of battle, and that the command was only temporary—Washington had been careful to make that point crystal clear—but he took it as a positive sign anyway. Right after his wing crossed the Hudson at Kings Ferry, New York, on July 20, he rendezvoused with Gates, and together the two generals conducted a thorough reconnaissance of the Connecticut shore along Long Island Sound. It didn't matter that there was no sign of D'Estaing's ships; just the fact that Steuben was doing things that commanding generals did was a tremendous boost to his ego. And if the French did indeed manage to land an expeditionary force, there would be action, and Steuben would be in the thick of it. High-ranking French officers would be there to see the army he had reformed and to see him in command.[4]

The Baron was so happy with this turn of events that he scarcely noticed that not everyone shared his joy. Washington's decision to give him the command was based on purely practical concerns, but that did not console many of the brigadiers, who complained that a foreigner with little time in rank had been given a responsibility that by right should have gone to one of them. John Laurens caught wind of the angry whispers that flitted through the officer corps, and they troubled him. "Unfortunately there is a prejudice against foreigners in many of our Officers," he wrote his father. "It is not without uneasiness that some of them see Baron de Steuben . . . appointed to the temporary command of a division in the absence of so many Major Generals."[5]

Such complaints embarrassed the idealistic Laurens, ashamed of his fellow officers for being so self-centered and parochial. Washington, on the other hand, did not have the luxury of taking the moral high ground. He had an army to run, and as the protests piled up on his desk, he could not ignore the sentiments of the aggrieved. The brigadier generals, he explained to Henry Laurens, did not mind that Steuben was inspector general, and "have said but little about his rank as Major General, as he had not had an actual command over 'em." But the temporary command, "tho' founded in evident necessity and not designed to produce to the Brigadiers the least possible injury, excited great uneasiness and has been the source of complaint."[6]

Steuben's own conduct did not help his case. Just as his division was setting out from New Brunswick, he arrested his divisional quartermaster, Capt. Reuben Lipscomb, for daring to take possession of a house in Paramus that Steuben had already earmarked for his personal headquarters. The transgression was trivial, but it ruffled Steuben's plumage. Charging Lipscomb with "treating [him] in a disrespectful manner," the Baron convened a court-martial on the spot. The court cleared Lipscomb of all charges with honor after giving him a mild reprimand for "Impropriety."[7] The court-martial was a poor political move on Steuben's part; it made him appear as an oversensitive, pompous martinet, and did nothing to improve his standing with his American-born colleagues.

So Washington wasted no time. On July 22, as Steuben's force approached White Plains, he ended the Baron's command—cordially, without the slightest hint of reproach, making sure to thank him for his "Care & Attention to the Troops during their March."[8]

The order devastated Steuben—not so much the termination of command, but rather the way in which Washington had worded it: "Baron Steuben will please to resume his Office of Inspector General & make his Arrangements accordingly." Steuben had demonstrated that he could lead troops, and had deluded himself that he was on his way to a field command, yet he remained a staff officer. If he could remain inspector general and still command troops in the field, as was the practice in the French and Prussian armies, he would have been more than satisfied. But the administrative side of the inspectorate, taken by itself, held no real interest for him. Picking through the contents of cartridge boxes and knapsacks, accounting for lost property, filling out reports—these were the duties of lieutenants and clerks, not of major generals.

Even those duties would have been more bearable if only Congress and Washington could agree on the limits of the inspector's authority, on what he could and could not do. When Steuben had submitted a plan for the inspectorate at Valley Forge, the other generals and the politicians had to meddle with it—they "mutilated" it, according to

Alex Hamilton—and as a result he did not have a clear mandate. It was hard to get fired up about a position when no one would tell him what that position entailed.[9] ·

Aggravating his frustration was a situation that had recently arisen in Gates's Northern Army. Gates had his own inspector, Louis-Pierre de La Neuville, another French import. Gates thought highly of La Neuville. So did Congress. The same committee that had recommended Steuben as inspector general deemed La Neuville a capable and valuable officer, appointing him to the post of inspector for the Northern Army at the rank of brigadier. Steuben was La Neuville's superior, but La Neuville would not accept a subordinate position, and when the Baron arrived at White Plains in July, he told Steuben so to his face, "My rank in France, the assurance that Congress gave me . . . does not permit me to serve second under baron Stubben's as Inspector." La Neuville vowed to resign if he were not made Steuben's equal. The Baron had no taste for a confrontation, but clearly he could not work with such a man. "I foresee some difficulties in the way," he told Washington. His irritation was directed less at La Neuville for his willful insubordination than at Congress for not clarifying the chain of command.[10]

Since Congress had not done that, since they had not given him a plan for action "that would comprehend all the essential Duties of my Office," the Baron explained to his commander, there was nothing he could do. "I beg your Excellency to postpone my entering into the Office of Inspector General untill [*sic*] Congress have you[r] Opinion & directions about the matter finally pronounced." In the meantime, he requested Washington's permission to "take this Opportunity of making a tour to Philadelphia to see my Friends."[11] Steuben's request was not as innocuous as it appears. Since he was unable to get what he wanted—both explicit guidelines and a field command—he intended to go over Washington's head and try his luck with Congress.

To further bolster his arguments for a strong, assertive inspectorship and his right to command troops on campaign, Steuben solicited written opinions from two European soldiers in the Continental service: Henry Leonard Philip, the Baron d'Arendt, and Martial-Jean-Antoine Crozat, Chevalier de Crénis—the first a veteran of the Prussian army, the second of the French army. He knew that Congress already thought highly of him, and armed with these affidavits, he hoped to convince the delegates, newly reconvened in Philadelphia, that his ideas should be accommodated whether Washington liked them or not.

And if reasoned argument didn't do the trick, the Baron would present an ultimatum: he would resign his commission and go back to Europe.

Washington knew for certain that Steuben was up to more than just visiting friends in the capital. Steuben *wanted* him to know, and let the sympathetic Hamilton in on his plans. The commander in chief was not pleased. He did not care for insubordination—he had experienced enough of that martial vice in the past two years—but mostly he was disappointed in Steuben, whom he had grown to value and trust. "I regard and I esteem the Baron, as an Assiduous, Intelligent and an experienced Officer," Washington told Henry Laurens. "The Baron's services in the line he is in can be singular."[12] Yet Steuben had put his pride ahead of his dedication to the Cause, like so many foreign officers, who

> in the first instance tell you, that they wish for nothing more than the honour of serving in so glorious a cause, as Volunteers—The next day sollicit rank without pay—the day following want money advanced to them—and in the course of a Week want further promotion, and are not satisfied with anything you can do for them.[13]

It was an accurate, if ungenerous, description of Steuben's behavior so far, behavior that offended Washington's sense of patriotic devotion. The worst part was that Steuben knew the furor that would erupt if Congress were to accede to his demands, and the headaches they would cause at headquarters. For Washington, that could not be tolerated.

With a plan to intercept Steuben before he could do any damage, and with no wish to hurt Steuben's feelings, Washington quietly contacted two trusted allies in Congress: Henry Laurens and Gouverneur Morris, the latter an unusually young and womanizing New York delegate who had proven at Valley Forge that he was one of the best friends the army had in Congress. Congress *must* do something, *anything*, Washington impressed upon Laurens and Morris, to create a functioning inspector general's department. For starters, La Neuville must be put in his place. Beyond that, Congress could not grant Steuben's requests, Washington insisted, even if the Baron threatened to resign.

> I am extremely sorry, that this Gentlemans situation and views seem to have determined him to quit the service. . . . [He] resolves not to continue in the Service unless he can hold an actual command in the line. . . . [T]he Baron has in every instance discharged the several trusts reposed in him with great Zeal and Ability. . . . I regret that there should be a necessity that his Services should be lost to the Army. At the same time I think it my duty to explicitly observe to Congress, that his desire of having an actual and permanent command in the line cannot be complied with.[14]

American officers, Washington pointed out—as if it really needed explanation—"will not submit much, if any longer, to the unnatural promotion of men over them, who have nothing more than a little plausability, unbounded pride and ambition." Giving the Baron a field command, Washington believed, would "have the whole line of Brigadiers in confusion."

Alex Hamilton tried to intervene, too, and without consulting his master. His loyalties were split. On the one hand, he owed his primary allegiance to Washington, but he was also one of the Baron's sansculottes from the long, cold nights at Valley Forge. And like John Laurens, Hamilton believed that Steuben's position was the reasonable argument of a professional, and that those who opposed him spoke only from envy and were men who, lacking the Baron's abilities, sought to snipe at him from the shadows. If lost to the army, Steuben would be irreplaceable. Hamilton wrote in confidence to his friend Elias Boudinot, asking him to find some way of placating the Baron. "Whether any expedient can be adopted, to reconcile difficulties, and retain him in the service at the same time, that no disgust is given to others, who ought not to be disgusted, I cannot certainly determine": maybe not a permanent field command; maybe, instead, a promise that Steuben could hold temporary commands from time to time. "Far be it from me to contravene [Washington's] views, you may be assured that they cannot be essentially departed from without serious inconvenience," Hamilton concluded. "But if anything could be done consistent with them to satisfy the Baron, it would be extremely desireable."[15]

A S HE RODE from White Plains to Philadelphia, Steuben's temper cooled. The prospect of visiting the city was in itself an exciting one. It would be his first extended stay in the largest and wealthiest city in the United States, and doubtless there would be much to take his mind off of his predicament in the army.

In Philadelphia, too, there were men who genuinely liked him, enjoyed his company, and—after Valley Forge—considered him a miracle worker. His closest personal bond was with Richard Peters, the brilliant Philadelphia lawyer who served as secretary on the Board of War. Peters and Steuben had first met at York in February, and had struck up a warm friendship in no time at all. When the Baron rode into Philadelphia at the end of July 1778, Peters insisted that he stay with him and his young family in Belmont, their spacious mansion. The Peters clan—Richard, his wife, Sarah, and their little son, Ralph—adopted him as if he were a much-beloved uncle. Young Peters, only a toddler, took a shine to the affectionate Baron, who in turn showered him with gifts and called him his "little aide-de-camp." Richard was infinitely indulgent of his Prussian friend. When Steuben left the city later that autumn, Richard paid the Baron's debts—he had racked up quite a set of bills with a tailor and a saddler—without complaint, and laughed it off when Carl Vogel inadvertently took off with some of the Peters family's silver.[16] Going to Philadelphia was as close to going home as Steuben could get.

Though he was put off a bit by the high cost of living—"How unmercifully We poor Strangers are flayed alive by the people of this country," Steuben grumbled to Richard Peters—the city did wonders for his mood. Best of all, Congress seemed to be taking him seriously, appointing a committee to review his proposals. Unaware that Washington had tried to undermine him, he wrote to thank the commander in chief for his support, vowing that he would work with Congress to create an inspector general's office "on such principles as may be agreable to your Excellency & the Army in general."[17]

In his quarters at Belmont, Steuben sat down with Ternant to draft a detailed proposal for the "constitution" of the inspector's office. Duponceau took notes and translated. The plan was based on the reports of Crénis and the Baron d'Arendt, but adapted to what Steuben believed were the guiding principles of the American republic. In France and in Prussia, inspectors wielded sweeping powers over all other officers. They could issue any orders they pleased concerning the discipline, training, and good order of the troops, and could countermand any orders given by another officer. In France, the authority of an inspector general superceded that of provincial governors. In both armies, inspectors were also field officers who commanded troops in accordance with their rank. Steuben was not about to ask for the right to order the state governors around, or to strike down Washington's orders at will, but he did believe, and fervently, that he should have the power to do anything necessary to make the army combat-ready, without regard for the objections of the other generals. In his proposal, the inspector general would also have the power to reorganize regiments and brigades as he saw fit, to maintain a uniform structure in the army. On the march and in battle, he would command troops like any other officer of his rank—therefore he, as a major general, would lead a full division.[18]

Steuben's proposal was based on proven principles that had served European armies well. It was also bound to fail, with or without Washington's subterfuge. As a Prussian, Steuben was raised in a political climate that put efficiency ahead of all other virtues. The science of public administration—often referred to as "cameralism"—was all the rage in German princely courts. While cameralism emphasized talent over birth as the principal qualification for holding office, it was not democratic. Democracies are inefficient, and hence democratic thought had no place in a well-ordered army. Steuben as yet did not grasp the subordination of military authorities to civilian control, a principle to which Washington was dedicated. He certainly did not fathom that there were those who believed that standing armies were in themselves a necessary evil at best, and a tool of tyranny, a direct threat to liberty, at worst. Many of the men with whom the Baron had rubbed elbows while at Boston and York, men like Sam Adams and James Lovell, felt this way.

Congress, strangely, didn't do much to discourage Steuben, though Gouverneur Morris had promised Washington otherwise. "The Baron has a Claim from his Merit to be noticed but I never will consent to grant what I am told he requests & I think Congress will not," he reported to Washington on August 2. "At least they wont if I can help it."[19] But for some reason, perhaps fear of an unpleasant confrontation with a popular man, Congress held back. The committee appointed to hear Steuben's proposals, dubbed the Committee of Arrangement, consisted of three men who were not likely to find fault with the inspector: Joseph Reed, Elias Boudinot, and Samuel Chase of Maryland. After a brief meeting with the Baron, they made only a handful of recommendations, and these were on the least controversial points: that the inspector should compose regulations for the use of the army, and that he should review the troops regularly. With regard to La Neuville, the committee sided with Washington and Steuben, asserting that Gates's inspector must submit to Steuben or else resign.* The

---

*La Neuville chose to resign, and departed for France immediately thereafter.

committee said nothing about the rest of the proposal, which they left to Washington's consideration. They, in short, passed the buck.[20]

But Washington had his hands full elsewhere. The strategic situation in Rhode Island was deteriorating rapidly. D'Estaing, his fleet damaged by heavy storms, retreated to Boston for repairs, leaving John Sullivan's makeshift force of Continentals and militia to fend for itself against the British at Newport. Congress panicked; fearing that failure at Newport would turn popular opinion against the French alliance, they sent Steuben packing for Rhode Island to help Sullivan in any way he could. Sensing the possibility for action, the Baron did not object, but Washington stopped him en route at White Plains. He was needed with the main army, and since when did Congress have the authority to order *his* staff about? Steuben, confident that approval of his proposal was a mere formality now, didn't object to this, either, even though the wasted trip had wreaked havoc on his personal finances.[21]

It wasn't long before his hopes were dashed. Washington finally reviewed Steuben's proposals and passed them along for his generals to examine. The generals—fourteen of them—were far from happy with the plan; in fact, they *hated* it. They "view[ed] with concern that resolves so dangerous in their consequences to the united States . . . should ever have been penned." The inspector's "inquisitional authority" would "form a new fangled system of powers . . . uncontrolled and unchecked." The only good thing they had to say about the proposal was that Congress had not approved it yet.[22] Washington was kinder, but not by much. His main concern was the reaction of the other generals, their "jealously and disapprobation." "The authority of those Officers in their respective Corps is reduced to a shadow [by Steuben's plan] and no man of spirit will continue in the service."[23]

A blind man could have seen this coming. Yet Steuben did not. He was taken by surprise by the universally negative reaction, and it dealt him a hard blow. What he had proposed reflected reason and experience, and established practice in the great armies of the civilized world. Americans, whether in Congress or in the army, were beginning to strike him as disingenuous: to his face, they praised his abilities and craved his advice, but none of his suggestions was ever good enough. As he saw it, his presence in the United States so far had meant nothing. He vented to the French resident ambassador in Philadelphia, Conrad-Alexandre Gérard:

> It is with pain that I tell you that our army finds itself again in the same condition as I found it upon my arrival [at Valley Forge]. The regiments are not complete, the troops are not clothed, there is no order, no discipline, no organization, and despite all my cries . . . I do not see even the smallest preparations made to remedy these deficiencies for the coming campaign. I had believed that the establishment of an inspectorate would lead us to make all of these important arrangements. But so far I have been unable to obtain a final resolution of this goal. We will be finished as soon as we begin this campaign.

What made this lack of discipline even more depressing, Steuben thought, was that it pointed to a certain complacency on the part of Congress and the American people, an unwillingness to see the war through. "It is said that Congress has given the order to suspend recruitment in all the states," he railed to Gérard. "Are we to believe that the war is already over? I desire it, but I very much fear that we are deceiving ourselves . . . I believe that a peace treaty signed at the head of a strong army is always more advantageous."[24]

The frustration was almost more than he could bear. "[W]hen I see that a solid formation of this army is so absolutely opposed," he groused, " . . . I put away my papers and reassert my regrets of having made a mistake when I left the position of lieutenant general in the service of the margrave of Baden, where I was fine in all respects."[25]

It was bad enough that the Continental Army was leading itself to its own demise by ignoring his prescriptions. What made it worse was the idleness. His resignation threat had been a bluff; he had nothing to do and nowhere else to go. He was stuck at his headquarters in the sleepy little hamlet of Fredericksburg, New York, miles from anything that even vaguely resembled civilization. "The inactivity in which I now live, and the little use made of my Military Talents makes me despair of ever having a Right to ask for so high a Reward as the Town Majority of Fredericksburg," he intimated to Richard Peters.

"Experience teaches me that Offered services do not always prove acceptable," Steuben continued. He had done all that he could. "If the Arrangements I have proposed for the Good of the Army are not accepted of, by having fulfilled a Duty I had imposed upon me I have acquitted what I owed to myself, as Well as to all the Military." He would "wait in respectful Silence for the Orders of Congress" and ride out the war until he could get a better offer elsewhere.[26]

T HE SKIES OVER NORTHERN NEW JERSEY were clear but moonless on the night of September 27, 1778, when the scarlet-clad soldiers emerged, silent as ghosts, from the woods and fields along the Kinderkamack Road, not far from the border-town of Old Tappan. Their features—indeed their very presence—were completely obscured by the impenetrable darkness. Unbetrayed by the soft glint of moonlight on polished musket barrels, or by the cry of an alarmed sentry, they crept stealthily toward a stone house and its outlying barns.

The Redcoats, twelve companies of elite light infantry, were on no ordinary night patrol. Nothing showed that better than the fact that the man breathlessly urging them along was one of most distinguished commanders of His Majesty's troops in North America. General Charles "No Flint" Grey was something of a legend in the British army. He had earned his chilling sobriquet the year before at Paoli, Pennsylvania, where he had caught Anthony Wayne's detachment completely unaware in the night, his men rushing into the American camp and bayonetting the slumbering Continentals in their tents. He had, it was said, ordered his men to remove the flints from their muskets so that they would not be tempted to shoot. They would have to rely on their bayonets and on the crushing force of musket butts swung by brawny arms.

Grey's men had a similar intent this night. In the barns and stone buildings that lay ahead of them in the thick darkness, near a stream crossing that bore the ominous Dutch name of Overkill, were around one hundred men of the Third Continental Light Dragoons. They were Virginians mostly, whose nickname—"Lady Washington's Guards"—gave them a chivalric air. Part of a larger mixed force of local militia and Continentals, they had been screening Lord Cornwallis's incursion into New Jersey.

Grey's advance toward Old Tappan had already scared off most of the militia, who had scampered away without alerting the men of the light horse. The dragoons were bedded down for the night in the six barns belonging to old Isaac Blauvelt. Their commander, Col. George Baylor, set guards on the bridge at Overkill to the south, and along the road north of the Blauvelt house—though the guards complained that the night was so black that the pickets were of no use. No one could possibly see an approaching enemy in that darkness.

Their reports proved to be tragically prophetic. The British took to the road at ten o'clock that night, enveloping the Blauvelt farmstead and cutting off any chance of escape. Sometime after one o'clock in the morning, the Redcoats materialized from the darkness. They were upon the hapless American pickets in a flash, dispatching them with bayonets and clubbed muskets before they even had a chance to utter a sound. Grey and a few men took possession of the Blauvelt farmhouse, where Colonel Baylor and his second-in-command, Maj. Alexander Clough, were quartered. According to local tradition, Baylor and Clough tried frantically to hide themselves in a chimney. Baylor escaped; Clough, who was discovered, was bayonetted repeatedly as he pleaded for mercy.

The rest of the British force closed in on the barns, forcing their way in, and the killing began in earnest.

A few of the Americans were alert enough to effect an escape, melting into the safety of the nearby woods. Most were not so lucky. Some were bayonetted as they slept, others as they searched clumsily for their weapons; some fought back with pistols or sabres but were quickly overcome. A great many of the Continentals, seeing the hopelessness of their predicament, surrendered. Some were granted quarter, while others were coldly taken outside and bayonetted anyway.

It was all over in a matter of minutes. Grey's men withdrew at daybreak, prisoners in tow, leaving the Blauvelt family to bury the dead and tend to the wounded left behind.

The Baylor Massacre, as the event came to be known, had no significant impact on British or American strategy—only about fifteen dragoons were killed outright—but, still, the "Butchery" appeared monstrous to many contemporaries, a sign of British barbarism. American leaders denounced the British officers for making no effort to restrain the bloodlust of their men.[27]

The Baron de Steuben was troubled by the incident, but not for the same reasons. The clash at Overkill was upsetting to him because it could have been prevented so easily. The real tragedy at the heart of the bloodshed was not the inhumanity of the attackers, but the carelessness of the Continentals, "the consequence of a bad discipline," Steuben observed to Henry Laurens. "The service of the guards, piquets & patrolls is totally neglected in our Army. Our Cavalry is without a Chief, without an Officer acquainted with the service—Brave, it is true, but bravery never made an Officer."[28]

Laurens thought Steuben's analysis cold. How could poor Baylor bear the responsibility when it was the British who had violated all the rules of civilized warfare? Yet the Baron had hit the nail on the head. Baylor had been criminally negligent—of his duty to the army, to the Cause, and above all to the men entrusted to his care. Steuben had been urging all along that the army pay greater attention to guard and outpost duty. He had been ignored, and Overkill demonstrated the tragic results that could ensue.

"I have acquitted what I owed to myself, as Well as to all the Military," he had told Laurens, apparently washing his hands of any responsibility for whatever fate might befall the Continental Army now that he had been so brusquely rebuffed by his fellow generals. Yet the truth was that the Baron cared about the army much more than his hurt pride would allow him to let on. He accepted, grudgingly, that he could not command troops in battle, and once he took this fact to heart, he became eminently useful. In the coming year, he would make his greatest, most enduring contribution to the Cause.

What Steuben realized at this moment, as he gave up on his dreams of battlefield glory, was that Congress, Washington, and the army brass did set great value on his counsel—so long as that counsel was not coupled with demands for augmented powers. And while this was personally disappointing, it was also liberating in a way. Since he was no longer angling for a more prominent role, he could offer his advice directly, without tact or restraint. The rebels needed this kind of guidance. Blunt advice, after all, is generally good advice.

Both Washington and Henry Laurens solicited the Baron's strategic insights—and he gave them, no matter how bleak the prognosis. And with French intervention temporarily out of the question, there was little good to say about the state of the war effort. His reflections on the condition of the army, written for Laurens at the beginning of October 1778, "would shock a feeble mind."

Lord Cornwallis is [in New Jersey] with perhaps Six thousand Men, & Lord Stirling with Three Brigades, I shall not say how strong for fear of afflicting you. But pray, is that number Sufficient to oppose the forces of the Enemy? You will say that they will be joined by the state Militia. But is that the same Militia America could boast of when she had yet no Enlisted Troops? Do they retain the same spirit which animated them at that Time? . . . Do not suffer yourself to be dazzled by the Accounts of the Strength of our Regiments and Brigades, at least a third part of them are unable to suffer the fatigues of a march, in this season when Nights begin to grow cold & damp & that for want of Cloaths, Even of Shoes or Stockings. . . . I think it my duty not to suffer you to be ignorant of the true state of our Army. And now Examine the Land forces of our Enemies in this Country . . . and then tell me if you dont think our Case somewhat hazardous?

What made the army's sad state even more depressing was that it stemmed from a deep-seated cause: the tendency of Americans, especially those who disdained a standing army, to eschew long-range planning and count instead on the occasional miracle.

How long will America suffer her Welfare to depend on the good or ill success of a day? Is it not certain that a greater loss will arise from the plundering of the Jersies, than it would have Cost to Keep the Regiments complete after the plan in Congress? . . . An Army too numerous, I own, is Expensive, but the Contrary Extreme is dangerous. It was, I think, in 1776, that Gen¹ Washington had the glory to keep the field at the Head of an Army of 1800 Men; I wish he mayn't have that glory again. Had a proper number of Soldiers been Raised, the War would probably at this time be at an End. Withal, Sir, if our Regiments are not completed, and put on an Equal footing, it is absolutely unnecessary to think of any Arrangement, Either in the Administration or Manœuvres, or Even of any Order or Uniformity in our Army.[29]

Washington asked Steuben for his opinions on the army's strategic options in light of the French withdrawal, and once again the Baron held nothing back. His written reply to the general-in-chief was a piece worthy of a great operational planner. Because the army was both pitifully small and in poor condition, Steuben pointed out, there were no options. The British, he argued, were likely to either attack Boston or to remain passively in New York. Either way, they had the advantage. Clinton was no fool; he knew exactly how weak the Americans were. If the British attacked Boston, they could do so with impunity, for they had enough troops to do it while still retaining a respectable garrison in New York. What could Washington do if this happened? Nothing. Any force he might detach to defend Boston would so deplete the main army that the Hudson Highlands would be vulnerable, and no matter how many men Washington sent to Boston, it would not be enough to save the city. The Continental Army was in no condition to do any-thing but sit tight for the winter and hope for the best.[30]

All the reforms in the world, Steuben had told both Washington and Congress, would not save the army or the country. Victory would require a substantial and lasting commitment in manpower, and that responsibility lay solely with Congress and the States. Steuben could do nothing about that. What he could do, within the few and limited parameters approved by both Congress and the generals, was to instill discipline, broadly defined. Discipline, as Steuben—and most Euro-pean soldier-philosophers—saw it, was the universal application of rules and procedures that came from following a common code of con-duct. The Continental Army had no such code. The incident at Over-kill stood as bloody proof.

Despite his jeremiads, the Baron had not yet given up. The best thing he could do in his present situation, as he told Henry Laurens, was to "put on a cheerful face" and hope that Congress would eventually see the necessity of enlarging the army. In the meantime, he had to define discipline, and that entailed creating that missing military code.

Washington agreed. He had known all along how badly the army needed a set of official regulations. So with the general-in-chief's blessing, Steuben set out again for Philadelphia, on November 13, 1778, to spend the winter working out the details.[31]

———

THE TIME WAS RIGHT. The Baron was not really needed at camp, even for drill. He had trained a competent group of subordinates, the sub-inspectors and the brigade inspectors, at Valley Forge. He could even spare Ternant, who was dispatched to spread Steuben's gospel to Gen. Benjamin Lincoln's badly organized Southern Army. Nor was there much possibility of action in the Northeast. Once D'Estaing removed his fleet from Boston Harbor in early November, choosing to spend the winter months in the West Indies instead, the campaign of 1778 came to an abrupt if anticlimatic end.

From his personal staff, Steuben assembled a team to help him draft the new regulations. Fleury knew the details of French military practice as well as anyone in the Continental service; Duponceau could translate, and Walker was conversant in American military terminology; L'Enfant, a skilled draftsman, could fashion the plates and figures necessary for a drill manual. Together, they entered Philadelphia at the end of November and set up cozy quarters at the Peters' Belmont. This in itself was a great attraction for the Baron. Here he would have the comforts of family life as well as direct access to the Board of War.[32]

Steuben was driven, and he wrote almost without letup from the time he set foot in Philadelphia until he departed the city in late April 1779. His mind, and his quill, moved much faster than the slow pace dictated by the translating and editing process. He had no intention of merely copying the Prussian military regulations. He admired the Prussian system, and overall believed it to be the best in all of Europe, but he also recognized that the center of military thought was not Prussia but France. The composition of new regulations would involve picking and choosing the best elements from the Prussian and French systems, and then adapting them to American conditions—and this required juggling a dizzying quantity of details and ephemera. Working from memory, Fleury's advice, and the few military texts he had at hand, he composed scores of short essays, written on a variety of topics, for his own use: on the proper formation of infantry units, on tactics, on the duties of officers in European armies, on the administration of entire military establishments.[33]

The five men worked at a furious pace. Walker and Duponceau, as translators and scribes, took up most of the drudge work, but Steuben and Fleury were no less busy. They frequently labored into the wee hours, sketching maneuvers in pencil and comparing notes by candlelight. There was little time for them to partake of Philadelphia's social scene. Steuben was content to take the occasional dinner with his hosts, to chat with Richard Peters about politics, and to play with little Ralph. Until the final chapters of the regulations were complete, in late March 1779, however, Steuben and his team did not take a single significant break, allowing little to interrupt or distract them.

There were unavoidable disruptions nonetheless. Steuben still had a score to settle with an old enemy: Charles Lee. Through his few remaining adherents in the army, Lee had spread the rumor that Steuben was a fake. Even Francy was taken in by the talk. "It is pretended that [Steuben] is nothing less than a great soldier, [yet] people really mock the Order he carries, which is regarded in Germany as worthless," Francy reported to Beaumarchais in early November 1778. Other Prussians in the Continental service claimed never to have heard of Steuben while in the army of Old Fritz. The Baron, Francy admitted, "infinitely embarrasses me."[34]

The dangerous thing about Lee's gossip was that it contained more than a kernel of truth, but it was meanspirited and unnecessary, intended only to sabotage the Baron's high standing in the army. Francy soon recognized this and repented. The damage, however, was already done. Des Epiniers, whose admiration for Steuben had bordered on hero worship, quit the inspector's staff, only telling Francy that he "would have nothing to do with the Baron." Steuben had done his best to ignore Lee up to this point, but he could do so no longer. At the time he left camp for Philadelphia, already there were whispers that the Baron would seek satisfaction in the way that any honorable gentleman would: by duel.

So when Lee made his next negative remark about him, Steuben was ready to pounce. Lee was in the process of appealing the sentence of his court-martial, refuting much of the written testimony, including Steuben's. He argued that Steuben had not been near enough to the action to judge Lee's conduct, and referred to the Prussian as a "very distant Spectator." It was a minor criticism, but it did impugn Steuben's honor, and the Baron was not inclined to be very forgiving. "Were I now in my own Country, where my reputation is long ago Established, I should have put myself about your Epigrams, and would have despised them," he shot back at Lee. "But here I am a Stranger. You have offended me. I desire you will give me satisfaction. You will chuse the place, time and Arms." It was not the first time Lee had been challenged to a duel, and it certainly wouldn't be the last. He was a brave soldier, but a coward and a bully in his personal life, and he backed down in great humility. He apologized profusely, assuring the aggrieved Baron that he had no intention of slighting him. Fortunately that was enough to satisfy Steuben.[35]

Steuben had challengers of his own, but over matters not of honor but of imitation. A young French lieutenant, William Galvan, was also writing a tactical manual. Coincidentally, he was working in Philadelphia at the same time as Steuben, but without making any effort to consult the Baron. Galvan submitted his text to Washington, unsolicited, hoping to impress the general. He did not get very far. For all of the trouble that Steuben had caused him, Washington was very protective of his inspector, and saw in Galvan's manuscript a direct affront to Steuben. "I do not perceive any utility that could be derived from encouraging the competition you seem to desire between you and the Gentleman who has already been appointed to superintend the instruction of the army," Washington wrote Galvan. "The specimens he has given of his zeal and knowlege entitle him to my confidence."[36]

Another foreigner, one Baron Knoblauch, also tried to cash in on Steuben's work. After Steuben had already finished, Knoblauch petitioned Congress for recognition, claiming that he deserved some credit for having lent his Prussian military texts to the inspector! Indeed, he would have written his own regulations if only he "had been Master of the English Language or could have had the steady assistance of a good Translator."[37] Congress ignored him.

Steuben's biggest headache was one largely of his own making: the emptiness of his wallet. Money problems had haunted him since the day he left the Prussian army; one gets the impression from his correspondence that he thought of little else. As a major general, his monthly pay was $166.67 in Continental scrip, which, thanks to rampant inflation, was worth no more than around $20 in gold. Maybe there wasn't much purchasing power in that salary, but then, Steuben did not have to pay for his meals—he received fifteen rations per day on account of his rank, while the members of his staff drew between three and five rations daily. Together, they could feed themselves quite well, and often they dined at the Peters' table anyway.

But the Baron was no good at managing his money. He was not greedy, for he spent lavishly on his friends and frequently lent huge sums to help his junior staff members when they were down on their luck. Yet money flowed through his hands like water. His taste for expensive clothes did not help. One time he purchased eight plumes and twelve cockades—hat ornaments, in other words, hardly necessities—from a Philadelphia tailor for the princely sum of $2,200, more than thirteen times his monthly pay! It was fortunate that he had such a good friend in Richard Peters. Peters lobbied Congress on his behalf, making the perverse claim that Steuben—who "appears to be frugal and moderate in his expences"—could not be expected to support himself on the money he could draw from his (imaginary) European incomes. At Peters's urging, Congress granted Steuben an additional $84 per month to cover his expenses as inspector.[38]

None of these matters was a serious interruption of the Baron's grand work. He had set an ambitious schedule for himself and his staff, for he wanted to have the regulations finished, approved, printed, and ready for distribution to the army in time for training in the spring. He wasn't too far off. The first half of the regulations was finished in February 1779. He submitted the second and more substantial half, the regulations for military conduct and administration, to Washington on March 5. Three weeks later, having addressed Washington's concerns and revised the text, the Baron tendered the completed manuscript to Congress for final approval. Congress gave the book its imprimatur, and Steuben its thanks, on March 29, 1779, ordering that the regulations be printed immediately. After four long years of fighting the British, the Continental Army finally had a standardized military code.[39]

‹————›

STEUBEN'S MAGNUM OPUS bore the inelegant title *Regulations for the Order and Discipline of the Troops of the United States*, but in common parlance it soon acquired another name, derived from the color of the pasteboard covers used for the 1779 edition: the Blue Book. The production standards were perhaps a bit crude, but the contents were pure gold. Many military manuals had been published in the colonies prior to the war, or during the early years. Timothy Pickering, Washington's adjutant general and one of Steuben's allies on the Board of War, had himself written one of the best. But none of them could compare with Steuben's in depth, concision, or originality. In a mere 150 pages of text and plates, the Baron had created one of the most significant and enduring documents in American military history.

The Blue Book's many chapters form three distinct and very different parts: a drill manual for the infantry, a set of official regulations for the use of the entire army, and a treatise on the conduct of officers and enlisted men. The drill manual is the most famous part, the portion of the Blue Book most commonly associated with the Baron's name. For its time and genre, it was uncommonly straightforward, easily grasped by officers with the most rudimentary literary skills.

The soldiers at Valley Forge commonly referred to Steuben's tactical lessons as "the Prussian exercise"—not that they had any way of knowing that the drill they were learning was Prussian, but they knew that the Baron was, and so it was an easy assumption to make. Steuben, offhandedly and partly tongue in cheek, labelled his "discipline" in the same fashion. "My good republicans wanted everything in the English style; our great and good allies everything according to the French fashion," he told a former Prussian comrade after the war. "And when I presented a plate of sauerkraut *à la prussienne*, they all came together to throw it out of the window. Nevertheless, by the force of proving by *God-dam* that my cookery was the best, I overcame the prejudices of the former; but the second liked me as little in the forests of America as they did on the plains of Rossbach."[40]

The style of Steuben's "plate of sauerkraut" was Prussian, but in nearly every other respect it definitely was not. The drill with which most Continental soldiers were already familiar—the British manual of 1764 and books based upon it—was much closer to what Prussian soldiers learned than the Baron's drill was. In the Seven Years' War, the army of Frederick the Great had performed remarkably well against incredible odds, and nothing inspires imitation like success. Since the secret to Prussian excellence seemed to come from discipline, it was only natural to assume that drill held the key. The British army was no exception; much of British drill was based on its Prussian counterpart.

Steuben did not copy the Prussian drill, or even adapt it. Rather, what he did was to incorporate the most important things about the way the Prussians fought—emphasizing firepower and speed of maneuver—and ideas from other tactical manuals into a cogent whole, while stripping it of all unnecessary ephemera, so it could be taught quickly and painlessly to amateur soldiers.

"I have rejected every thing which tended only to Parade," he explained to Congress, "and confined myself to what alone appeared to me absolutely necessary."[41] The "manual exercise," though the least important part of the regulations, clearly showed the Baron's common-sense approach. A good example is the command "Order . . . FIRE-LOCK!"—the simple act of carrying a musket from its upright position at the left shoulder down to the right side, so that the butt of the musket rested on the ground near the right foot. In British and Prussian drill, this command was executed with needless complexity. It took six distinct motions.* Certainly it looked impressive when done correctly and in unison by a whole battalion of crack troops, but was it *necessary*? Steuben didn't think it was, and so he reduced the process from six motions to two: one to seize hold of the musket with the right hand, one to carry the musket to the right side and plant it on the ground. No superfluous flourishings of the musket, no pointless movements of the feet. It illustrated one of the primary tenets of Steuben's gospel: keep it simple. In the Blue Book, form took a backseat to function.

---

*One to rotate the musket inward, one to bring the musket held upright in front of the body, one to step back with the right foot and bring the musket to the position of "Present," one to carry the musket to the right shoulder, one to raise the right hand to grasp the musket near the muzzle, and one to bring the musket straight down to the ground while bringing the right foot forward again.

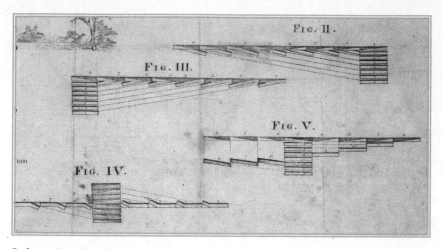

Infantry battalion deploying from column to line of battle by Guibert's method, from *Regulations for the Order and Discipline of the Troops of the United States* (Philadelphia, 1779).

The most important elements of that function, though, were to be found farther along in the drill manual. Again, Steuben steadfastly refused to be constrained by the narrow horizons of his Prussian experience. In the Prussian infantry, columns deployed into line, and shifted back into column, through a process of wheeling: individual smaller units, like platoons within a battalion, would wheel ninety degrees in the same direction to form a line from a column, or vice versa. It worked well enough with highly trained troops, but even then it was cumbersome and time-consuming. A brilliant French tactician, the Comte de Guibert, proposed a much improved method in the early 1770s. In Guibert's system, individual subunits arranged in a column would simply face to the right or left without wheeling, and march obliquely, one behind the other, in order to make the line. The method was far more efficient and faster than wheeling, and more flexible, too (see Figure 2).

An army trained in Guibert's method of deployment could also—with relatively little training—change formation during battle as required, and not just into lines or marching columns. It could form assault columns, called "columns closed in mass," which were broader and shallower than marching columns but deeper than lines of battle, useful for short-range, rapid bayonet charges. Guibert's system retained the firepower of traditional linear tactics while allowing a tactical flexibility that went beyond the capabilities of the Prussian army at its height. Guibert's ideas were radical; even the French army rejected them initially, and did not adopt any of them until 1791. Yet in 1779, Steuben adopted these very same ideas for the Continental Army.[42]

The remainder of the tactical portion of the Blue Book gave basic instructions for dealing with different kinds of terrain while on the march or in battle: how to pass safely through a narrow defile, how to march across an open plain in the presence of enemy cavalry, and so forth. To experienced commanders, such procedures might not have required explanation, but then, Steuben was not writing for them. His intent was to provide novice commanders with a time-tested set of tactical instructions. By ensuring that all commanders would approach similar problems in the same way, little was left to chance.

The second part of the Blue Book, the regulations for military conduct, was not quite so pathbreaking but was equally vital. Here Steuben set forth basic procedures for the daily administration of the army: how to conduct a court-martial or inspect troops, what kinds of records all officers should keep, how public property was to be accounted for. Other sections addressed the safety and well-being of the troops. The Baron gave explicit directions on the manner in which regimental camps were to be laid out. He knew from experience that raw troops were lazy in matters of hygiene and sanitation, that untrained men were often inclined to eat inside their tents and to urinate or relieve their bowels immediately outside. This was why infectious diseases like smallpox and measles spread like wildfire through the ranks. That could not be tolerated. Officers and men alike would have to avail themselves of specially constructed "sinks"—pit latrines—for their bodily functions. Livestock would have to be slaughtered in designated butchering areas, and the offal appropriately disposed of some distance from the camp. Every activity had its place, each man his specific duty.

The improper execution of guard duty was one of the Baron's pet peeves, and so it received a single large chapter all to itself in the Blue Book. All the details of regimental guards were included: how and where guards should be placed, how passwords and countersigns were to be given, how officers should make their "grand rounds" to test their guards' vigilance.

Steuben devoted the last third of his book to a more philosophical purpose: to clarify the duties of all ranks in the army, and to imbue officers with a sense of the nobility of their calling. Despite the fearsome reputation of Prussian officers as brutal martinets, the Baron insisted that the secret to successful leadership was not fear but love. He could never forget the image of his men digging trenches through that churchyard in Breslau on a sweltering June day, the stench oppressing them as they toiled in the foul earth, or the overwhelming sense of concern and responsibility for their welfare that he felt as their lieutenant.

There was something paternal about Steuben's vision of officership. The ideal officer was an ideal father, as measured in that era: stern, certain to punish when disobeyed, but patient, protective, and caring toward his "children." He was not their friend and should never get too close to them, yet neither could he treat them with contempt or arbitrary severity. And he must share in their privations. This is the predominant theme in the final portion of the Blue Book. "The preservation of the soldiers health should be [the] first and greatest care" of regimental commanders. For a captain commanding a company, "His first object should be, to gain the love of his men, by treating them with every possible kindness and humanity."

The tome was not as complete as Steuben would have liked—it did not, for example, include brigade or divisional maneuvers—yet it was a remarkable achievement in that its significance went way beyond its intended primary function. It imposed order on an army that had very little order. It introduced the very latest in European tactical thought, some of which would not be tested in Europe until the armies of Revolutionary France swept away the detritus of the ancien régime and ushered in a new era in the history of warfare. And by establishing common procedure and a common professional ethos, it imparted uniformity. It made it possible for the Continental Army to be something other than a collection of small state armies under one command—to be *the* army of the United States, the only institution that brought together common folk from all of the states to work toward a common purpose.

Washington was delighted with the final result. He, too, had a hand in the writing of the book. As Steuben fed him the initial drafts, Washington went over them line by line, and passed them along to Generals Stirling and Arthur St. Clair for comment. The three men disagreed with the Baron only on minor matters of language or on extremely trivial issues. Washington didn't like the command for aiming muskets—Steuben used "Present!" while his superior much preferred "Take Aim!" Stirling thought the distance between the officers' tents and the cooking fires in Steuben's model regimental camp was too short. Stirling and St. Clair were a tad confused by the concept of the oblique marching step. But all agreed that the Blue Book was a superior work, ideally suited to the American army. Washington was eager to see it put to practical use. "You will, I flatter myself, shortly have the satisfaction, so rarely enjoyed by Authors, of seeing your precepts reduced to practice—and I hope your Success will be equal to the merit of your work," he wrote in final approval to Steuben.[43]

The Baron would indeed see his "precepts reduced to practice" very soon, though it could not be said that he would find much satisfaction in it.

CHAPTER 9

The True Meaning of Discipline

[MAY 1779—JULY 1780]

> If I still had the Prussian spirit, such a delay would
> exhaust my patience, but now I am so used to such
> negligence that very often I feel disposed to become
> negligent myself.
>
> STEUBEN TO BENJAMIN WALKER,
> FEBRUARY 23, 1780[1]

I T WAS THE VERY END of April 1779 when Steuben reunited
with Washington and the army at Middlebrook, New
Jersey. The army was just beginning to stir from the leth-
argy of winter quarters. The winter of 1779 had been one of
comparative luxury: the weather had been mild, the supplies
more bountiful. For the generals the season had been most notable for the fine living and the number of parties and balls;
and nearly every one of the generals' wives had shared in the
revelry. The prevailing mood was one of guarded optimism.
The French, it was presumed, would shortly be on their way to
American shores. The end of the war couldn't be too far away.

The Baron was anxious to return to the army. His prolonged
stay in Philadelphia was starting to get to him. He had assumed
that since he could talk face-to-face with the Board of War at
leisure, the organization of the inspector general's office would
be worked out in no time at all. But it wasn't, even after General

Washington prodded Congress to do something. "The immediate establishment of the Inspectorship on some definitive plan," he reminded them in early January, ". . . is a matter of the utmost importance." Yet Congress did nothing, and Steuben's hands were tied. "Indeed this Department may be said to be only tolerated," he complained. "It wants that Authority & support necessary to penetrate into the Abuses."[2]

Congress also dragged its feet when it came to money. Steuben had asked for compensation for his work, and that of his staff, on the Blue Book. The amounts were perfectly reasonable, he thought: $4,000 for himself, $1,000 for Fleury, $600 for Ben Walker, $500 for L'Enfant, and $400 for Duponceau. The Board of War agreed; Congress did not. Steuben's main worry was for his staff, especially Fleury, who was deep in debt. He could think of only one explanation for Congress's refusal: there must be a plot to discourage foreign officers and force them to return to Europe. The Baron had heard rumors to this effect, rumors that implicated Silas Deane's many enemies in Congress . . . including Henry Laurens.

Since Steuben had taken up residence in Philadelphia that winter, French and German officers by the score had sought him out, asking for his intercession with Congress and Washington: Could the esteemed Baron get them a commission, obtain for them a transfer to a cavalry regiment, help them win a promotion? He became an unofficial advocate for the expatriates in the Continental Army, and he could not help but sympathize with their sad tales of neglect at the hands of Congress.

As he stewed over his predicament, the Baron became convinced that Henry Laurens must be behind Congress's refusal to pay bonuses to his staff. One cool April evening, Laurens invited Steuben to dine with him, and Steuben could not restrain himself from challenging the former president. Just before dinner, he confronted Laurens: Why wouldn't Congress pay his expenses, as they had promised him at York? Why wouldn't they help his staff?

Laurens, who was entertaining several friends besides the Baron that evening, was a bit put off by Steuben's tone of voice. Patiently, he tried to explain that the Treasury was practically empty, so Congress just couldn't hand out cash to everyone who felt he deserved it. He advised Steuben to wait, and not to press his demands until the country's financial affairs were in better order.

Steuben allowed that he could wait, but his assistants could not. Fleury was so strapped for cash that if Congress did not pay him for his work on the Blue Book, he would have to return to France. "If the case be so, that Colonel Fleury cannot stay with us unless Congress will do something for him . . . the consequence will be that he must go home," Laurens responded testily. "I shall be very sorry for it."

The Baron, his face darkened and distorted by "Choler & rage," snarled, "Then *I* shall go home. I will not stay."

Laurens tried to turn the conversation to something less serious, joking with the Baron, but with no effect. Steuben felt betrayed. He remained silent through dinner, and left the table much earlier than he usually did.

It saddened Laurens to "upbraid a Man with whom I wished to have continued in friendship," as he later told his son, almost apologetically. "But the times are distempered & the Divide of avarice & ambition are indefatigably improving them to their own advantages."

The friendship between Steuben and Henry Laurens ended when the two men parted company that night. Laurens scarcely ever mentioned Steuben's name again, and Steuben continued to hold Laurens responsible for driving away foreign talent. "Doth yet Mr. H___y L___ns," he asked Richard Peters several months later, "send back the Officers who have come over here to defend his Country?" He added in a cold, oblique, but unmistakable reference to the Carolina shipping magnate: "I believe that in order to reconcile Heaven to us we should begin by hanging some Merchants who have troubled our affairs in such a manner by their mercantile spirit."[3]

AMONG THE MILITARY HEROES of the Revolution—Washington, Greene, Knox, Wayne, Lafayette—Steuben stands out as more flawed than most. It was not difficult to befriend him. "I was much pleased with the Baron," said Polly Duane, daughter of New York politician James Duane, upon meeting Steuben for the first time in 1783. "There seems to be so much candor & honesty in his composition."[4] It took, however, a very patient and tolerant soul to sustain a friendship with him over the long haul. Fortunately there were such people in his life. Steuben's friends saved him repeatedly, not just from his enemies, but also from himself.

The Baron had neither home nor family to speak of. He had very limited written contact with his parents or his siblings, and he remained a lifelong bachelor. Without a conventional family to lend him emotional support, Steuben learned to assemble a makeshift family as he drifted through life. The friends he made—almost effortlessly—in Europe and in America became his surrogate family. In America, he attracted scores of admirers, men and women drawn to him by his wit and his frank, open manner, and by the way in which he seemed to embody the literary sophistication of the Enlightenment. Relatively few of these admirers, though, got to know the Baron as a man of flesh and blood.

This was because he let very few people see him that way, for despite his sociability he was actually a very guarded man. Everyone in the army knew Drillmaster Steuben: a showman, loud and brash, who was both sharp-tongued and clownish at the same time, yet dedicated and hardworking. His friends in the high command—Knox, Wayne, Greene, Washington—knew him as a military expert of unparalleled learning, and as a bon vivant who enlivened raucous parties and elegant high-society gatherings alike with his deep, easy laugh. They knew, too, that he could be sensitive and short-tempered, and was prone to grandstanding, but they accepted this. When critiquing the first drafts of the *Regulations*, Arthur St. Clair and Lord Stirling suggested that the inspector general might benefit from incorporating portions of William Galvan's drill manual into his own. They soon thought better of it. "Whether this could be recommended without hurting the Baron's delicacy may be a doubt," they concluded.[5]

That delicacy could be very trying to those who became convenient targets for Steuben's occasional angry outbursts, which were all too often directed at those he trusted most. Richard Peters was such a target on more than one occasion, but he was quick to forgive, just as Steuben was quick to apologize for his misdirected wrath. After a minor disagreement over the printing of the Blue Book, a dispute caused by Steuben's paper-thin patience, Peters observed:

> I have the strongest Hopes . . . that Time with its lenient Hand will administer some Drug which will conquer the Irritability of your System. When this happy Day arrives I am clear that the little feverish Flights which have induced you to censure where no Blame was merited will no longer disturb your Rest or hurt the Sensibility of your Friends.[6]

No one was more familiar with those "little feverish Flights" than Steuben's two principal aides, Ben Walker and William (Billy) North. North, a young Massachusetts Yankee who was fluent in French, joined Steuben's staff sometime in the autumn of 1779. Walker and North stayed by the Baron's side to the end of his days, sharing his table and managing his finances as best they could. Steuben treated them like sons.

Loyalty was the quality Steuben treasured most of all in any of his friends. But he was not so egocentric that he demanded blind devotion. Walker and North did not hesitate to tell him when he was unreasonable, ignorant, or wrong. He wanted and needed this kind of advice. Once, when North rebuked him for his financial carelessness, Steuben reassured his protégé: "I would be as sorry to have my friends blind to my faults as to have them insensible to my good qualities. No, my Friend, never cease to tell me the truth and I shall never cease to love you sincerely."[7]

But those who betrayed him were never readmitted to the inner circle. Henry Laurens was one of these; Beaumarchais's nephew Des Epiniers was another. When the Frenchman sided with Charles Lee in the fall of 1778, quitting Steuben's staff, he lost his master's affection

LEFT: Nathanael Greene, by Charles Willson Peale, from life, 1783. One of Steuben's foremost friends among the Continental Army generals, Greene hoped to have Steuben at his side during his campaigns in the Carolinas. The British invasions of Virginia, however, kept Steuben busy elsewhere. *(Independence National Historical Park)*

RIGHT: Capt. (later Major) William North. Billy North joined Steuben's staff in 1779. Along with his best friend, Ben Walker, North looked after the Baron in his declining years, and tried in vain to keep Steuben from spending extravagantly. *(Emmet Collection, Miriam and Ira D. Wallach Division of Art, Prints and Photographs, The New York Public Library, Astor, Lenox and Tilden Foundations)*

LEFT: Anne-César, Chevalier de la Luzerne, by Charles Willson Peale, from life, 1781–1782. Gérard's successor as French ambassador to the United States. Steuben tried hard to impress Luzerne, hoping that it would lead to recognition in France. Luzerne was impressed, but was unable to move Vergennes to generosity after the war. *(Independence National Historical Park)*

forever. He later repented and tried to reconcile, but Steuben rebuffed him with cold silence. Not even appeals from Francy and Beaumarchais would move the Baron to clemency. After reading one of Des Epiniers's self-abasing pleas for forgiveness, Steuben wrote to Ben Walker: "I received a particularly stupid letter from M. des Epiniers. . . . He asks my advice as to whether he should come back as my aide or take care of his uncle's business. You may be sure I recommended the latter."[8]

There was also a secret Steuben, a man not even Walker or North would ever know. This Steuben was scared, full of self-doubt, a man who so feared mediocrity that he fibbed to cover his inadequacies— even to those friends who accepted him unconditionally. From his closest companions in Europe, notably Chancellor Frank, he hid the truth about his new life in America. He spun elaborate yarns about his glorious adventures in the Revolutionary cause: how he had led the army to victory at Monmouth and Yorktown, how Congress and the States had heaped laurels upon him. He even told Frank, while sparring with Congress in the spring of 1779, that Congress had appointed him to a seat on the Board of War![9]

His American friends, conversely, would never know the full details of his previous life in Europe. To his dying day, Billy North believed that the Baron really had been a lieutenant general and a wealthy landowner. Steuben was ashamed of his checkered past in Europe, and felt that his current condition in America stank of failure. He did not measure up to the goals he had set for himself, and the sad result was that he could not be truly intimate with anyone.

Steuben protected himself with an impenetrable shell of fabrications. Undoubtedly it affected his romantic life. The Baron said nothing about his loves, if indeed he had any, and therefore this murkiest aspect of his personality remains shrouded in mystery.

It has been claimed that Steuben was a homosexual. Indeed he may have been, and there is circumstantial evidence to suggest it: his friendship with Prince Henry, the accusations of pederasty at Hechingen, his undisguised affection for Walker, North, and Francy. But there is also circumstantial evidence to the contrary. While traveling through New York near the end of his life, Steuben once dropped a miniature portrait of a beautiful young woman. His personal assistant asked him about her identity, and the Baron choked up. "She was a matchless woman," he finally managed to say, but would speak no further about her.[10]

There is little to prove one or the other. Steuben enjoyed the company of women, in social settings at least, but like many soldiers of his day he spent nearly all of his time in the exclusively male society of the army. Whether Steuben was homosexual or heterosexual, or asexual, for that matter, may never be known with any certainty. But his inability to let down his guard suggests that he may have been incapable of forming an intimate romantic bond with anyone, male or female.

THE TRAINING of the army was not over and done with in 1779, but at least the process no longer required Steuben's daily personal attention. The Baron retrained the army in 1778; 1779 would be the year he reorganized it. That was the plan.

When he rejoined the army and set up his headquarters in the "low, rambling" house of Abraham Staats at Bound Brook—or, as Steuben wrote it, "Baum brok"—he made the transition from author-scholar to inspector general smoothly. His first task was to arrange a suitably impressive display of American martial prowess for the French ambassador, Conrad-Alexandre Gérard, who would be visiting Middlebrook at the beginning of May. The Baron was happy to do so, for he still hoped to impress the French and guarantee himself a position in King Louis's army.

On May 2, instead of a feu de joie, Gérard was treated to mock battle. Four battalions of handpicked men paraded in front of the viewing dignitaries, split into two separate columns, and marched to opposite ends of the Parade. The columns deployed, snapping smartly in seconds from column to line using the new method introduced by the Baron. The two forces took turns launching stately but brisk bayonet assaults upon one another. The austere Gérard clapped his hands in delight as he watched the staged battle from the sidelines. He congratulated Washington and Steuben on the perfect execution of the spectacle, but said nothing more, and gave no hint to Steuben that the Baron's American exploits had been noted at Versailles.[11]

No matter. Steuben had much to occupy his attention. The army needed a thorough spring cleaning, so that it could look and perform at its best when the French finally arrived in force that year. The only thing holding him back was the Blue Book itself, which was not yet available in printed form. The war drained Philadelphia of skilled labor, leaving the city's printers and engravers shorthanded. "Here under the present scarcity of hands you can place no dependence on your workmen," Timothy Pickering had explained to him. "To-day they are with you, & tomorrow on board a privateer with hopes of making their fortunes."[12]

Production problems dogged the book. The printer, Charles Cist, did a remarkable job considering the shortages of paper, ink, and labor; the engraver, one John Norman, did not. He botched the copper plates badly, and a replacement engraver had to be hired. And since only one bookbinder could be found to assemble the finished product, the project dragged on well into June 1779, without a single copy ready for distribution.

Peters and Pickering did their best, hounding the workmen, which was supposed to be Duponceau's job, but Duponceau was no taskmaster. Effete and unprepossessing, the secretary was incapable of intimidating anybody, let along rough-spoken Philadelphia artisans. "I have a real Esteem for Duponceau," Peters quipped to Steuben, "but think him the worst Person you could have left here as he was unaquainted with the Customs . . . of our Country. . . . As to stimulating the Work<u>man</u> (for Work<u>men</u> we could not get) he was of no more use than if you had left him to observe an Ecclipse without a Telescope."[13]

Steuben didn't care whose fault it was, or why there were problems. He was furious that such an important matter had been permitted to slide, and that for six weeks he had been compelled to dictate the *Regulations* line by line to regimental clerks so that they could be entered into the orderly books. He lashed out without thinking, and nearly lost his two most valuable allies in Congress as a result. Without consulting either Peters or Pickering, he went over their heads, lodging a formal complaint with President John Jay that the Board of War wasn't doing its job. For once Congress acted quickly, handing the Board a stinging rebuke for a delay that was not at all its fault.[14]

No sooner had he made the complaint than Steuben realized he had made a big mistake, for with Peters and Pickering lay the only chance of getting the *Regulations* finished. Almost too late, he tried to make amends. "I know I have already given you a Considerable deal of Trouble," he wrote Pickering. He was still convinced that he was in the right—"the Board of War has hurt me considerably by the delay of the Regulations," he blurted to Peters—but after his falling-out with Laurens he had no wish to lose any more friends. "Altho' I give to the Devil the Honorable Board of War, I still always Except my dear friend[s] Mssrs Peters & Pickering," he tried to joke with Peters. "I beg, my dear Sir, you will make a similar distinction between the Inspector General & Baron Steuben. You may damn the first as much as you please, but pray, preserve your friendship to the Latter."[15]

Peters and Pickering *were* offended, but they also understood the Baron and let his anger pass. Peters, though, made him suffer first. Observing that the country air had not improved Steuben's temper, he jabbed at his friend,

> I am sorry that Carpenters, Tailors, smiths, Wheelwrights & what has now stirred your Wrath, a damned Book binder . . . should call forth the Exercise of a Virtue which ought not to be drawn forth but upon great Occasions—such as bearing the undeserved Reproaches of the Inspector General. . . . You tell me to make a Distinction between the Baron Steuben & the Inspector General. I will make another Distinction. I will distinguish between the Baron Steuben uninformed & the Baron Steuben acquainted with Facts & Difficulties. A third Difference I will also observe and that is between the Baron Steuben

in good Humour & the same Gentleman . . . angry and fretted. You see how readily I obey your Injunctions.[16]

The disagreement was soon smoothed over, the bookbinder and the new engraver caught up on their assigned work, and less than a week later the Blue Book was on its way to the army. Congress commissioned special leather-bound presentation copies for Louis XVI and Washington. Between June and August 1779, some fifteen hundred copies of the *Regulations* were printed for and distributed by the Board of War.[17]

———

WITH OR WITHOUT THE BLUE BOOK, Washington wanted an immediate and accurate report on the condition of the army. This was Steuben's job, not only because he was the inspector but also because he was the only officer in the army capable of doing it on such short notice.

Annoyed but undeterred by the truant *Regulations*, the Baron threw himself into the task with the same frantic energy he had displayed at Valley Forge, working late into the night each night, rising before sunup each morning. He expected no less from his assistants. In the army-wide inspections, which began in mid-May 1779, he was a regular terror, far more exacting than he had ever been. Each brigade, every single regiment, had to be inspected not annually but monthly, and since Steuben insisted on conducting the inspections himself, it was a punishing experience for him.

The inspection of a brigade would normally take up an entire day. Typically, a brigade of three or four infantry regiments—roughly one thousand to fifteen hundred men—would form up on the Parade first thing after breakfast. All of the men would form themselves in a single long rank, carrying their full marching gear: muskets, packs, and all of their impedimenta. Steuben, followed by Walker, perhaps, or Duponceau—the Baron no longer needed a translator all the time, as he was growing comfortable with English—would stride along the front of the line from end to end, moving surprisingly fast on his stumpy legs, making an initial visual assessment of the brigade's strengths and faults. Then he would pass by a second time, now examining each and every soldier individually. He halted in front of each man, took each musket in hand, his sharp eyes searching relentlessly for rust, fouling, any trace of unsoldierly neglect. With his thick fingers, which barely protruded from the immaculate white lace of his shirt cuffs, he opened each man's cartridge box, examining the condition of the ammunition inside; he tugged at clothing, rattled canteens, and readjusted uniforms and equipment with his big rough hands. Each man had to drop his knapsack to the ground and open it so that the Baron could rifle through its contents. Any slovenliness, any missing piece of equipment, drew instant reproofs from him, but he was equally liberal with his compliments to men who presented a soldierly appearance. From time to time he interviewed soldiers picked at random. What had they received for rations? How did they prepare them? When were they last issued shoes? How often did they drill, and who led them?

The process became yet more painstaking that summer. Steuben had been horrified to learn that the army had no system to account for weapons, uniforms, or equipment issued to individual soldiers. The men could leave camp at the end of their enlistments taking their muskets and gear with them, and no one was the wiser. No wonder there was such waste! So the Baron created a system: company officers would have to keep "company books," listing each item of government property—every coat, hat, knapsack, musket, pair of shoes, everything—issued to each soldier. Each soldier, likewise, had to keep what Steuben called a *livre du soldat*—a "soldier's book"—listing what he had been issued and when. Now when the Baron inspected a brigade, he would take the extra time to check each soldier's actual belongings against the records in his soldier's book.

Then it was the officers' turn. They had good reason to quail in the Baron's presence, for nothing escaped his eye. Individual soldier's books were checked against the company account books for accuracy; on-the-spot head counts of each company were compared to the official muster rolls. Woe to the captain who could not account for a missing knapsack or for a soldier listed as present but not actually there, for Steuben demanded to know the whereabouts of every man and every article of clothing and equipment. Regimental and brigade officers were ultimately accountable for everything that was amiss, and Steuben did not hesitate to reprimand them for the failings of their subordinates. He interviewed surgeons, visited the sick in the regimental hospitals, and examined camps to look for signs of untidiness or disorder. Not a stone was left unturned. Overtly negligent officers were arrested on the spot.

No one, except perhaps the Baron himself, enjoyed the inspections. Many a soldier, one man recalled, felt a "trembling in [his] limbs" when confronted with "the keen eye and piercing countenance of the Baron." Officers dreaded the possibility of a confrontation with the inspector should he happen to find a problem they might have overlooked. The Baron's staff hated the process most of all, the mind-numbing procession of red tape, the endless compilation of reports and statistics. Duponceau's chief memory of the "bloodless campaign" of 1779 was that it was "anything but pleasant . . . a tedious business."[18]

But the results were worth the effort. Property losses dropped significantly; morale soared, for the inspections helped to breed esprit de corps and a healthy spirit of competition among the regiments. The men wanted to look their best for the Baron and earn his praise. The officers paid much closer attention to the appearance and whereabouts of their men. Company officers bartered their own surplus rations for clothing and equipment to keep their men in fighting trim. And as with the training regimen at Valley Forge, Steuben consciously set an example for other officers to follow. If a major general could take such an interest in the condition of each individual soldier, so could they.

A ND SO THE INSPECTIONS CONTINUED throughout the summer: first in New Jersey, then in the Hudson Highlands, where Washington had relocated the army in June, and finally with Gates's army in Rhode Island. Steuben kept up with the demanding pace—indeed, he thrived on it—and Washington rewarded him with a pleasant and relaxing assignment. The new French ambassador to the United States, Anne-César, Chevalier de la Luzerne, had just arrived in Boston that summer; the general-in-chief delegated Steuben to escort Luzerne from Boston to army headquarters in the Hudson Valley. The Baron jumped eagerly at the task, for the chevalier undoubtedly would have letters for him from France or Germany.

The arrival of Luzerne, presumably with further word of French help on the way to America, was just one of several developments that lightened the mood in the army and in Congress that summer. As Steuben himself knew, the army was still far from operating at peak efficiency, but when it came to tactical proficiency the Continentals had not regressed since Monmouth. "If we understand by Order & Discipline only what regards the Manœvres prescribed in the Regulations," Steuben conceded, "I will venture to say that the Army in general is well Disciplined, that there are some Regiments which have more precision than the English Infantry."[19] This was no small praise from a man who was his own worst critic.

And it showed in combat. Washington had no intention of risking a "general action"—an all-out battle with the British—but he could engage in smaller actions. That May, Clinton had threatened American-held West Point, a vital stronghold, key to the Hudson Valley and up-state New York. British troops took possession of Stony Point, an outpost on the west bank of the Hudson that controlled Kings Ferry. Clinton hoped to draw the Americans out of the security of West Point; Washington obliged him, but not quite in the way Clinton had anticipated.

On July 15, 1779, Anthony Wayne led a corps of thirteen hundred Continental light infantry toward the modest earthen fortification at Stony Point, which was situated on a forbidding bluff overlooking the river. Late that night, part of Wayne's force launched a diversionary attack on the landward approach to the fort, drawing British fire in that direction, while the two remaining American columns silently scaled the rocky heights on the northern and eastern faces of the Point.

They achieved almost complete surprise over the fort's defenders, leaping into the upper works with fixed bayonets and overpowering the garrison without firing a shot. The entire British force was either killed or taken prisoner. American losses were trivial. And the first American to enter the upper works was none other than Lieutenant Colonel Fleury.

Only a month later, Washington struck again, and from a different direction. In the early morning hours of August 19, 1779, Maj. Henry "Light-Horse Harry" Lee led a tiny mixed force of infantry and cavalry in a raid on the British fort at Paulus Hook, immediately across from New York City, in present-day Jersey City, New Jersey. Lee was unable to gain possession of the fort, but he managed to escape with nearly 160 British and Hessian prisoners—and all practically within cannon-shot of Clinton's main army.

Stony Point and Paulus Hook did wonders for American morale. No one was prouder than Steuben, who was so overjoyed about Stony Point that he personally arranged for a triumphal entry when Wayne's aide-de-camp brought the news to Philadelphia. "I came into the City," the aide reported, "with colours flying, trumpets sounding, and hearts elated, drew crowds to the doors and windows, and made not a little parade. . . . These were the Baron Steuben's instructions, and I pursued them literally, although I could not help thinking that it had a little the appearance of a puppet show."[20]

Certainly the consensus among Washington's generals and the delegates in Congress was that Steuben's reforms had given the Continentals the discipline and proficiency with the bayonet that allowed them to take Stony Point and raid Paulus Hook. Even the Baron was cautiously optimistic. As he wrote to Benjamin Franklin early that autumn,

> I leave it to your other correspondents to give you an Account of the present State of our Army; if they tell you that our Order & Discipline Equals that of the French and Prussian Armies, do not believe them, but do not believe them neither, if they

compare our Troops to those of the Pope, & take a just medium between those two Extremes. Tho' we are so young that we scarce begin to walk, we can already take Stoney Points & Powles Hook with the point of the Bayonet, without firing a Single Shot.[21]

THE BARON DID NOT DELUDE HIMSELF. The Continental Army was still incapable of outmastering the British in sustained operations without substantial French help, and without further improvements, the Americans would be shamefully dependent on the French—if, that is, the French ever came to their aid.

A year and a half had passed since Valley Forge, and nearly a year since the painful object lesson of Overkill, but many of the problems of military discipline had still not been addressed. Guard duty remained neglected, soldiers were free to wander about camp—or out of camp entirely—without constraint, "the natural consequence of the Regiments being without Officers." Independence might be the heart of the Cause, but independence had no place in the ranks. When the Baron wrote to Ben Franklin in September 1779, he added in a cautionary tone: "We have still many Weaknesses which bespeak our Infancy. We want, above all, the true meaning of the Words *Liberty, Independence,* &c. that the Child may not make use of them against his father, or the Soldier against his Officer."[22]

Steuben was not just bewailing individual acts of insubordination within the army. The problem went much deeper than that: not only the discipline of the soldier, but also of the *nation* and the *people.* The states were unwilling to fill their assigned recruitment quotas, and Congress was unwilling or unable to compel them to do so. Until this changed, the army would be undermanned and undersupplied, and the British would hold every advantage over them. If the Americans wanted to win the war, they would have to commit everything they had. Steuben had said as much to John Hancock and Sam Adams back in 1777. It was no less true now.

As the months rolled on and 1779 drew to an anticlimactic close, the condition of the army didn't get any better. It did, in fact, get much worse.

Actually, *everything* got worse, and the weather itself was in large part to blame. The winter of 1779–80 was the worst since the war began. Storms pelted the army with snow and sleet in late November, as the troops converged on Morristown, New Jersey, to settle in for the winter. The serious snowfall began shortly after Christmas, before huts could be built to accommodate the men. A three-day blizzard in early January dumped upward of six feet of snow on the ramshackle tent city at Jockey Hollow, burying soldiers as they slept. The army was paralyzed; roads were shut down by the drifting snow, making travel to and from the camp impossible. Fierce winds tore through the men's tattered clothing and ripped tents apart as if they were made of paper. At Valley Forge, the weather had been unpleasant; at Morristown it was lethal.

The army was as close to complete dissolution as it had ever been or would ever be. Enlistment terms for many soldiers were about to expire; starvation would have compelled many more men to leave were it not for the snow-blocked roads that prevented them from deserting en masse—a dark blessing for the army, as Nathanael Greene would observe.

Many officers left as soon as they could, but Steuben stayed on. Washington, ever the optimist, wanted a frank assessment of the army's strength so he could plan operations for the spring—therefore the inspections continued, snow or no snow. The general-in-chief had no idea just how bad things were until Steuben showed him the stark arithmetic on paper.

The Baron had not pulled any punches in the spring inspections, but the observations he made in December 1779 were absolutely scathing by comparison. The underlying problems had not changed since the army came to Jockey Hollow. It was the magnitude of those problems—absenteeism, low morale, inadequate clothing, lax discipline—that had ballooned.

No regiment was up to strength—not even close. One company of Moses Hazen's Canadian Regiment consisted of nothing more than a

The army inspections at Morristown, December 1779. This is a typical report from the inspections done by Steuben himself. Evaluating the condition of Sherman's 8th Connecticut Regiment, the Baron writes: "Four companies of this Regiment are left without Officers too many being on furlow. This Regiment has near Thirty Men dispersed in the Country in improper Commands. Some near two years absent and many of those returned Sick absent have been absent two even three Years. [signed] Steuben, inspector General." *(National Archives)* drummer and two privates, and two other companies had no officers whatsoever. Edward Hand's brigade, "the worst composed in the Army," contained two Pennsylvania regiments that Steuben pronounced "almost ruined for want of care." Some of the many absent men in the brigade had been missing for two years. The New Yorkers "exhibit the greatest picture of misery that ever was seen"; the average New York Continental did not have clothing "sufficient to cover his nakedness in this severe season," while their officers looked so shabby they were "ashamed to appear even in Camp."[23]

Washington was already overburdened with paperwork, so it took him some time to sift through the mountain of reports that Steuben and his sub-inspectors had piled on his desk. When he did get to them he was shocked. "I am extremely disappointed to find," he wrote Steuben, "that most of the corps in the army are in worse shape than I had flattered myself." Some units had even "gone backward."[24]

Many of the problems, Steuben knew from experience, could be remedied with hard work and the return of better weather. But the real evils, the things that truly threatened the army's continued existence, were beyond the powers of the high command to fix: numbers, recruitment, and organization. Organization had been the chief concern at the time of the spring inspections. There was too much disparity between unit sizes, as there had been at Valley Forge. Then, as now, Steuben advocated reducing the number of regiments and collapsing them into fewer but larger units of a standard size—preferably around five hundred rank and file per regiment. It would not be a popular solution, especially among the officers who would lose their posts. But it would be brutally effective, for both administrative and tactical purposes.[25]

That was in the spring. Since then, the individual states had become increasingly negligent in meeting their assigned manpower quotas. The national economy, if it could be called that, was headed toward complete collapse, as Continental currency depreciated in value faster than anyone could have imagined. In January 1779, one gold dollar was worth eight Continental dollars; by December, it took forty-two

Continental dollars to equal one in specie. One Connecticut soldier remarked that the currency issued by Congress was "fit for nothing But Bum Fodder."[26] The army deteriorated as the economy did, and by the time the first snows fell at Morristown, the army was already dying.

Organization, therefore, took a backseat to numbers. Washington and Steuben were of one mind on this issue. Performing a sort of institutional triage, they temporarily pushed reform to the side in order to focus on bringing the army up to strength.

Unfortunately, the prevailing sentiment in Congress had come around to Steuben's previous proposal: the consolidation of the army into fewer but larger units. In the Board of War this had come to be known as the "incorporation plan," and it was sponsored by New York delegate and Board of War member Robert R. Livingston. It was an attractive solution for a Congress lacking money and to command authority, where so many delegates distrusted the simple notion of a standing army. The plan required no outlay of cash, and did not compel them to press the states for more men. And it had the blessing of the inspector general himself. If French aid was so close at hand, why would it be necessary to keep anything more than a skeleton army in the field?

This was a dangerous way of thinking. It assumed that the British would remain passive, and that the French would be true to their word—and the survival of the country could not be gambled on either of these dubious conditions. The army had to be restocked with men, and for that, Congress would have to act.

Congress was not quite the same animal in 1780 as it had been two years before. Relatively few of the delegates who had greeted Steuben at York still actively represented their states in Philadelphia, and the acrimonious dispute over Washington's leadership had by now subsided. The main thing keeping Congress from supporting the army was not ideological division or personal spite, but "the grand cause of all our misfortunes, the bad state of our finances."[27] It would be difficult to cajole Congress into spending more on the army when the delegates perceived everything in terms of dollars and cents.

The army needed its own voice to be heard in Philadelphia. Washington decided that Steuben would be that voice. No soldier but the Baron had so much experience in dealing with Congress and still held Washington's trust; no other officer commanded such professional respect in Independence Hall. And certainly no one else knew the facts and figures of Continental military strength as Steuben did.

At the commander's request, Steuben and Duponceau left Morristown for Philadelphia on January 16, 1780. After six days of pushing through snowdrifts the height of a man and riding precariously along treacherous, icy roads, the two men arrived in the city, setting up their headquarters at a boardinghouse on Front Street. They did not so much as pause to catch their breath. Steuben presented his written report on the state of the army only four days after his arrival.

That report made for doleful reading, though the members of the Board of War couldn't have been too surprised. Using the devastating statistical evidence of the army's weakness to make his case, the Baron attacked the notion of "incorporation." Incorporation might save money in the short term, but it would not make the army any more capable of defending the country. It would sap morale, sacrifice experienced officers, and send a message of encouragement to the British and the Loyalists: that the rebels were tiring of the war and were no longer capable of supporting an army. The only possible solution was to enlarge the army through vigorous recruitment, to a minimum strength of thirty thousand men, including a larger cavalry arm.[28]

The Board weighed Steuben's new proposal against the incorporation plan for more than a month. In the meantime, its members wanted more specific figures on manpower, showing just how many troops would be available when the new campaign began in the summer. Hence a hefty delay, as the sub-inspectors scrambled to compile accurate returns from each and every regiment, at a time when much of the army was scattered around Morristown and the foul weather made routine headcounting an arduous chore. Steuben became so impatient that he could barely contain himself. If recruiting did not start soon, there would be no time to prepare new troops for combat. "We shall

Certainly lose two months at a Time when we ought not to lose two Days," he grumbled to Washington.[29]

These were not his only headaches. Unbeknownst to him, Congress and Washington had added yet another set of tasks to his department's unmanageable workload. In mid-January, Congress abolished the office of the mustermaster general and assigned its duties to the inspector general's office. The mustermaster had supervised recruiting and kept tabs on regimental strengths. That department had been defunct for quite some time. Steuben and his assistants had already been taking up the slack for several months, and the merger of the two departments had been under discussion for just as long. But the Baron resented the final decision all the same, because it was presented to him as a fait accompli, "without my knowing any thing of the Matter." He did not have enough assistants to handle the added labor, he was not allowed to appoint assistants, inflation had diminished his pay to almost nothing, and Congress had not seen fit to give him an expense account to cover the costs of his necessary travel.

Sick at heart—the Board was inclining perceptibly toward Livingston's incorporation plan—and physically ill as well, Steuben lapsed into a despair almost as deep as that he experienced after Monmouth. He felt that he had been backed into a corner. "My dear friend," he wrote in French to Ben Walker at the end of February, "there is a letter on my table for the Honorable Congress, which has been sealed for a week. It contains my resignation from the office with which America has honored me. The bad state of my private finances compels me to quit a game which I can no longer play."[30]

By vowing to resign—something he had done before, but without result—Steuben shook Congress more than he could have imagined. Unlike his earlier threats, this was not an empty one. He did not say he would resign his commission and return to Europe. Instead, he swore that he would resign his "office," meaning the inspectorship. If he did so, he would remain a major general, but without the extensive travel and extra duties that came from being inspector general. And since Nathanael Greene had also tendered his resignation as quartermaster general, it must have seemed as if the entire army staff was about to abandon ship.[31]

Congress took him at his word. Only two days later, the Board of War received congressional authorization to negotiate Steuben's finances. A few days after that, Congress voted to grant the Baron two bills of exchange: one for his expenses in coming to America in 1777, another for his expenses in office to date, for a total of 796 louis d'or. The amount was not huge, given the circumstances. Steuben had to accept a 40 percent discount when he cashed the first bill; the second was given to him at face value, as just over $150,000 in Continental scrip. Yet it was satisfactory, and far more than Steuben had a right to expect from a Congress that had devoted itself to pinching pennies.[32]

Steuben had not only saved himself—temporarily—from financial ruin, but he had also saved the army.

Early in February, Congress had given its stamp of approval to one of Steuben's recommendations, setting the size of the Continental Army for the 1780 campaign at thirty-five thousand troops. This was five thousand more than Steuben had recommended. The Baron was pleased, though he knew that the number meant nothing if Congress didn't strong-arm the state governments into disgorging their assigned quotas. The Board of War, in the meantime, was not quite so accommodating. On March 16, before harried Ben Walker could get all of the regimental returns forwarded, the Board voted to accept Livingston's incorporation plan. If Congress approved, which they almost certainly would, 25 percent of the army's regiments would disappear in very short order.

This was sheer madness, Steuben thought. Even if the army were increased in size, consolidating the army at this stage of the game would only cause confusion, absorbing all the attentions of the high command at a time when training and preparations for the coming campaign should be the paramount concerns. For all of the effort he had put into showing the Board the disadvantages of incorporation, he might as well have been arguing with the walls.

That was the last straw. The Baron told his opponent Livingston so, adding that he would return immediately to Morristown, where he was needed. If the Board of War would not listen to him and to reason, then he certainly was of no further use there.

Coming so close on the heels of his February letter, his statement to Livingston might as well have been a resignation threat. The Board was afraid of just that, and they had no desire to alienate a man who had earned for himself the reputation of miracle worker. Livingston himself begged Steuben to stay on in Philadelphia for a little while longer, promising him that he could present his arguments against incorporation directly to Congress. And the Baron, with just a trace of smugness, assented.

To Congress the Baron brought his best and most eloquent arguments against incorporation, citing the damage it would do to morale and to the discipline of the army. The regiments should instead be left intact, and new recruits fed into them until each regiment reached a standard size of 315 rank and file.

Congress listened. Only five days after Steuben's plan was introduced, on March 25, the delegates voted to table the incorporation issue altogether until December 1780 at the earliest. There would be no incorporation that year. The army could focus on recruitment and training, on working with the French, and on beating the Redcoats.

Steuben remained in Philadelphia for another two weeks, hounding the Board about recruiting and looking after Duponceau, who had taken quite ill. The Baron was not entirely satisfied, for despite his qualified victory over the Board of War, Congress had taken no positive steps to bring new recruits into the army. There were, however, signs of hope. In the first week of April, Congress decided to dispatch a special committee to Morristown, to observe the army and discuss the strategic situation with Washington.[33]

Something else of value came from Steuben's protracted stay in the capital that winter. The fight over the incorporation plan forged a new relationship between the inspector general and the commander in chief. The two men had corresponded throughout the season with a warmth and candor absent from their earlier letters. On an almost

THE TRUE MEANING OF DISCIPLINE ➔ 221

weekly basis Steuben poured out his frustrations, all of the details of his exasperating exchanges with the politicians, to Washington. Washington reassured him and gave friendly encouragement. To be sure, Steuben did ask for more money, but his principal business in Philadelphia was the fate of the army. Steuben put the Cause ahead of his personal interests, and that made a tremendous difference to Washington. Now Steuben was a friend and a trusted adviser. After two years of working side by side, Washington and the Baron had finally become partners in the stewardship of the army.

S TEUBEN WAS GLAD to leave Philadelphia behind, but the journey back to Morristown was not one of his most pleasant travels. For starters, he had to leave Duponceau behind and make the trip alone. The secretary was still confined to his bed, too sick to travel, which worried Steuben to no end. Despite his crusty exterior and his casual attitude toward his own health, when it came to the members of his staff, the Baron was a doting nursemaid. He left $10,000 Continental behind to cover Duponceau's medical expenses. But life just wasn't the same without his exuberant twenty-year-old translator by his side.[34]

Nor was Morristown itself a welcome (or welcoming) sight. The snow had just recently receded, leaving a muddy, pestilent wasteland in its wake, populated by hollow-eyed shadows who had once been soldiers in the full vigor of their youth. Clothing and food were not yet reaching the camp in satisfactory quantities, and would not for some time to come. Even a full month after the Baron's reunion with the army, the lack of food was so acute that two entire regiments of the Connecticut Line mutinied, threatening to go home if not fed. The prevailing mood at Valley Forge had been lively compared to this, but then, these men had suffered far more from every conceivable discomfort than the soldiers at the Forge had.

Yet for all that, Steuben resumed his duties as inspector with cautious optimism, or at least a feeling of resignation that came from a realistic appraisal of the limits that had been imposed upon him by

Congress. He could not fix everything that needed to be fixed; he had come to terms with that fact. Without once bemoaning the circumstances of his position, he launched into what by now had become a familiar routine: a showpiece review of the army, followed by intensive training.

The occasion for the review was the visit of the new French ambassador Luzerne. Steuben had only a couple of days to cobble together an appropriate spectacle for the diplomat. Luzerne, Washington, Steuben, and other dignitaries watched from a specially constructed reviewing stand as about twelve hundred infantry staged a mock battle for their benefit. It "made a great noise, if nothing more," according to one participant. Luzerne was impressed, and that had been the intention. That evening, Luzerne and the generals attended a ball and were entertained by a fireworks display orchestrated by Henry Knox's artillerists. The men and the junior officers engaged in festivities that were more their style. Washington had rewarded them with a gill of rum per man. The raw liquor "took violent hold" of men with empty stomachs, who caroused, sang, and fought with all of the gusto that one would expect from drunken soldiers.[35]

There was little time for further levity, though, even if the British army remained inactive in New York and Clinton himself was occupied with the siege of Charleston, where Benjamin Lincoln's pitiful remnant of an army sat bottled up and without hope of relief. Soon the Continental camp at Morristown bustled with activity again, much of it the Baron's doing. Regular inspections of the army began anew in the first days of May, as Steuben resumed his twelve-hour, seven-to-seven work schedule. The inspections revealed nothing new, just the customary absenteeism and the perennial neglect of guard duty, and that expiring enlistments would soon whittle the army down from around ten thousand effectives to eight thousand.

Still, Steuben would work with what he had at hand. The task of training the remaining troops began in mid-May. There were few raw recruits in the army, so Steuben and his inspectors could skip over the elementary levels of the *Regulations* and proceed straight to brigade and divisional maneuvers. By month's end, Steuben introduced mock battles as part of the training program—not for show this time, but with the intent of demonstrating just how the grand maneuvers would actually work in combat. He tried to simulate battlefield conditions, employing cavalry and artillery in the scenarios, while the field music lent the skirling of fife and drum to the din.[36]

The only real blow to morale came from Charleston, where Lincoln's battered command finally fell to Clinton on May 12. This was no minor setback. It was, in fact, an absolute disaster, perhaps the worst American defeat of the entire war. Any despondency over the loss of Charleston and its defenders, however, was quickly offset by much more encouraging intelligence, news that Washington, Congress, and indeed anyone with rebel sympathies had longed to hear: the French were coming. Six thousand royal troops, under the command of the Comte de Rochambeau, were already en route to America. There was no questioning it this time; Lafayette himself, having just returned from his trip to Paris, brought the good word to Congress. Another six thousand French soldiers, the marquis reported, would shortly follow Rochambeau's corps.

The imminent arrival of French forces electrified both Congress and the high command. Congress, rather belatedly, pressured the states to fill their recruiting quotas and bring their Continental regiments up to strength. Washington's thoughts turned again to the attack. But before he could make any definite plans, the British made up his mind for him. On June 6, 1780, six thousand Redcoats and Hessians left the safety of their camp on Staten Island, crossed into New Jersey, and began to march toward Morristown.

THE BRITISH PROVED STEUBEN RIGHT. Steuben had told Congress and the Board of War, again and again, that their neglect of the army was bound to encourage the enemy. It did. Deserters from Morristown, picked up by British patrols in New York and northern Jersey, told their captors of how badly the Continental Army had suffered that winter and spring. There were only four thousand troops left in Morristown, they said, and those few were themselves on the verge of desertion, and had no fight left in them. The British commander in New York took this to heart, deciding that he would be irresponsible if he sat by and did not capitalize on the rebels' misery.

The British commander in New York was not actually British. He was Wilhelm, Reichsfreiherr zu Innhausen und Knyphausen, lieutenant general under Sir Henry Clinton and the ranking officer of all the German mercenaries commonly (if inaccurately) known as Hessians. Clinton had left him in command at New York while he went to reinforce Cornwallis in the south. He really had very little independent authority—Clinton treated him as just another division commander—but Knyphausen took it upon himself to take the initiative in Clinton's absence.[37]

Knyphausen anticipated an easy expedition. He would march toward Morristown, take up a position near Springfield on the first day's march, and force Washington to come out of his encampment and give battle. Since the Continentals had so few horses—so the Hessian general had heard from his informants—Washington would have to abandon most of his supplies.

The British-Hessian-Loyalist force did not quite reach their destination. Jersey militia turned out in unexpectedly high numbers, leaving their homes with musket in hand to contest the invasion. After hot fighting and a difficult march, Knyphausen withdrew his men back to Elizabethtown to observe the Americans and wait for a better opportunity.

Washington reacted quickly to the enemy incursion. On June 7, while the New Jersey militiamen were making life difficult for the Hessian light infantry, he prepared his army for battle. He would not abandon Morristown, but neither would he wait passively for the arrival of the enemy. Especially not for the Hessians. Deserved or not, the German auxiliary troops had earned a reputation for barbarism, and few things seemed to anger the rebels more than the imagined depredations of Hessian troops—except, perhaps, for those of the perfidious Loyalists.

The Baron de Steuben on horseback, ca. 1780–83. Steuben was a knowledgeable connoisseur of fine horses. His favorite stallion, Cincinnatus, attracted admiring comments in Virginia even when the Baron did not. The Baron sold Cincinnatus in late 1788 to pay off some of his debt. *(Library of Congress)*

Washington mobilized several brigades for the march toward Springfield and Elizabethtown, grouping them into three divisions. The first line of troops was divided into two wings, one under Nathanael Greene, the other under Lafayette. The second line, consisting of the brigades of Edward Hand and John Stark, he entrusted to Steuben.[38]

The ensuing campaign was brief but not pointless, for Knyphausen, even if poorly served by his sources of intelligence, presented a real threat to the undermanned American army. The French had not yet arrived, and there was no guarantee that the French fleet would be able to penetrate the cordon of warships with which the British had sealed off the American coastline. If Knyphausen could deal Washington a stinging blow, he just might be able to shift quickly northward and wrest West Point from Washington's grasp.

After two days of marching, Steuben's division was handed over to the command of Lord Stirling, while the Baron himself was transferred to a position of greater responsibility and risk: commanding the advance guard, a mix of Jersey militia and Continental troops, including William Maxwell's brigade and Light-Horse Harry Lee's legion. With this force, Steuben was to scout Knyphausen's positions outside Elizabethtown. Washington anticipated that Knyphausen would either attack the Continentals outright or make a mad dash for the Hudson and West Point. Either way, Steuben would act as his eyes and ears, and—in the case of an attack on the Continentals in New Jersey—his first line of defense, too.[39]

This was not a promising assignment. The Baron was firmly convinced that the real target of Knyphausen's onslaught was West Point, not Morristown, and he knew well that West Point was in no condition to withstand a determined assault. That was where he wanted to be, where he felt the decisive blow would fall.

The worst thing, however, was that he found himself commanding forces that did not quite live up to the standards he expected from soldiers. Within a few days of Knyphausen's retreat to Elizabethtown, the Jersey militia grew restless and bored, and soon they were straggling back to their homes. While making his rounds of the American advanced posts on the morning of June 20, the Baron found that two of these posts had been completely abandoned by the militia assigned to man them. He was dumbstruck that the militia could be so careless and negligent while Loyalists and Hessians were burning homes and farms in the countryside. "With a very inferior Force I have hitherto labor'd to keep at Bay an Army very respectable in their Numbers & prevented their ravaging your Country," he wrote to the state governor, William Livingston. "I am liable however every moment to be defeated by those few Men who constitute my Command." Feeling very ill, and fearful that his reputation as an officer would be destroyed not by his own actions but by the incompetence of the men under his command, Steuben begged Washington to send him to West Point instead. Washington, who agreed with the Baron's assessment of British intentions, complied immediately.[40]

Steuben's instincts were dead-on. While Knyphausen was holding tight at Elizabethtown, Clinton and his troops returned from Charleston, sailing into New York Harbor on the very same day that the Baron requested a transfer. Sir Henry was not the least bit pleased with Knyphausen's independent action, but he thought it wise to turn the New Jersey invasion to good use. He would reinforce Knyphausen's force, presenting an even greater threat to Morristown, and so enmire the Continentals that a thrust up the Hudson toward West Point could be executed. Again Knyphausen's army surged forward, and again the offensive failed. Washington moved with the main body of the army to West Point, where Steuben was already helping to organize the small garrison and beef up the defenses. Greene's division remained behind, alone, in New Jersey. At Springfield, on June 23, the intrepid Rhode Islander and his men held off Knyphausen's assault in fine fashion, convincing the Hessian to give up and retreat to New York.

Greene was the one who took most of what little glory was to be gleaned from the anticlimactic Knyphausen invasion. The battle at Springfield, perhaps the most unjustly forgotten clash of the war, was a telling demonstration of the effectiveness of the revamped Continental Army in the hands of one of its star generals. It was also the only real pitched battle of the entire campaign. Steuben, by contrast, could not count himself quite so fortunate.

But it was not without significance. Washington had given him a field command, and not just the responsibility of moving troops. It was a sure mark of esteem from the commander in chief, a sign that Steuben had finally earned the trust that he thought he had won at Monmouth. Even better: none of the brigadier generals had complained about the Baron's preferment. He was no longer an inspector general with the rank of major general; he was one of Washington's generals, a bonafide and permanent battlefield commander in the Continental Army.

In a mere six months, Steuben would come to regret this with every fiber of his being.

CHAPTER 10

Tormenting the Governor

[July 1780—May 1781]

I must confess that I have not yet learnt how to beat
regular troops with one third their number of militia.

STEUBEN TO GEORGE WASHINGTON,
JUNE 11, 1781[1]

W HILE CONDUCTING INSPECTIONS at West Point in
early October 1780, the Baron de Steuben ran
across a name in the muster rolls of the 3rd Connecticut Regiment that caught his eye. Inspection days were
busy ones, without much time for idle banter, but Steuben
found the man's name so intriguing that he simply had to investigate. As the regiment stood stiffly at attention, the inspector general summoned the man to report front and center.
Jonathan Arnold, a twenty-three-year-old tenant farmer from
East Hartford, stepped nervously to the front and saluted.

Only a couple of weeks before, the name "Arnold" would
not have merited a second glance, but that had changed. On
September 25, Benedict Arnold, one of Washington's favorite
generals and the unsung hero of Saratoga, had tried to sell out
West Point to the British. Arnold's treason was detected before
any real damage could be done, but the act devastated Washington and infuriated the entire army. Steuben shared in the

communal, visceral hate. He sat on the court that tried Arnold's British accomplice, Maj. John André, as a spy. Like most of his comrades, Steuben admired the cultured, gentlemanly André, and would have far preferred to have seen Arnold, and not André, dangling from the gibbet at Tappan.

Somehow it struck Steuben as odd that another man from General Arnold's native state could possibly bear the same surname as the perfidious traitor. When Jonathan Arnold came before him that day, the Baron asked him how he could stand having such a name, as if it were a matter of choice. The terrified young soldier stammered out that he hated the name but didn't think he could do anything about it. Delighted at the response, Steuben put Arnold at his ease. Assuredly the name could be changed, he said, and offered "Steuben" as a substitute.[2]

Neither man forgot the episode. As soon as he was discharged from the army in 1783, Jonathan Arnold petitioned the Connecticut General Assembly to change his name. "Pitying the misfortune of any person Friendly to the American cause" with that unspeakable name, Steuben supported the petition, and further asked the state of Connecticut to pay Arnold a lifetime pension of two dollars per month. The Baron and the Connecticut farmer, now Jonathan Arnold Steuben, would remain linked for the rest of their lives.[3]

This kind of informal fellowship with the common soldier came easy to Steuben, especially now that he had accepted the fact that America was likely to be his permanent home. Two years before, the notion that he might never leave the New World would have struck him as inexpressibly depressing. His gentleman's agreement with St. Germain, assuring him of a commission in King Louis's army, had been his hope and his comfort. Only gradually did he come to realize that that hope had been but a phantom.

The sad truth was that France had forgotten him. St. Germain had died in January 1778, and any arrangement he had made with the Baron went to his grave with him. Beaumarchais no longer held much influence at court. Of those men privy to the deal, only Vergennes remained, and Vergennes did not care what became of Steuben.

The Baron searched both Gérard and Luzerne for any sign that he might have a future in France, but in vain. After escorting Luzerne from Boston in the summer of 1779, it finally dawned on him: "I saw that he knew nothing of me," Steuben confided to his memoirs, "and that the French ministry had not informed him how it happened that I came to this country. . . . They had set me adrift and . . . I was to manage for myself as well as I could."[4]

That was a discouraging epiphany, but things could have been worse. Steuben had to admit that he *liked* America and Americans, and he had come to think of their Cause as his own. Historians and a few hostile contemporaries would later describe the Baron as a "mercenary" to whom the concept of liberty meant little. Such an assessment is both unfair and wrong. Like many educated Europeans of the Enlightenment, Steuben idolized Montesquieu, Rousseau, and Voltaire, men who sincerely believed in the equality of humankind and the sanctity of freedom. To him, as to Lafayette, the American bid for independence was a great experiment, one that would, he hoped, prove that these were not the mere musings of abstract philosophy.

The political progressive in him thought very highly of the *idea* of America. He was nobly born and proud of it, yet he found the lack of class distinctions in the New World wondrous. "What a beautiful, happy land is this, without kings, without high princes . . . and without idle barons. . . . Here we are in a republic and a baron does not count for more than any James or Peter," he explained, with evident pride, to Chancellor Frank. "Our general of artillery [Henry Knox] was a book-printer in Boston—a worthy man who understands his craft from the bottom up, and who carries out his present position with much honor."[5]

He liked most politicians, too, but as individuals and not as officials. As a body, Congress left much to be desired, he thought: there were too many idealogues and self-seeking businessmen, too few realists who understood war. Congress's lack of authority perplexed him. What perplexed him even more was the unwillingness of the states to cooperate with one another when solidarity was vital for America's survival. "In the moment when the most Vigorous exertions are necessary," he ranted in exasperation in 1780, "the States instead of vying with each other [to see] who should do the most, observe a Contrary Conduct & calculate only to furnish the least to the general good."[6]

Steuben's assessment of American politics was not far off the mark. Nothing, however, could have prepared him for his firsthand experience of American democracy in 1781, when the shortcomings of American politics nearly resulted in the loss of an entire state.

A s Knyphausen's army receded sullenly from northern New Jersey, burning farmsteads as it went, Washington concentrated his forces in the Hudson Valley. Steuben was already in the mountains at West Point, helping Maj. Gen. Robert Howe to train new recruits and prepare the Point's defenses for a possible British attack. He reunited with Washington and the main army before the summer was out.

Steuben made his headquarters near Fishkill, New York, in the modest, one-story stone farmhouse of Hendrick Kip. There, he and the core of his staff—Walker, North, and Duponceau's replacement, Lt. James Fairlie—inspected the small bands of recruits trickling in from New England and New York, and resumed the training that had been so rudely interrupted by the Hessian Knyphausen. But the Baron didn't mind the brigade drills and inspections that started each morning at five o'clock. He loved the Hudson Valley above all the places he had fought or camped; the views of the broad river from Fishkill Landing, and of the mountains to the west beyond, calmed and invigorated him. And at the Kip house he had plenty of room for entertaining guests, which he did almost nightly. "Notwithstanding the scarcity of provisions in the camp," one of those guests noted with approval, "the Baron's table continues to be well-supplied; his generosity is unbounded."[7]

More exciting than the idyllic landscape and the social life was the promise of action to come. Rochambeau's first expeditionary corps of French royal troops had made landfall in Newport in mid-July. There would be battle soon—maybe not this year, but undoubtedly in the spring—and as a division commander, a *real* major general, Steuben would be in the thick of it.

As eager as Washington was to oust the British from New York, he and his generals agreed that the time was not yet right. The British fleet still controlled the seas, trapping Rochambeau in Rhode Island, and the Continental Army remained quite small. Developments in the south were not at all encouraging. On August 16, Horatio Gates, the darling of Congress, fled in terror as Lord Cornwallis destroyed his army just north of Camden, South Carolina. The battle ruined Gates's career, but more important, it all but gave the Carolinas to the British.

Content, and with time on his hands, Steuben drew up plans for the creation of a corps of light infantry based on the ideas of the French tactician Guibert: selected from the most agile, physically fit, and intelligent veterans in each regiment, the light infantry would be specially trained as shock troops for special operations like Stony Point. He also tried to fine-tune the administrative procedures practiced by the army. In the Prussian, Austrian, and French armies—the only armies worthy of emulation, in Steuben's view—the commanding general met daily with all of his subordinate generals as a group, but in the Continental Army "the Commander in Chief . . . does not see the General Officers as often as he should." This bad habit came from British practice, and just because the British did it "certainly cannot justify any thing which is in itself absurd." Henry Knox, who had come to be Steuben's best friend among the generals, warned him that Washington might take "umbrage" at the blunt criticism of his leadership style, but Steuben was unconcerned. He knew he was secure in the commander's esteem, and saw no reason to mince words.[8]

But the pleasant late summer could not last forever. Congress had just resurrected the incorporation plan. That might have been alarming news in other circumstances, but the Board of War had taken a different approach this time. The loss of Charleston and Gates's disgrace at Camden had humbled Congress, so when Washington dictated his ideas on army reorganization, Congress hushed to listen. In

Washington's plan, the number of infantry regiments would be reduced only slightly, the number of men per regiment increased, and the army—not Congress—would determine which officers would have to be dismissed. Retired officers, like their brethren who served throughout the war, would be granted half-pay for life. And Congress *must* pressure the states for more recruits. It was a bold proposal. Anticipating a fight, Washington sent Steuben back to Independence Hall in October 1780 to defend the plan.

Steuben went, with a certain amount of dread, but much to his surprise there was almost no wrangling except over the issue of half-pay. After only a few days of negotiation, the Baron could report back to Washington that Congress had accepted the proposal "without Alteration."[9]

On the very same day, Washington had news of his own for the Baron. The commander in chief had made a decision that would radically alter Steuben's role in the war. On October 22, 1780, Washington nominated Nathanael Greene to replace Horatio Gates as commander in the Southern Department, where he would rebuild the army and try to slow the northward advance of Lord Cornwallis. Accompanying Greene as his second-in-command would be the Baron de Steuben.[10]

W ASHINGTON WAS WILLING to part with two of his most prized subordinates because he was deadly serious about the southern theater of operations. There was nothing to keep Cornwallis from sweeping through the Carolinas and into Virginia—and that would be a catastrophe. If Virginia fell, then Clinton and Cornwallis could envelop Washington's army in a giant pincers, crushing it and ending the war. Of all of Washington's generals, only Greene had the command instinct and the fire to take a swing at Cornwallis, and only Steuben had the ability to fashion a functioning army out of virtually nothing.

"To the Southward there is an army to be created," Washington informed Steuben, "the mass of which is at present without any formation at all."[11] It was no exaggeration. Most of the Continental troops in the South had been lost with Savannah and Charleston, and the small remainder had been chewed up and spat out by the British at Camden. It would be Steuben's assignment to raise and train a new Continental force, and—more challenging—to get some useful service out of the southern state militias.

Orders in hand, General Greene went to Philadelphia to receive Congress's blessing and to consult with Steuben. Four days later, on November 3, 1780, the two men and their staffs set off for Virginia as quickly as they could. Joining them, over Steuben's initial objections, was Duponceau. The young Frenchman had been suffering terribly from consumption, and his doctors had condemned him to death, but he insisted on accompanying his master anyway. "Very well," Steuben conceded, "you shall follow me, and I hope that you will either recover your health or die an honourable death."[12]

The group paused briefly at Mount Vernon, where Martha Washington greeted them as old friends. Steuben loved Mrs. Washington, whom he knew well from many gatherings at the Potts house in Valley Forge, but he was unimpressed with the Washington estate. "If General Washington were not a better general than he was an architect," he told the ailing Duponceau with a wink, "the Affairs of America would be in a very bad condition."[13]

Actually, the affairs of America *were* in a very bad condition, and the greatest troubles were within Virginia.

Greene and Steuben did not plan to stay very long in Washington's home state, for their tasks there were very simple: assess the strategic situation, make sure that local defenses were adequate, take whatever Continental recruits and supplies they found, proceed to South Carolina. But from the intelligence they garnered along their journey to the new state capital at Richmond, it appeared that their business in Virginia might be a bit more complicated than they had anticipated. Before they had even left Philadelphia, Maj. Gen. Alexander Leslie

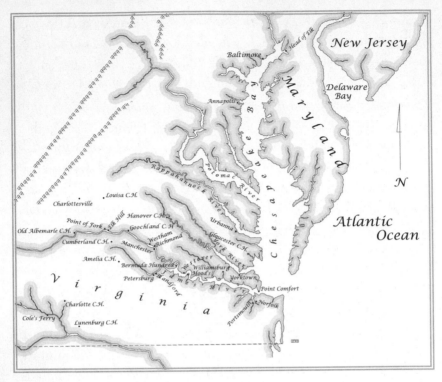

Map of Virginia, 1781

and 2,200 Redcoats had sailed into Chesapeake Bay, disembarked, and seized the towns of Portsmouth and Suffolk. The British "invasion," if it could be called that, caused little damage and did not last for very long. On November 16, the very same day that Greene and Steuben rode into Richmond, Leslie's corps boarded their transports again and left for Charleston.

The real reason for Leslie's precipitous withdrawal was that Cornwallis, clamoring for reinforcements, had ordered Leslie to leave. No one in Virginia knew that, however. Leslie's invasion had prompted a groundswell of patriotic fervor. The state militia, poorly organized and worse armed, had turned out in force. From the rebel side, it certainly looked as if the British had withdrawn because the militia had convinced them to.

The whole episode gave the Virginians and their governor, one

Thomas Jefferson, a false sense of security, a conviction that the militia alone was sufficient to protect the state. This was dangerous. For as Greene and Steuben clearly saw, Virginia was in no condition to fight a protracted campaign against even a small force of British regulars. The state owned few muskets and little ammunition, not even enough to equip the militia who had been called up to defend against Leslie.

Inevitably, Leslie's invasion had an impact on the Continental Army, too. There were at most eight hundred Continental recruits in Virginia in November 1780, and—untrained, lacking weapons and clothing, all but destitute of provisions—they were not even ready to march south. The Continental quartermaster's department in Virginia was, in Greene's words, "totally deranged," without any organization or personnel.[14]

Greene desperately needed men, equipment, clothing, and food from Virginia, but neither could he tarry in the state much longer. Before he left for the Carolinas on November 21, he decided to leave Steuben behind in Richmond to organize recruits and supplies for the Southern Army. He did so reluctantly, for he needed Steuben's personal assistance, too. But it would be only a temporary assignment. As soon as a critical mass of Continental recruits could be clothed, armed, and formed into regiments, Steuben could march south with them and take his place at Greene's side.

Easier said than done, as the Baron soon discovered. "All the Wheels of the Machine are Stopt, and all the Departments in the greatest Confusion," he reported to Washington in dismay. The eight hundred Continental recruits—inactive, half-naked, and without food—were deserting in droves. Because of the invasion scare in October and November, the Virginia General Assembly was much less concerned about meeting Greene's requirements than it was about the defense of the state. "Your Affairs are very little more advanced than when you left this town," Steuben told Greene at the very end of November.[15]

Steuben took charge. On Greene's recommendation, he delegated the task of recruiting and supply to Col. William Davies. A rough-spoken man with "an uneasy disposition," as Timothy Pickering described him, Davies was nonetheless highly dependable and intelligent, and he knew how to work with the Baron: he had been one of the original sub-inspectors at Valley Forge. Davies quickly constructed a recruiting depot at Chesterfield Courthouse, complete with barracks, a hospital, a clothing manufactory, and storehouses. Here Steuben made his headquarters. A Continental "laboratory"—a facility for manufacturing ammunition and repairing weapons—was established at nearby Westham. Davies somehow managed to find enough clothing and equipment for four hundred men. Within days, more than a full battalion of fresh Continental troops was on its way south to Greene.

Better yet: the next month, the state government gave every sign of willingness to cooperate with Greene. At Jefferson's urging, the General Assembly authorized the recruitment of three thousand men for Continental service, promising cash bounties, gold, silver, and slaves to men who volunteered for three years' or more service.[16]

At this rate, Steuben could count on sending off a battalion to Greene every month or so, maybe even every couple of weeks, and perhaps he, too, could leave the state by February. But the obvious strategic vulnerability of the state troubled him. Entrusting the defense of the state to the militia was in itself a risky proposition. Geography, too, made eastern Virginia difficult to defend. The network of rivers, the James and York estuaries in particular, could serve as a highway for an invading enemy. If the rivers were not properly guarded, a seaborne army could stab deep into the state.

One very inexpensive measure, Steuben saw, would go a long way toward forestalling invasion. Just downriver from the mouth of the Appomattox, the tidal estuary of the James narrowed sharply at a place called Hood's Landing. A simple earthen fort there, properly sited and bristling with ship-killing cannon, could keep a British fleet at bay indefinitely. Steuben could find the cannon, and he already had a competent engineer: Col. John Christian Senf, formerly chief engineer to Horatio Gates. All that was wanting was labor.

Steuben laid his plan for Hood's on Thomas Jefferson's desk at

Richmond. Nothing came of it. Neither Jefferson nor the Assembly thought that an enemy force would attempt to ascend the James. Virginia did not have the money to waste on guarding against every remote strategic possibility. The militia would have to suffice—if indeed there was any invasion at all.[17]

On December 29, 1780, a British fleet of twenty-seven sail dropped anchor off Old Point Comfort. On board were sixteen hundred British regulars and their commander, a familiar figure who had returned to plague his former comrades-in-arms. Benedict Arnold was back.

STEUBEN HAD GUESSED that another invasion was coming soon. At the first sign of trouble he took measures to safeguard what little Continental property he had, transferring men and supplies from Chesterfield to safe locations farther south, away from the James. The state government, on the other hand, "was never more taken off its Guard" than by Arnold's sudden appearance that December.[18] Even then, vague and conflicting intelligence as to Arnold's intentions lulled the government in Richmond into indecision. The state's executive council discounted the Baron's warnings—that Arnold would invade—until late in the day on January 2, 1781, four days after the fleet had been sighted. And by that point it was too late to stop him. Arnold's ships were already on the James.

The fleet did not stop to unload its menacing cargo at Portsmouth, as Leslie had done, but taking advantage of a fair wind, it drove straight upriver. The British encountered virtually no resistance. To Arnold's amazement, there was nothing more at Hood's Landing than a small band of militia, which a British landing party quickly swatted aside as if they were flies. On January 4, the fleet dropped anchor at Westover, where nine hundred Redcoats went ashore and set out on foot for Richmond.[19]

Richmond, then an unspectacular river port of less than four thousand souls, had served as the capital only since the previous April. It could not compare to its predecessor, Williamsburg, in size or stately elegance; its chief advantages over the colonial capital were its more central location—Virginia's population was shifting steadily westward—and its lesser vulnerability. But little had been done to defend it. The General Assembly had called out four thousand militia before adjourning and fleeing. Few men, however, had yet answered the call.

Jefferson scrambled to impart some order, while the inhabitants of the Virginia Piedmont panicked and took to their heels as the traitor Arnold and his men drew close. Jefferson detailed the state's commissioner of war, Col. George Muter, to grab what military supplies he could and take them out of Arnold's path. The overall defense of the state he entrusted to Steuben.

The Baron did what he could. He rounded up what few militia troops he could find near Richmond, sending most of them downriver to slow Arnold's advance by land. The militia commander flagrantly disobeyed the order, and instead retreated to the Chickahominy River. Steuben did not have enough men left to defend Richmond—and most of them were unarmed, thanks to Muter's mishandling of the state-owned muskets—so he, too, retreated. At Manchester, across the James River south of Richmond, he intended to make a stand.[20]

Arnold ignored him. On January 5, his nine hundred Redcoats marched into Richmond. Half of his force proceeded to Westham, where they wreaked havoc with the Continental laboratory. The following day Arnold's men torched a few public buildings and some tobacco warehouses in Richmond before withdrawing to their base at Westover. In less than a week, the British had marched with impunity into the heart of Virginia, terrorized the population, and burned much of the capital, almost without firing a shot or losing a single man. And it had all been done with an army less than one thousand strong.

Steuben fell back on Petersburg. The small battalion of Continentals from Chesterfield were there, but they were so badly clothed as to be of no earthly use and had to be sent back to their barracks. The Baron rallied a few militia and advanced carefully on Westover to observe Arnold from a safe distance. In a few days, Arnold's troops boarded their transports and sailed back downriver to Portsmouth, where they landed again and dug in. Steuben pursued cautiously, finally establishing a defensive cordon around Portsmouth.[21]

Throughout the state, the reaction to the invasion had been a near-fatal mix of poor planning, panic, and complacency. Even state military leaders were aghast at the abject failure of the militia to come to the aid of their native state. "My God!" one of them wrote to Steuben in shame. "What could have occasioned this total Departure from Virtue on the Part of the People?"[22]

Steuben didn't have an answer. He wanted only to leave, to be with Greene. "He had rather Obey in an Army," Billy North intimated to Greene, "than Command in Virginia."[23] And Greene wanted Steuben to join him, but he also believed that the Baron would be far more valuable in Virginia at the moment. "As reenforcements and supplies are more important than Generals without them, I wish you not to leave Virginia," he wrote to Steuben in January. "I fear that when you leave it nothing will be done."

Greene added, with uncanny foresight: "The state is lifeless and inactive unless they are often electriced."[24]

So the Baron would stay. His primary responsibility was to support Greene—or, as he put it, "tormenting the Governor" into supplying what Greene needed.[25] Initially, he had promised Greene that he would send along one infantry battalion every fortnight, and additional clothing, weapons, and horses as opportunity allowed. This soon proved impossible. So long as Arnold remained on Virginia soil, the state government was loath to part with a single man or musket that could be employed by the militia. Steuben was unable to raise so much as a solitary infantry battalion between late December and late February. "My Situation here is really very embarrassing," he reported to Washington on February 18. "Genl. Greene's whole dependance is on this State."[26]

Unable to raise troops for Greene, yet stuck in Chesterfield anyway, Steuben became by default the man principally responsible for the defense of Virginia. The charge was more demanding than he could have anticipated. He had several excellent combat commanders beneath him, men like John Peter Gabriel Muhlenberg, the Prussian-educated

Lutheran parson who had led most of the Virginia troops in the Continental Line. Governor Jefferson, not a military man by any stretch of the imagination, nonetheless worked untiringly to keep a militia army in the field. But to Steuben fell everything else.

The workload nearly overwhelmed the Baron. Each day his desk was piled high with requests and petitions. Militia officers begged him to supply them with muskets, cartridge boxes, shirts, canteens, all from Continental stores; at the same time, the Board of War scolded him for distributing Continental property to state militia. Quartermasters wanted his advice on requisitioning horses from farmers unwilling to part with them. Greene wrote to him nearly once a week, asking for more men and supplies to be shipped south. Well-meaning Jefferson was the worst offender, sometimes writing to the Baron three or four times in a single day, and usually about trivial issues. The militia lacked proper hats, he once informed Steuben. Would it be acceptable to issue them cloth caps instead? Could Steuben come to Richmond to model a cloth cap for the governor?[27]

VIRGINIA SORELY NEEDED THE TOUCH of an experienced, nononsense soldier. Steuben, as the Continental Army's resident miracle worker, was perfect for the job. But he was not perfect for Virginia. With the state's defenses in such profound disarray, and with so little time to spare, he saw no choice but to be autocratic in his undesired role. His intolerance of mediocrity and false pride—qualities he would find, and to spare, among his subordinates in Virginia— made him appear insufferably overbearing. This had landed him in trouble before, among his fellow Continental officers, and they were men who were accustomed to being ordered about. Virginia civilians were assuredly *not* used to this kind of rough treatment.

The result was that Steuben clashed with just about everyone. He upbraided militia officers for trying to recruit young boys when so many eligible men were shirking their civic duty. He publicly rebuked Commissioner Muter for his incompetence in providing the militia with weapons, ammunition, and equipment. In mid-February 1781, he unleashed a storm of protest by giving George Weedon an upper-level command. Weedon was a former Continental brigadier who had resigned his commission in 1778; Steuben found him to be a talented commander, but many Virginia officers—even William Davies—were offended that a man who had voluntarily stepped down should be promoted over them.[28]

In his quest for efficiency, the Baron did not hesitate to criticize those who put their self-interest above the common good. While his better subordinates praised him for his forthright, critics-be-damned approach to leadership, as time went on he alienated a growing number of political leaders, militia officers, and ordinary citizens.

Steuben's sharpest conflict, however, was with Governor Jefferson. Jefferson admired the Baron for his talent and zeal, but when it came to the governor's role in the defense of the state, the two men had very different ideas. Jefferson insisted upon the strict observance of state laws; Steuben put military efficiency and effectiveness before rights and liberties.

The first sign of trouble came from a project that Steuben considered essential: the fortification at Hood's. After the smoke had cleared from Arnold's raid up the James, the Baron pushed Jefferson to get the necessary labor to construct the fort at Hood's, and pushed hard. Jefferson agreed that the fort was necessary and dutifully put the proposal before the General Assembly for approval, telling Steuben that work would begin no later than February 7. The appointed day came and went without so much as a single spadeful of dirt being turned, and the Baron was furious. Hadn't Arnold demonstrated just how necessary the fort was? It was also a matter of personal honor, for if the enemy took Richmond again, it would look bad for him. "The shameful Opposition made to the last invasion falls in some measure on me as the Commanding Officer in the State," he wrote to Jefferson with only a thin veneer of tact. "My wish is to prevent a Repitition of the Disgrace."[29]

Jefferson would not give the flustered general a reason why the fort *shouldn't* be built, only why it *hadn't*. As governor, all he could do was present the plan to the legislature; he was powerless to make them act. He could not order the militia to do manual labor, he could not force ordinary citizens to work, he could not force slaves to work. To Steuben, this was sheer nonsense. An executive who could not bend the rules a bit for the sake of the common good was no executive at all. As the Baron put it to Washington, uncharitably but accurately, "The Executive Power is so confined that the Governor has it not in his power to procure me 40 Negros to work at Hoods."[30]

As the burden of command pressed more heavily on Steuben's shoulders, the relationship between him and the governor, between him and the entire state, grew progressively worse.

First, some alarming news from Greene: the Southern Army was in full retreat through North Carolina and approaching Virginia, with Cornwallis in hot pursuit. Jefferson and the General Assembly called out an additional three thousand militia to guard Virginia's southern border, which meant that recruitment for Greene's Continentals would come to a "total stop." "Evry thing here is totally in Confusion," Steuben told Washington. If Cornwallis actually invaded Virginia, or if Arnold were reinforced, then "without some speedy assistance, our affairs in this Quarter will go very badly."[31]

Then a glimmer of illusory hope. On February 14, rebels scouts witnessed an amazing sight near Hampton Roads: a French naval squadron had dropped anchor off the Virginia coast, presumably to help Virginia evict Arnold from his base in Portsmouth. "Now is our time," wrote Thomas Nelson, Jr., general in the militia and soon-to-be governor of Virginia, to Steuben. "Not a moment is to be lost." Steuben agreed, rushing immediately to Richmond to talk strategy with Jefferson. But the high hopes were soon dashed. The French commander, Capt. Arnaud le Gardeur de Tilly, had not brought any troops, only a ship of the line and two frigates. He had been informed by sources in Virginia that French troops were not needed. Once he found that all Virginia could muster for an assault on Arnold was three thousand militia, many of them unarmed, he prudently decided to withdraw rather than risk his ships and his reputation. "The forces with which you intend to assist me," Tilly stiffly informed Steuben, "are completely insufficient."[32]

There were many people and factors at fault for the failure of Tilly's expedition. Steuben, however, blamed Jefferson and his government. The negligence of that government, he felt, had made him look very much the fool. He did not intend to let it happen again.

TILLY'S RETREAT to Newport had triggered no small amount of popular hostility toward the French. No one in Philadelphia or at Washington's headquarters wished to see the French alliance fall apart because of a simple misunderstanding. Another and a better French fleet was soon on its way to Virginia to do what Tilly could not.

This fleet was much larger, and this time it brought with it twelve hundred French royal troops. It sailed from Newport under the command of Admiral Destouches. The planned assault on the Virginia coast was simple and bold: while the French fleet set sail, the Marquis de Lafayette would march at the head of twelve hundred elite Continental light infantry to the top of Chesapeake Bay. The French fleet would sail up the bay, rendezvous with Lafayette at Annapolis and Head of Elk, Maryland, take the Continental troops aboard its transports, and then sail to Portsmouth. Together, the Continentals, the French, and the Virginia militia would crush Arnold, with the French fleet preventing the traitor's escape.

Now the pressure to perform was really on Steuben. He was annoyed that the younger and less experienced Lafayette—his senior—would take charge once he was in Virginia, but only a little. The Baron's chief concern was seeing to it that everything was ready for the arrival of the Franco-American force. Horses, small boats, provisions, and fodder would have to be available, and of course the militia would be expected to do its part. Jefferson, delighted that a major victory over the British was just around the corner, promised the Baron that the state would provide everything necessary for success.

Once again, Virginia didn't make good on Jefferson's promises, at least not to Steuben's satisfaction. Much of the militia Jefferson sent on to Portsmouth was unarmed, thanks to Muter's consistently bad performance as commissioner. Farmers refused to surrender their horses, and ferrymen and fishermen their boats, to Steuben's quartermasters, and Jefferson hesitated to coerce them into compliance.

This time the Baron let the stress get to him. He had been prone to outbursts of bad temper in less trying circumstances; in Virginia, he was at his worst. Even the deputy quartermaster in Virginia, a fellow Continental officer, remarked with some distaste upon Steuben's "fits of execrating every body and every thing."[33] Those closest to him sympathized. John Walker, Jefferson's personal friend and liaison at Steuben's headquarters, understood better than anyone why the Baron might snap. "The difficulties & Embarrassments that have been thrown into the Baron's way in the Course of this Business," Walker reported to the governor, "have perhaps transported him beyond the bounds of moderation, but were you acquainted with them all you would make great allowances on account of his Situation."[34]

With the unpleasant memory of the Tilly fiasco still rankling deep within him, Steuben lashed out at the governor. "In the Assurances I rec'd from [the] Government" he had guaranteed to Lafayette and to Washington that "every thing was ready for the Expedition," he wrote to the governor on March 9. He had trusted Jefferson, and that had been a mistake. "My Credulity however is furnished at the expence of my honor and the only excuse I have is my Confidence in [the] Government." If Jefferson could not do what he had promised, "if the powers of Government are inadequate to the furnishing [of] what is indispensably necessary, the Expedition must fail." Steuben refused to take responsibility for the failings of the state. If Jefferson could not give him what he needed, what *Virginia* needed, then the Baron would have to apprise both Lafayette and the French commanders so "that they may not engage too far in an Enterprize which there is no prospect of carrying through."[35]

Passionate words from a passionate man, but impolitic words, too, which Steuben immediately regretted. Jefferson deserves some credit for tolerating Steuben's outburst with equanimity. But the governor's response confirmed what the Baron thought of him as a wartime leader. "We can only be answerable for the orders we give and not for their execution," he wrote to Steuben the next day. "If they are disobeyed from obstinancy of spirit or want of coercion in the laws it is not our fault."[36]

To a military man like Steuben, Jefferson might as well have been speaking Greek. Even generals in the army were held responsible for the execution of orders. Why couldn't the highest civil authority in the state hold his subordinates similarly accountable?

THE HEATED EXCHANGE between Steuben and Jefferson, jarring as it was, had no lasting significance. Whatever his faults as a war leader, Jefferson was still a great man, and did not take Steuben's fulminations personally.

As it turned out, the planned assault on Portsmouth never happened anyway, and not through any fault of Jefferson's. The French fleet never arrived at its destination.

The final plans for the operation were being made in mid-March. Lafayette came to Yorktown, without his troops, to discuss strategy with Steuben. But before the marquis could return to his troops in Maryland to await the coming of the French transports, disturbing news arrived. As Destouches's fleet approached the Chesapeake, a superior British fleet under the command of Adm. Marriot Arbuthnot caught up with it and gave it a severe beating in the battle of Cape Henry. The entire French force, troop transports and all, had to limp back to Newport. Virginia would receive no assistance from France.

This was indeed bad news, but it got worse. On March 26, Arbuthnot's fleet anchored in Chesapeake Bay. And it was escorting transports. Shielded by the guns of Arbuthnot's eight ships of the line, two thousand Redcoats landed at Portsmouth to reinforce Arnold's men. Maj. Gen. William Phillips, one of Clinton's senior generals, replaced Arnold as the British commander in Virginia.

The strategic situation reversed overnight. Just a few days before, it was almost certain that the Franco-American coalition would drive Arnold's 1,600 troops into the sea. Now, the British numbered some 3,600 men. Even with French help it would have been difficult to dislodge Phillips, but without that aid it would be impossible. Sensing the futility of his presence in the state, Lafayette returned to Annapolis the very next day.

<hr />

THE NEW DEVELOPMENT CRUSHED STEUBEN, and not just because "the preparations we had made with so much trouble & Expence" were now proven "useless." Mainly, he felt that he had let Greene down by allowing Virginia to fall into enemy hands. Muhlenberg's defensive cordon around Portsmouth could not possibly hold firm against Phillips. If Phillips were determined to push into Virginia's undefended interior, there was nothing the rebels could do to stop him.[37]

Desperation, however, drove Steuben to concoct a brilliant stratagem. Virginia had about four thousand militia in the field, statewide. Even if all of them were concentrated around Portsmouth, it would still not be possible to keep Phillips and Arnold bottled up. There was, in short, nothing to lose, because Virginia was already beaten. So what if Steuben were to take half of the militia and make a forced march south to join Greene in North Carolina?

There was much to recommend the plan. Greene's army had just met Cornwallis's in a hard-fought battle at Guilford Courthouse, and while the rebels had suffered a minor tactical defeat there, Cornwallis's army was so badly mauled that the British general had to retreat toward the coast to repair his shattered command. If Greene were reinforced with two thousand Virginia militia, he would enjoy numerical superiority over Cornwallis, and there was a good chance he could then crush Cornwallis. At the very least, the move would compel Phillips to go to Cornwallis's aid, effectively removing the British threat from the Virginia coast.[38]

Steuben shared his idea with every general officer in the state, including Lafayette. And every one of them approved. Lafayette gave the plan his official endorsement just before leaving for Annapolis. Generals Muhlenberg, Weedon, and Nelson praised it without reservation. Richard Henry Lee, one of the most influential politicians in the state, saluted it as "one of those Master strokes which are productive of great effects, but which if neglected lay the train for much future evil," comparing its potential for victory to that of Rome over Hannibal.[39] There was not a single dissenting voice to be heard. The illustrious Baron had found a way to save the state and help Greene at the same time.

Everyone liked it—except the executive office in Richmond. Jefferson submitted the plan, together with its glowing official endorsements, to the Virginia State Council. The Council rejected it out of hand with almost no debate. While the proposal seemed to be "founded upon very probable principles," the fact that it would take so many men and weapons from the state made it unacceptable—even though many of those weapons had been initially intended for Greene's use, and even though the state had not provided Greene with anywhere near the number of men it was supposed to.[40]

The Baron did not lose his temper. He did not fire off angry letters to the governor. He had expected as much from the government, as did his supporters. "I was fearful," George Weedon commiserated, "our Scheme would be rejected by the Executive who has not an Idea beyond local security." Steuben only wished for Greene to summon him to his side, and to be done with Virginia forever. "If I preferred my own inclination to the public interest," he wrote to Greene in resignation, "I should immediately set out to join you."[41]

STEUBEN WASHED HIS HANDS of Virginia. He really did intend to leave this time. Virginia was as good as lost, and for reasons of honor he did not want to be in the state when it collapsed. But he also felt duty-bound to delay his departure until he could accomplish something positive for Greene. He was fairly certain, he informed Greene, that he already had five hundred Continental recruits waiting at the Chesterfield barracks. Once he had these men armed and ready, plus a handful of cavalry, he would lead them to the South and be rid of Virginia forever.

Greene pressed him to stay as long as he could. "I see and feel for your disagreable situation. . . . But if you leave Virginia everything will run into confusion," he wrote to Steuben at the beginning of April. "I am greatly in want of your aid here as well as there; but it is my opinion that you can be more extensively useful there than here."[42]

Greene could have spared his breath, for the Baron had been overly optimistic about Continental recruitment. As if the pace of recruiting hadn't been slow enough already, the arrival of Phillips's corps had brought it to a complete halt. When Steuben returned to Chesterfield at the end of March, he found a grand total of five new Continental recruits housed in the barracks, and three of these deserted within a couple of days.[43] The Baron was not destined to leave Virginia anytime soon.

That was just as well, maybe not for his sake but certainly for Virginia's. For Phillips was preparing to make his move.

Phillips had no intention of sitting passively at Portsmouth. As soon as he landed there, the British commander put his men to work constructing barges for carrying the Redcoats upriver. To keep the rebels guessing, Phillips sent a few smaller warships and some troops up the bay toward the Potomac and the Rappahannock, raiding the coastline as they went—burning houses, seizing tobacco, freeing slaves.

Steuben was convinced that this was just a feint, that Phillips's real target would be the upper James River, specifically either Richmond or Petersburg. And at least the raids caused enough panic to compel Jefferson's government to act. Finally Hood's Landing would be fortified. When no one showed up to dig the fortifications, Jefferson came up with an ingenious expedient: men who volunteered to work at Hood's for twelve days would be credited for six weeks of militia duty.

Perhaps, if Jefferson had thought of this a month or two before, it might have staved off the impending invasion, but like so much of the

Virginia war effort, it was too little too late. The militia was faltering, too. Many had been serving since January, and their three-month terms were beginning to expire, so they were deserting by the score. Muhlenberg reported that on just one night in early April, one hundred militiamen unceremoniously left their posts and went home. The new levy of militia, slated to relieve those currently on duty in April, would not be ready for a few weeks. Throughout the state, there was open opposition to militia duty, even violent riots. Muhlenberg's force outside Portsmouth was down to seven hundred militia—with another five hundred on the opposite side of the James—and the numbers were dropping rapidly.

Washington was well aware that trouble was brewing on the Chesapeake. He ordered Lafayette to return to Virginia. By the first week in April, Steuben knew that Lafayette's light infantry were en route, and one thousand Pennsylvanians under Anthony Wayne were not far behind. By the twenty-first, Lafayette's corps was at Alexandria, where the marquis intended to dump all unnecessary baggage so that he could come to Steuben's aid in time. "For Gods sake try to get us some shoes," he wrote to Steuben, "or we cannot advance principally at the rapid rate we are now going."[44]

On April 23, 1781, Phillips struck.

The sight of the British squadron working its way up the James estuary was breathtaking and menacing at the same time. Thirteen warships, black cannon muzzles jutting from each port and the Union Jack snapping from their mastheads, escorted twenty-three flat-bottomed barges. Most of the barges were crammed stem to stern with red-clad infantry, close to one hundred per barge. The vessels crowded the broad estuary, and were in no great hurry. The mere sight of the British force was enough to set the Peninsula in a panic. Richmond, though still some distance away from the danger, became a ghost town in very short order.

The militia had all but vanished, so the British encountered little or no resistance. At noon on the twenty-fourth, the squadron passed the half-dug fortification at Hood's, the one place where the rebels—had they been prepared—might have been able to cause Phillips some trouble. The British found the place deserted. A few local men had answered Jefferson's call for volunteer labor on the twentieth, but they had scampered off the very next day without having accomplished much.

The British ships hove to at Westover. Steuben rode from Richmond to Westover to watch the British from a safe distance, fully expecting a repeat performance of Arnold's actions. But Phillips decided not to disembark his force there. Instead, the squadron and the transports pressed on to City Point, on the south bank of the James, dropping anchor shortly before sunset.

Steuben knew it would be impossible to defeat Phillips outright, and therefore did not want to risk open battle. Still, he hoped to make a "demonstration"—namely, to slow Phillips's advance, buying precious time so that Richmond and Chesterfield could be evacuated before the British arrived, ready to torch anything of value. He also understood that if the British crushed the militia, it would devastate Virginian morale, but so, too, would giving the British free rein to terrorize the countryside unopposed. No matter what course he decided to take, though, the Baron did not dare concentrate his forces until he knew what Phillips was up to.

When the British ships came to rest at City Point, and the Redcoats leaped out of their barges to regroup on shore, Steuben could make a very accurate guess about their intentions. Though the British might attack Richmond later, that was not their primary target. First they would march on Petersburg, where state and Continental military supplies awaited their torches.

———

THE VIRGINIA MILITIA along the James was formed in two bodies: one on the north side, under Col. James Innes, and a second, larger one on the south, under Steuben's old friend General Muhlenberg. Innes could be of no immediate help; his force had moved to the north and west, having evacuated supplies and patients from the military hospital at Williamsburg.

Muhlenberg had been shadowing Phillips, marching his militia along the river and monitoring the British general's every movement. Steuben caught up with Muhlenberg, and together they decided not to attack the British as they disembarked. The warships were too close, and their guns would play havoc with the militia. The Virginians would instead make their stand in Petersburg itself, twelve miles up the Appomattox River from City Point. Leaving a few men behind to observe the enemy, Steuben and Muhlenberg led their citizen-soldiers down the road that wound along the river to Petersburg.

The sky that night was moonless, so when the first men of Muhlenberg's command reached the village of Blandford, just east of Petersburg, the darkness was already thick around them. Here Steuben halted them for the night. Though exhausted from the long forced march from the James, they slept fitfully, their muskets close at hand. Few, if any, had been in battle before, but they sensed from the urgency of their movements that they would not have to wait long for their baptism by fire. Most had received nothing but the most elementary training. Three days before, the Baron had issued orders that all militia—men and officers alike, with no exceptions—were to train constantly in the drill prescribed by the official *Regulations*. During those three days there had not been much time for drill.[45]

Steuben gathered Muhlenberg and his other officers for a council of war. They would hold here, at Blandford, when Phillips arrived the next day, withdrawing when necessary across the Appomattox via the long, narrow Pocahontas Bridge.

Rebel pickets first spotted Phillips's corps a couple of miles east of Blandford, around noon on Wednesday, April 25. They fired on the scarlet columns advancing toward them on the river road, and then fell back to the first line of militia.

The Baron had picked the overall positions to be held, while Muhlenberg—who was better acquainted with his militia and its officers—made the specific dispositions for the individual units. Two of the five battalions of militia infantry were formed in line of battle along high ground on the eastern edge of Blandford; two more held the next ridge at Petersburg, just west of the first line. Steuben was very concerned about the line of retreat—he knew that he would have to retreat, no matter how well the militia fought—so securing the Pocahontas Bridge, the only easy route across the Appomattox, was of the utmost importance. Accordingly, he positioned the fifth militia battalion inside Petersburg at the foot of the bridge. His small band of cavalry, plus two brass six-pounders that had been dragged laboriously upriver from Portsmouth, were situated on a commanding rise across the bridge, on the north bank of the river. Here they could cover the eventual retreat, but without having to retreat along with the infantry across the bridge. It would be difficult enough to perform an orderly withdrawal from Petersburg; if the panicked infantry had to share the bridge with horses and guns, the result could well be catastrophic.

Phillips deployed his marching columns as soon as he made con- tact with the American pickets. The bulk of his force, consisting of some light infantry and His Majesty's 76th and 80th Regiments of Foot, pressed steadily onward with bayonets fixed toward Muhlen- berg's first line. The Queen's Rangers, an elite Loyalist unit under the command of the talented Col. John Graves Simcoe, moved quietly around the British rear and arced south around the American right flank. Phillips was facing only militia, but he was a competent com- mander and knew better than to assume that militia couldn't fight if pressed. If he could envelop the Americans on the flank and crush them against the river, so much the better.

Steuben and Muhlenberg had no intention of letting the British get close enough to use their bayonets, where they would have an over- whelming advantage. The dispositions of the American units were carefully chosen to allow the militia to rely on firepower instead of cold steel. To get at the first line, the British infantry first had to ad- vance over a broad stretch of swampy low ground, cross Poor's Creek, and move uphill toward Blandford. Phillips's force was large enough to smother the American first line by sheer weight of numbers, but the militia held its ground, pouring volley after volley into the British lines as the Redcoats slowly plodded through the soggy morass around

Poor's Creek. Just when the British threatened to overtake the American right flank, Muhlenberg ordered the first line to withdraw to the second line. The movement was perfectly timed, the withdrawal executed without panic or disorder.

Now the oncoming British faced a more formidable obstacle. Once again they had to advance across low, marshy ground and cross yet another creek—Lieutenant's Run, which separated Petersburg from Blandford. Ahead of them were four battalions of Virginia militia, all of which unleashed devastating volleys of musketry. Artillery on both sides came into play, five British light guns as opposed to the Americans' two, but it was the British, not the Virginians, who reeled and staggered from the blows. The militia beat back two determined assaults before Muhlenberg decided it was a good idea to withdraw again, before Simcoe's Rangers could take them flank and rear.

The Americans had done enough for the day, in Steuben's eyes. They had not panicked, they had disputed "every inch of ground to the bridge." Now it was time to leave before it was too late. The militia had fought hard for nearly two hours and were beginning to run low on ammunition. The four embattled battalions drew back through the streets of Petersburg, firing as they retreated, toward the Pocahontas Bridge. The British were hot on their heels now, there being no real obstacles to slow their pursuit. Phillips did indeed catch up to the American rear guard, but even as the British closed in for hand-to-hand fighting in the narrow lanes and alleys of Petersburg, the militia did not panic. They fought back, with fists and clubbed muskets and even a few bayonets, while the remainder of the American troops made their way across the bridge to safety on the north bank. Finally the rear guard was able to break off the action, but did not run in fear. On Steuben's orders, the last militia to set foot on the bridge maintained their composure long enough to rip up the bridge's planking as they withdrew, safeguarding their retreat.[46]

Steuben's little militia army had achieved about as much as it could. The Baron and Muhlenberg retreated north as Phillips's men searched Petersburg, in vain, for the military supplies they hoped to find there.

The next day, Phillips marched his force to Chesterfield, where they burned the Continental warehouses and barracks. Steuben, wisely, stayed out of reach.[47]

Blandford was a magnificent little battle regardless. Steuben commended Muhlenberg for his role, but above all he praised the militia for their "particular good behaviour," for executing "their manoeuvres with great exactness." "The General . . . assures the militia, that from this day forward he shall always think himself honoured to have such deserving men to command." Jefferson was equally delighted, his previous spats with the Baron forgotten. "I cannot but congratulate you on the initiation of our militia into the business of war," he wrote to Steuben the day after the battle.[48]

The action at Blandford did indeed accomplish something of value: it kept up morale in the beleaguered state, and it held up Phillips just long enough to keep him from doing real damage. For while the British commander marched his men, with impunity, on to Richmond to destroy the capital, he was stopped dead in his tracks by unexpected news. On April 29, Lafayette's Continental light infantry, one thousand strong, had entered the town of Manchester, Virginia, and Steuben was on his way to join him. Wayne's men of the Pennsylvania Line would not be far behind. Vexed by this unwelcome development, cursing Lafayette for his impeccable timing, Phillips grudgingly retreated to Bermuda Hundred. After loading up on fresh provisions, the Redcoats piled back into their barges and set sail for Portsmouth. Along the way, they paused occasionally to raid farms and kill livestock.

Reversal followed reversal, and if Lafayette and Steuben celebrated the British withdrawal, they soon had cause to reconsider their jubilance. Phillips's squadron sailed as far down the river as Burwell's Landing, and then—inexplicably—hove to and reversed course. It stopped at Brandon on May 7 to unload its soldiers, who promptly marched back to Petersburg the following day. Phillips was again on the warpath.

Phillips knew something that his enemies did not. Cornwallis, having patched up his army after its bludgeoning at Guilford Courthouse, settled on a course that Nathanael Greene had not anticipated. He drove his army north from its base in Wilmington, North Carolina, to invade Virginia. He would meet up with Phillips at Petersburg to crush the Continentals before the French could intervene. After all of the heartbreak and sacrifice in Virginia, after all of the rebels' improbable success in the Carolinas, the very thing that Greene and Steuben had toiled to prevent was about to take place regardless.

CHAPTER 11

From Virginia to Fraunces Tavern

[MAY 1781—DECEMBER 1783]

When I drew my Sword for the Liberties of this
Country, it was with a determined resolution that
nothing but Death should make me sheathe it before
G. Britain had acknowledged the independence of
America.

STEUBEN TO ELIAS BOUDINOT,
DECEMBER 5, 1782[1]

STEUBEN HATED VIRGINIA, and Virginia hated Steuben
right back.

Despite the brief period of mutual admiration after
Blandford, the frictions and misunderstandings between the
Baron and the Old Dominion were neither forgotten nor for-
given. Virginia wanted him gone. In part this was because
Steuben represented the clutching, unwanted authority of the
Continental government, asking Virginia to sacrifice its sons
and treasure to defend other states. But largely Steuben's per-
sonality was to blame.

Whether dealing with the governor, or militia officers, or
ordinary civilians, the Baron found it impossible to be subtle.
In late February 1781, as Steuben's latest Continental battalion
was preparing to march south to Greene, a colonel in the Virginia militia showed up at the Chesterfield barracks. He

brought with him a young man whom he intended to present as a recruit for Continental service. Steuben and William Davies had had a devil of a time trying to find suitable recruits, so even a single volunteer was welcome. The Baron was genuinely pleased to meet the colonel—that is, until he met the prospective recruit. He was a mere boy, far too young for military service. Steuben had a sergeant measure the boy's height, and when his shoes were removed in order to obtain a more accurate measurement it was discovered that they had been altered in an attempt to make the child appear taller than he really was. "The Baron's countenance altered," North recalled; "we saw, and feared, the approaching storm." Steuben stooped down to the boy and tenderly asked him his age, while patting "the child's head with a hand trembling with rage."

Then he turned on the colonel. "You must have supposed me to be a rascal," he bellowed. The colonel, visibly frightened, blurted out a denial, but Steuben would not listen to him. Calling the colonel a "scoundrel" for "cheating" his country, the Baron ordered that he be forcibly enlisted in the boy's place. He told the young lad to go home and tell the colonel's wife "that her husband has gone to fight as an honest citizen should, for the liberty of his country."

His immediate subordinates approved. After his encounter with the militia colonel, Davies observed, "the people seem afraid to bring in the little dwarfs and children they formerly counted upon." Few could argue with the Baron's principles. It was his manner that got him in trouble. North summarized the incident neatly: "Nor did the Baron's zeal permit him . . . to act with the mildness and caution, proper to be observed by military commanders in the service of a Republic."[2]

CORNWALLIS'S INVASION spelled disaster for Virginia, but Lafayette's long-overdue appearance was a godsend for the Baron. In other circumstances, he would have resented being replaced, but the stress of command had sapped him in body and spirit. "I heartily wish his exploits may be more brilliant than mine have been," he wrote to Greene in mid-May.[3]

Not that Lafayette's arrival guaranteed victory. Far from it. The marquis had only around nine hundred Continentals plus three thousand militia. The main British force, now commanded by Benedict Arnold—William Phillips having succumbed to disease on May 15—numbered four thousand. Cornwallis marched into Petersburg with around fifteen hundred Redcoats and Loyalists, and a further fifteen hundred reinforcements sent by Clinton arrived in the Chesapeake the next day. Facing seven thousand seasoned enemies, Lafayette was seriously outgunned.

No longer in charge of field operations, Steuben resumed the preparation of troops for Greene. All he had at the moment was the newly raised battalion of Col. Thomas Gaskins, Jr., numbering around five hundred men. Certainly they could be of use in their home state, but both Steuben and Lafayette—like most military men in Virginia—still labored under the mistaken impression that the real war was going on in the Carolinas, not Virginia. As soon as Gaskins's men were made ready to march, they would go south.

Steuben would go with them. "My presence in this State has become entirely useless," he wrote to Greene. "Never was a man more disgusted than I am at the conduct and proceedings in this quarter." His prayers were answered immediately. On the very same day he wrote these words to the Quaker general, he received orders from Greene to join the Southern Army. "I find myself so beset with difficulties that I need the counsel and assistance of an officer educated in the Prussian school, and I persuade myself I shall find in you both the friend and the General I want."[4]

When he wrote these orders, Greene had no way of knowing that Cornwallis was going to lunge into Virginia. Not until May 23 did he learn otherwise, and once he found out, he immediately countermanded his latest orders to Steuben. Neither the Baron nor any of his troops should leave Virginia, Greene told Steuben. Unfortunately, Steuben never received the order. A British patrol intercepted it. The last Steuben had heard from Greene, he was supposed to march to the Carolinas.

Steuben needed no urging, but he hesitated anyway. He could not move. Not yet. Gaskins's battalion was "Neither cloathed nor equipped."[5]

On May 24, Cornwallis's heavily reinforced army set out from Petersburg, crossing the James and marching on Richmond. Lafayette retreated north, hoping to link up with Anthony Wayne's slow-moving corps, and all of central and western Virginia lay open to the invaders. As the people of Richmond fled from the British for the third time in five months, it struck Steuben that Gaskins's ill-equipped battalion was the only American force in the region. The new temporary capital, at Charlottesville, was vulnerable. So, too, was the only significant stockpile of state-owned military supplies. Since the time of the Phillips invasion, this stockpile was stashed away on the narrow, triangular jut of land at the confluence of the Rivanna and upper James rivers, forty-five miles northwest of Richmond. Locals called this the Point of Fork.

Steuben had no great desire to do any favors for the state of Virginia, but he understood that the stores at Point of Fork needed to be moved or guarded, and only Gaskins's men were available to do the job. He sent them from the "new" Continental recruit depot at Albemarle Barracks, a former prisoner-of-war camp near Charlottesville, to Point of Fork on May 28, catching up with them the next day.

The Baron was wracked by uncertainty. Greene's orders for him to move south made little sense in light of the current situation. "Please let me have news of you," he begged Lafayette on June 3. "I do not know where you are or what has become of Cornwallis." The sorry state of Gaskins's battalion immobilized him. A recent shipment of newer French muskets from Philadelphia allowed Steuben to arm the Virginians, but they were lacking in every other necessity. "There is this poor battalion camped in the forest, perishing without the power to employ it in the service," Steuben appealed to Archibald Cary, speaker of the Virginia Senate, "without even the power to drill the men, because they lack shoes and shirts." Inadequate accommodations at Point of Fork—the men were lodged in "two very bad Negro Quarters"—exacerbated the rate of sickness among the men, which was already disturbingly high. "Two-thirds of [the men are] very bad cases."[6]

Cornwallis did not wait for the rebels to prepare for battle. The aggressive Briton had been on Lafayette's tail for a week. He gave up the chase on June 1, but not before sending out two raiding parties to the exposed west. One, led by the ruthless cavalry commander Col. Banastre Tarleton, was ordered to raid Charlottesville, capturing Governor Jefferson and the members of the General Assembly if possible. The other, under John Graves Simcoe, was to seize Point of Fork.

As Gaskins's men loaded the state's military supplies on the few wagons they could find, Simcoe pushed his corps mercilessly forward in a series of forced marches that wore the men's shoes to nothing. But because they moved with extraordinary stealth, taking prisoner every soul they encountered to ensure secrecy, Steuben did not have any idea that the enemy had been on the move until June 3.

The details came the next morning, and they were not reassuring. Just before dawn, a Continental dragoon officer galloped into Point of Fork, his horse winded and frothed after a long chase. He had nearly been captured by a mounted British patrol but had seen enough in the meantime to give him a good fright. Two columns, he informed Steuben, were rapidly converging on Point of Fork: a small force of British cavalry coming from Goochland Courthouse to the east, and nearly a thousand enemy infantry from Louisa Courthouse to the north-northeast. Cornwallis himself was approaching Goochland with the main body of troops. Goochland was only twenty miles away from Point of Fork; Louisa, a mere fifteen. The British would be upon Point of Fork in no time at all.

Right then and there, Steuben decided to retreat. From what he had been told, the entire British army in the state was headed toward him from two different directions. Even with the addition of Gen. Robert Lawson's command of 250 militia, who arrived later that day, Steuben's position was untenable. The British far outnumbered and outclassed him; Point of Fork had no fortifications, no high ground worthy of mention; and the James was swollen to flood stage. There could be no escape once the Redcoats got close. "I thought it absurd to be making a Bravado with a small number of bad Troops against such a force," Steuben wrote in his official report.[7]

Hoping at least to save his men, Steuben ferried most of them across the James. Simcoe's four hundred infantry and one hundred cavalry crossed the Rivanna early on the morning of the fifth. By noon, they occupied the Point in plain view of the rebels on the opposite bank of the James. Only one hostile exchange of fire occurred that day, and it quickly confirmed the wisdom of Steuben's decision to retreat. Simcoe directed his men to fire a three-pounder cannon at one of the American picket posts. The rebels, to a man, fled in terror as the small projectile whizzed harmlessly overhead. "It was with much persuasion and threats [that] they were brought back again," the Baron noted sourly.[8]

The Baron waited for the cover of darkness and then retreated as fast as his men could move. Simcoe awoke early on the morning of the sixth surprised to discover the rebel camp deserted. He had fought against Steuben at Blandford, and he expected another fight now.

Steuben was right to be prudent. Mere hours after the rebels withdrew, Tarleton's dragoons returned from their raid on Charlottesville and joined Simcoe near Point of Fork. The next day, Cornwallis brought the main army to Elk Hill, only five miles downriver. Had Steuben delayed his retreat by a few hours, his troops would have been destroyed. All of the truly valuable stores had already been evacuated. The loss of the few supplies left—a modest quantity of cloth and a few hogsheads of rum—would hardly have justified the sacrifice of his entire command.

Cut off from Lafayette by a much larger and highly mobile British force to his north and east, the Baron led his men south. He did his best to raise the alarm as he went, sending letters to the county lieutenants to call out their militiamen. Leaving Lawson's militia at Charlotte Courthouse, he took Gaskins's battalion to Cole's Ferry, on the

Staunton River, a march of seventy miles in five days. At Cole's they paused for a couple of days so the men could catch their breath and tend to their blistered feet. Steuben tried to relax, too, enjoying a local culinary delight that he had just discovered: he had acquired a taste for black snakes, and he detailed several of his men to scour the woods around Cole's for the reptiles.[9]

Here Steuben first found out about Greene's lost order, that he was to stay in Virginia and help Lafayette as best he could. Abruptly changing course, he drove his troops back north toward the James, even faster than he had retreated. On June 19, less than two weeks after the evacuation of Point of Fork, the bone-weary Baron reported in person to Lafayette, then encamped on the South Anna River northwest of Richmond. With Steuben were precisely 408 of Gaskins's men and about 500 militia.

S TEUBEN'S CAUTIOUS ACTIONS in May and June 1781 may not have been glorious, but they were militarily sound. There could be no comparison with Blandford. There he had good ground and enthusiastic troops; at Point of Fork he had neither.

These facts made little difference to those in the state government who already had cause to dislike the Baron. To them, Steuben's conduct before and after the incident at Point of Fork smacked of cowardice and incompetence. Benjamin Harrison, speaker of the lower house of the Assembly, asked congressional delegate Joseph Jones to try to get Steuben cashiered. The Baron, he asserted, had "600 fine men" who "lay Idle" because he refused to lead them against the British. "I believe him a good officer on the Parade," Harrison concluded, "but the worst in every other respect in the American Army."[10]

Six hundred "fine men"? Had Harrison seen Gaskins's half-naked, disease-ridden troops—"more ragamuffins than soldiers," as Steuben described them—he might have whistled a different tune. But once the news of the loss of Point of Fork, and of Steuben's retreat, came to the new capital at Staunton—the next in line of Virginia's ad hoc wartime capitals—the criticism got much, much worse.

The mood at Staunton was understandably black in mid-June. Virginia had been ravaged, and the Assembly was hungry for scapegoats. One of them was Jefferson himself, whose term as governor expired in early June. Gen. Thomas Nelson was elected in his place the following week. Although Nelson had been one of Steuben's most vocal supporters, he made no effort to deflect the barrage of criticism the Assembly was firing at the Baron. The members of the Assembly did not know exactly what had happened at Point of Fork. They assumed that Steuben had fled before an inferior force, and in doing so lost thousands of muskets and tons of ammunition. The State Council opined that the Baron should be hanged for negligence of duty. The Assembly then demanded an inquiry into Steuben's conduct, asking the Marquis de Lafayette to take the lead.[11]

Lafayette refused, correctly noting that he was too busy to attend to the affair. He understood that the Virginians' fury at Steuben came in part from their deep dislike of the Baron's methods, even if they had done much to earn his scorn. He reassured the Baron publicly that he did not share the prejudice of the state officials at Staunton, but in private he expressed much different thoughts. Even after Steuben told the marquis his side of the story, Lafayette wrote in confidence to Washington that the Baron's conduct at Point of Fork had been "unintelligible." The American force at Point of Fork, he asserted, was larger than Simcoe's corps, and could easily have held the Point for another twenty-four hours—enough time to evacuate the remaining stores and still retreat in good order. Steuben's retreat from the Point was a panicked one, alienating Lawson and the Virginia militia, who deserted him in protest.[12]

On every point, Lafayette's recounting of the affair at Point of Fork was wrong. Over time, he modified his views, once he came to realize that the lost stores were inconsequential and that Steuben had no hope of holding out at the Point. One cannot help but sense, however, that a strange and uncomfortable relationship existed between the two Euro-

pean nobles, and that if there was indeed bad blood, it came from Lafayette's side and not Steuben's. When the marquis wrote his account
of the American campaigns years later, his assessment of Steuben was
not a kind one. He saw the Baron as little more than a drill sergeant,
"an old Prussian whose methodical mediocrity perfected the organization and tactics of the army."[13]

Even those who supported Steuben in everything he did, however,
knew that his feud with the civil authorities was far past the point
where it could ever be patched up. As William Davies informed
Greene, "The Baron has however become universally unpopular, and
all ranks of people seem to have taken the greatest disgust at him. . . .
A very little, however, has raised all this Clamour; but at all events his
usefulness is entirely over."[14]

STEUBEN WOULD NOT DISPUTE Davies's prognosis. He no longer
had a purpose in Virginia, nor even the possibility of one. And he
was truly sick. "The heat of the season, uneasiness of mind and a thousand other things" worked their cumulative effect on his body and
spirit. For a couple of weeks he tagged along with Lafayette, but had
nothing to do. In mid-July his strength left him completely, and with
Lafayette's permission he took up residence in a "country house near
Colonel [John] Walker's," in the vicinity of Charlottesville. Tended by
Walker's physician father, he remained in bed for much of July and
August, suffering from a serious "skin eruption," recurring flare-ups of
gout, and general exhaustion.

He was too weak and listless to even be a bystander as the young
marquis, who had been spared the tribulations of preparing Virginia
for war in the first half of the year, garnered the glory of a successful
campaign against Cornwallis. He could only fulminate against the administration that had robbed him of his chances of winning some of
that glory. "I have seen so many atrocious villainies since I have been
in this state," he intimated to Richard Peters, "that I can no longer be
surprised at anything." The final straw was the uproar over the evacu-

ation of Point of Fork, which he attributed to "the dastardliness of the government, the absurdity of the laws and the pusillanimity of those who should have executed them."[15]

Greene summoned him to join him in the South, which the Baron intended to do, though a painful recurrence of the gout delayed his plans. A letter from Lafayette then changed everything: Would the Baron care to join the army at Williamsburg?[16]

Though a half-invalid and more than a hundred miles distant from the army, Steuben knew that Lafayette and Wayne had been gradually wearing down Cornwallis, who had since withdrawn his forces toward Yorktown in hopes of being rescued by sea. But the British general, in George Weedon's pungent words, was caught in a "pudding sack." Washington had been counting on a Franco-American assault on Clinton in New York, but Cornwallis's predicament was too good an opportunity to be missed. Washington and the overall French commander, Rochambeau, decided on a joint expedition to Virginia. By great good luck, the French royal fleet, under the Admiral François-Joseph-Paul, comte de Grasse, came up from the West Indies, ran into the British fleet of Sir Thomas Graves, and on September 5 the French admiral bested Graves in a slugging match off the Virginia capes. Admiral de Grasse landed 3,200 French troops, Washington and Rochambeau were on their way with 7,000 Continental and French soldiers, and the French controlled the seas off the Chesapeake. "It will be a miracle if [Cornwallis] escapes," Steuben exclaimed in delight to Ben Walker on September 9. "If he saves himself from this, Cornwallis will be immortal in his homeland."[17]

The summons from Lafayette lifted Steuben's spirits as nothing else could. "My gout was cured at once," he told Walker. He set out immediately for Williamsburg, with Billy North and John Walker in tow, arriving there on September 10. Washington and Rochambeau had not yet appeared, but already the French, Continentals, and Virginia militia vastly outnumbered Cornwallis's 7,500-man army.

The Baron had little to do there, at first. He could not consult with Lafayette, who was himself sick in bed and not taking visitors. But for two months now, Steuben had been bored and desperately lonely. Fairlie had been taken prisoner by Simcoe's patrols at Point of Fork, Ben Walker was in Philadelphia, and there were few friends in Virginia. There was only Billy North, who had also taken ill while still on the road. Steuben feared that his "poor lad" might not survive his serious fever.

Washington's arrival on September 14 at least brought Steuben another friend, a much-missed one, and the Baron easily slipped back into the familiar role of inspector. At last he was surrounded again by soldiers, and not by carping, vindictive politicians. "This, my dear General," he wrote to Greene, "is the decisive moment—the happiest time I have spent in America."[18]

Washington, however, had other plans for his inspector. As French and American engineers started to dig siege works around Yorktown, tightening the noose on Cornwallis, the general-in-chief reorganized his forces. He divided the Americans into four divisions: one of Virginia militia under Thomas Nelson, who had just resigned as governor, and two Continental divisions under Lafayette and Benjamin Lincoln. A third division of Continentals, consisting of the Pennsylvania brigade of Anthony Wayne and the Maryland brigade of Mordecai Gist, he entrusted to the Baron de Steuben.

One gets the sense that Steuben's appointment was a consolation prize of sorts, given to him as a token of friendship from Washington. Nathanael Greene felt bad for his would-be collaborator who had so damaged his own career in his earnest efforts to support the Southern Army. He hoped that Washington would do something to reward Steuben. "Baron Steuben seems to have got into some kind of disgrace, and I believe it without cause," he wrote to Washington in mid-September. "I wish your Excellency would write him a letter to console him." The general-in-chief did not wholly exculpate all blame from Steuben. He had heard too much damning, if inaccurate, testimony from Lafayette to do otherwise. "The Baron from the warmth of his temper had got disagreeably involved with [Virginia], and an inquiry into a part of his conduct must one day take place," Washington responded to Greene. But for all that, "I have for the present given him a command in this army which makes him happy."[19]

Regardless of the motives that lay behind Steuben's new assignment, it did indeed make him happy. It was also a vindication, in his eyes. His commander in chief, a son of Virginia, had made a public demonstration of his regard for the Prussian, with a command in Virginia no less.

Siegecraft consisted of a series of highly stylized routines, which once set in motion required very little in the way of tactical skill on the part of the attacker, or of leadership on the part of the commanders. Steuben really had very little to do besides lead his troops into and out of the parallel trenches once every three days after the first parallel was opened on October 6. The Pennsylvanians and Marylanders of his division did their duty in the siege works much the same as the men of the other American divisions, manning the lines by day, digging new and closer parallels by night, and under enemy fire. They witnessed the great allied bombardment that commenced on the ninth, the awe-inspiring cannonade that lit up the sky and shook the ground, cannon and mortar shells all but destroying the town within the British lines. The Baron's men were on duty on October 17, when a single drummer boy and an officer waving a white handkerchief mounted the British parapet to signal Cornwallis's heart-wrenching decision to capitulate.

Steuben's division was still in the trenches two days later, on the nineteenth, the day designated for the surrender ceremony. It was actually Lafayette's turn to man the works, but the Baron stubbornly refused to be relieved. Tradition, he told Lafayette, dictated that those on duty in the trenches when peace overtures were first made should remain at their posts until the surrender was signed. The Baron planted the American flag on one of the captured British redoubts with his own hands. A small satisfaction, perhaps, but satisfaction nonetheless. After he had done so much to make this day possible—both by training the victorious army and by holding Virginia until Lafayette could take his place—Steuben no doubt felt that he deserved the honor.[20]

In the midst of one of the most dramatic moments in American history, the triumphant climax of the War for Independence, Steuben was at his most relaxed. He wrote very little about his time at Yorktown, but every account that mentions his presence at the siege invariably depicts him as lighthearted and jovial. During a British artillery barrage, Steuben was seen standing up—fully exposed—and chatting with Anthony Wayne as he watched the bombardment. Suddenly a shell arced through the air toward him, its sputtering fuse spiraling a telltale corkscrew of smoke as it came. Steuben instinctively threw himself into the nearest trench, and Wayne fell on top of him. Surprised, the Baron swivelled his head to see what had happened. Discovering his brigadier lying on top of him, he roared in laughter. "I always knew you were a brave general, but I did not know you were so perfect in every point of duty. You cover your general's retreat in the best manner possible."[21]

Many in the ranks of the Continentals believed that Yorktown was the last battle of the war; Steuben seems to have sensed that this was the last of his life. It was fitting that he should end his career as a soldier in the way it had begun, almost forty years before, when as a wide-eyed young lad he had stood in his father's commanding presence in the trenches at Breslau.

ONCE THE SIEGE drew to its glorious conclusion, once the pageantry of Cornwallis's surrender was over and the muskets of the British and Hessian soldiers lay piled in heaps where their teary-eyed owners had thrown them, Steuben came back down to earth. He could no longer forget about his problems, and at the moment the worst of these problems was money. He could no longer hide from his poverty or hide it from others.

His stint in Virginia had wrecked him financially. During his time there, he had drawn more than $220,000 in Continental and state currency to cover his expenses. It sounded like a great deal of money,

The Baron de Steuben. One of two known (and extant) color portraits of Steuben, this one painted by Ralph Earl in 1786. Note that Steuben wears not only the star of Fidelity (*Bruststern*) on his coat, but the medal of the Order as well, suspended by a ribbon from his neck. *(Fenimore Art Museum, Cooperstown, New York. Photo credit: Richard Walker)*

but in specie it translated to only about $750 or so. That would not go very far. Steuben's host for much of the time he spent in Chesterfield, one Henry Winfree, charged him nearly £53—roughly $130 in specie—for the use of two cramped rooms and one bed for him and his staff over an eleven-week period. The Baron wore out three horses because of his constant travel and had to purchase replacements out of his own pocket. When North took ill, Steuben had to pawn a gold watch and much of his silverware to pay for his aide's medical care.[22]

The social scene at Yorktown turned his private money woes into public embarrassment. For days after the surrender, the officers of all three armies took turns entertaining one another with lavish parties. To Steuben, as a senior commander, this was no matter of choice—it was a social obligation that befell him as a gentleman. But he could not afford to. "We are constantly feasted by the French," he remarked to North, "without giving them a bit of *Bratwurst*, I can stand it no longer. I will give one grand dinner to our allies, should I eat my soup with a wooden spoon for ever after." Ultimately he was able to host a dinner, but only after pawning one of his favorite mounts to his friend Col. Walter Stewart, commander of one of Wayne's Pennsylvania regiments.[23]

Nor did Steuben have the money to follow his heart and join Greene. Instead, he would have to go to Philadelphia to wring more pay from a bankrupt Congress. His prospects for success there were not good and he knew it. If need be, he would quit, though he didn't quite know what he would do then, either. "I sacrifice my time, my Interest & my Health & what is more than all these, I risk a reputation gained by twenty seven years service in Europe," he sadly wrote Greene. "Can you blame me for quitting when all my Zeal & . . . my Military Experience is attended with so little success & procures me so little Satisfaction?"[24]

Greene didn't blame him. "A terrible picture of the Rewards of Long Service," he scribbled on the Baron's letter after reading it.

The Baron said his goodbyes, reluctantly taking leave of Billy North, still too sick to travel. "I must leave you, my Son," he told North. "The instant you are able, quit this deleterious situation." He gave North what little he had left: his two-wheeled sulky and one of the two Portuguese gold coins, known as "half Joes," that constituted his entire wealth. With a single half Joe, worth less than ten dollars, in his pocket, he set out alone for Philadelphia.[25]

<hr />

A T PHILADELPHIA WERE FRIENDS who were glad to see the Baron, rich or poor. He spent the winter there, mostly at Belmont, where the growing Peters family—Richard and Sarah now had three "little aides-de-camp"—happily took him in.

To his friends at Hechingen, Steuben described the money, land, and honors heaped upon him by a grateful nation. "I am not lacking in the good things of this life," he wrote. But any rumor that "I lead an existence like one of the chief princes of the Empire is a little exaggerated. I live more as a good republican than a German baron. My table is simple, I have no unnecessary servants."²⁶ It was a brave attempt to mask his financial embarrassment. All of the Continental officers suffered from the fiscal inadequacy of Congress, but it was worse for Steuben.

The members of Congress, ecstatic that the war seemed to be drawing to a close, were looking to save money, not to spend more. They proposed—with Washington's blessing—a reduction of the inspector general's office, collapsing the intricate network of sub-inspectors and brigade inspectors down to two assistants, one for Greene's army and one for Washington's. Steuben did not raise any serious objections. Most of the army's officers knew the Blue Book by heart, and did not need constant tutoring as they once had.²⁷

His main concern was his pay. He did not ask for riches—that, presumably, would come later—and was happy to get enough to last him through the next campaign. Congress obliged. An audit of his accounts in January 1782 revealed that the Treasury did indeed owe him some $8,500 in back pay, one fifth of which he was allowed to withdraw in cash. Living expenses and payments to creditors ate up that $1,700 in no time flat, reducing Steuben once again to begging. Washington interceded, prevailing upon Robert Morris to forward the Baron a small sum so that he could return to the army. By the summer of 1782, that money, too, was used up, and Steuben had to return to Philadelphia for a couple of weeks to plead for another advance from his back pay.

In the meantime, he still had a job to do. The war was not yet over.

———

THOUGH ALL BUT FORGOTTEN by historians of the Revolution, the Continental Army's training program in 1782 produced results that were even better than those of Valley Forge. There was not much likelihood of an attack on British-held New York. As Steuben pointed out to his general, Admiral de Grasse's fleet had been humbled by the British in the West Indies that winter; even if the Yorktown coalition of French, Continental, and militia forces did converge on the Hudson, an assault on a place as "naturally fortified" as New York City would be unwise. Still, Washington intended the army to be ready just in case.

Washington, who had also wintered in Philadelphia, rejoined the army at Newburgh, New York, at the very end of March 1782, with Steuben following a few days later. A thorough inspection of the army began immediately; large-scale maneuvers commenced in June.

Steuben's team of assistants—his "kids," as North called them—had changed a great deal from the early days. Sickly Duponceau, much missed by his master, had resigned after the retreat from Point of Fork; Fairlie was in British captivity; Washington had raided Ben Walker for his own staff. A new face, Capt. William Popham of New York, joined the Baron's family. Pennsylvanian Walter Stewart took over the new position of assistant inspector for the main army.

The Baron and his "kids" whipped the army into the best shape of its entire history. The emphasis was on constant large-unit drills, along with the introduction of exercises of a very different but very practical sort. At the end of August, for example, when Washington decided to move the army down the Hudson from Newburgh to Verplanck's Point, Washington and Steuben orchestrated a mock amphibious assault. Five full infantry brigades piled into flat-bottomed boats, aligned in perfect order by brigade, and hit the beach at Verplanck's. Jumping out of the boats onto shore in full gear, the men formed brigade lines of battle in minutes. If only the French had been in a position to cooperate, Washington could have made a very dramatic entrance into New York City.[28]

The most exacting test came in September and October 1782. Rochambeau's army, having served its purpose, marched north from Virginia toward Boston to begin its long sea voyage home. En route, the French stopped for a few days' rest near the Continental encampment to bid farewell to their American comrades. Amid the feasting and drinking, Steuben took the opportunity to show just how adroit his army had become.

In a series of reviews held in honor of their valiant allies, Steuben and Walter Stewart led the army through all sorts of complicated maneuvers for Rochambeau's benefit. Steuben took the visit as a personal challenge, and was not about to let the French brass find anything wrong with *his* men. Before one review, one of the French generals dropped by Steuben's marquee to go over the upcoming maneuvers. One of the proposed movements caught the Frenchman's attention. He had seen it performed before, by the Prussian army, "but with a very complex addition." "You will recollect," Steuben pointed out, "that we are not quite Prussians." The Frenchman conceded, "This is true, but that will come with time." It was not an unkind response, but Steuben took it as patronizing. As soon as the French general left, Steuben muttered angrily to North, *"This is true, this is true, but that will come with time!* I will let these Frenchmen know that we can do what the Prussians can, and what *their* army cannot do." Wheeling around to Popham, he barked, "Get the order for review. Set down and add as I dictate. . . . They may come to Verplanck's Point next week for instruction with their *that will come with time!"* Steuben amended the proposed maneuver, replete with the "complex addition," and the review went off without a hitch.[29]

The French generals took note. "We went to watch the American army, which drills extremely well," observed Rochambeau's aide, the Baron de Closen. "Both its direction and the ease and precision of its movements really astonished us." Another general said to Steuben in utter amazement, "I admire the celerity and exactitude with which your men perform, but what I cannot conceive, is the profound silence with which they maneuver!" (To which the Baron replied that even his brigadiers "dare not open their mouths, but to repeat the order!") Steuben received all the credit. The army "owes all its improvement . . . to the labors and zeal of General Steuben, and to his subordinate, Colonel Stewart . . . who has learned M. de Steuben's style perfectly."[30]

And then the ultimate compliment, straight from Rochambeau himself: "You must have formed an alliance with the king of Prussia. These troops are Prussians!"[31]

The Baron, for once, took the compliments at face value. "The French connoisseurs," he announced proudly to General Greene, had assured him that "the British never had an Infantry comparable to ours."[32]

B Y THE END OF THE YEAR, Steuben had again run dry on funds, so it was off to Philadelphia to beg for a few more scraps from Congress's table. He had learned, from experience and from the counsel of his politician friends, that it did little good to demand large sums of money to compensate all that he had lost by leaving Europe. That argument had clearly worn thin, and Congress just didn't have the funds to make good on such claims. Instead, he emphasized what he had done for the army recently. "I dare assure you that your Enemies cannot oppose to you an Infantry equal to your own," he boasted to President Elias Boudinot in early December 1782. And it didn't hurt to remind the money-conscious delegates that his administrative reforms had "produced the most important savings to the Public."[33] The approach worked. On the recommendation of a committee chaired by the Baron's loyal friend Alexander Hamilton, Congress forwarded him $2,400 in back pay and a monthly allowance of $300 to cover expenses.[34]

So, with any luck, Steuben would have enough money to see him through the next campaign . . . if, indeed, there would be one. Rumors of an imminent peace with Britain flew thick and fast through the streets of the capital. He might be preparing the army for another operation; he might be supervising the dissolution of the army.

Peace, and with it British recognition of American independence, would be a good thing. But there was also good reason to be highly apprehensive of peace. Once the war was officially over, Congress could no longer justify the expense of maintaining an army in the field. But demobilization could also result in fiscal disaster. The soldiers' pay was long in arrears, and would have to be made good; the officers expected half-pay for life or a reasonable lump-sum payment in lieu of a pension. And those obligations simply could not be met, not anytime soon at least. The Treasury was empty, and the prospects of solvency were quite dim.[35]

At New Windsor, New York, where the army had encamped for the winter, officers and men alike feared that Congress would welch on its obligations to the military. Egged on by the disaffected in Congress and malcontents in the officer corps, a growing number of army leaders began to toy with the idea of a move against Congress, to force the delegates to meet the army's demands, at bayonet point if need be. Washington, the one man who seemed to have understood the ugly ramifications that would result from a violent clash between army and civil government, defused the more destructive passions of the so-called "Newburgh conspiracy" by mid-March. But even the great general could not drive away the underlying feeling that the politicians were within a hairsbreadth of betraying the army to which they owed everything.

Steuben, who remained in Philadelphia until the end of March, kept his distance from the controversy. But as someone who had himself felt the sting of ingratitude, he could not help but sympathize with his fellow officers. He felt passionately, too, for the men he had trained and led, who had done all that had been asked of them and more. They had done so without pay, food, or clothing, and now it seemed likely that they were going to be sent home without so much as an expression of thanks.

The black, poisonous atmosphere that hovered over New Windsor cantonment and Independence Hall also permeated Steuben's temporary residence outside Philadelphia near Belmont, a country house he dubbed "Bellisarius Hall." The Baron and his staff lived in dread uncertainty, not knowing if the discipline that they had tried so hard to instill in the Continental Army would completely unravel. "We are frequently in town but receive no pleasure," Billy North wrote to Ben Walker from Bellisarius Hall. "We dine & suspect. . . . We go. We return. This is a most infamous world. . . . Whether troops will be kept up or disbanded, a monarchy or our present government—What will be the event nobody knows."[36]

One wonders if anyone in Congress read a deeper meaning into the appellation with which Steuben christened his Philadelphia house. It was named for Belisarius, the great Byzantine general, who had led his armies to victory without a shred of support from his government.

───────

IN MID-FEBRUARY 1783, General Washington summoned Steuben to the main army. Peace was not yet a fact, he told the Baron, so the army must be kept prepared for war. Steuben reported to Washington at Newburgh at the end of March.

Though he inspected and drilled the troops as he always did in the spring, it seemed a hollow and pointless enterprise now. Definite word of the conclusion of peace came at the beginning of April. Congress signed the treaty on the eleventh, and Washington—after pondering the wisdom of announcing the peace to his disgruntled troops—proclaimed the formal end of hostilities on April 19. It was precisely eight years, to the day, after the first clashes at Lexington and Concord.

Steuben spent much time that spring at Washington's Newburgh headquarters, discussing with the general the future of the army and not infrequently staying for dinner. He had the unaccustomed luxury of time on his hands, and at Newburgh he could reacquaint himself with the Washingtons and with his old aide Walker. The Washingtons likewise enjoyed the lighthearted banter that the Baron brought to the table; Martha in particular found his accent and his occasional difficulties with the English language highly amusing. The Baron knew when he had an appreciative audience, so he pretended to be clumsier with the language than he actually was. One evening Martha asked him how he passed the time now that his military duties were somewhat reduced. Steuben replied that he read, wrote, played chess, and—for the first time in his life—went fishing. But he knew he wasn't a very good angler, he confessed, for he had sat in a boat in the Hudson for three hours and had caught only two fish. One of them, he said, was a whale. "A whale, Baron, in the North River?" Lady Washington asked. "Yes, I assure you, a very fine whale." Turning to his staff, he demanded with a wink, "It *was* a whale, was it not?" Billy North corrected him: "An *eel*, Baron." Steuben shrugged his shoulders and pretended to be mortally offended by the correction. "I beg your pardon, my Lady, but that gentleman certainly told me that it was a whale."[37]

The Baron's main duty, when he wasn't fishing for whales in the Hudson, was working out the details of demobilization. He had hoped for a dramatic send-off. The men deserved that much, he believed. He envisioned a ceremony that would demonstrate to the soldiers that their leaders, their Congress, and their nation regarded them as heroes. A grand review, perhaps, like that at Valley Forge, just one last time, before the individual regiments marched off to their home states. They would do so with colors uncased and flying proudly, fifes and drums ringing out the lilting tunes that had led them into battle at Brandywine, at Monmouth, at Yorktown.[38]

It would have been a fitting end to eight years of heartache and sacrifice, but it was not to be. Congress could not afford to keep the army a day longer than was absolutely necessary, but with the British still in possession of New York, it would be risky to get rid of the troops altogether. The compromise arrangement was to be a mass "furlough" of the army. Those men who had enlisted for the duration of the war were to disband and go home, taking their muskets with them. If their country needed them before the British departed American soil, they could be recalled to the colors, ready to fight if need be. A handful of men, whose enlistment terms had not yet expired, would remain at West Point until all affairs were settled.

On Congress's order, Washington began the process on June 2, 1783. There was none of the ceremony that Steuben had envisioned, only the sadly undramatic spectacle of a camp breaking up as the men said their goodbyes to their brothers in arms and went their separate ways. During the first two weeks of June, they took to the road in small bands, with little in their pockets but promissory notes for back pay and a few scraps of food.

It was difficult for Steuben, or any officer, to part with the army for good; it was even harder to see it trickle away to nothing, man by man, without the satisfaction of viewing his creation on parade one last time. Years later, a former Continental officer recalled the very last drill session conducted by the Baron. His bitter melancholy came through that day at Newburgh. After giving his men the order to "March!" he added in a growl loud enough to be heard by everyone, ". . . into the river and drown yourselves!"[39]

Yet there were consolations. The men did not forget him. Disillusionment was rife in the now-defunct army, as many were convinced that the furlough system was just a clever way of disposing of the army without paying it. Washington, rather unfairly, took much of the blame for the circumstances of the disbandment. Steuben did not, and in fact he received unrestrained accolades. The officers of the New York and New Jersey regiments expressed their affection in a heartfelt but florid letter. The testimonial, written soldier to soldier, could not have failed to move the Baron.[40]

Your unremitted exertions on all occasions to alleviate the distresses of the Army—and the manner in which you have shared them with us, have given you more than a common title to the character of *our Friend*—as our Military Parent we have long considered you. Ignorant as we were of the profession we had undertaken, it is to your Abilities & unwearied assiduity, we are indebted for that Military Reputation we finally attained.

THE BARON had better luck memorializing the contributions of the officer corps. That May, while still at Newburgh, Henry Knox had the idea of forming a fraternal association of officers, to perpetuate the friendships forged over eight long years of war, and to honor those who had given so much in the service of their country. The result was the Society of the Cincinnati, named for the Roman citizen-soldier *cum* political leader Lucius Quinctius Cincinnatus. Cincinnatus, who had reluctantly put aside his plow to serve as dictator of Rome in a moment of national emergency, only to shed his political powers as soon as the crisis had passed, had long been held up as a model of selfless republican virtue and civic duty. This made him a perfect namesake for this new society, which saluted the Continental officers for exactly the same qualities.

The first formal meeting of the Cincinnati was held at Steuben's Fishkill headquarters, the Verplanck house, on May 13, 1783. Washington was elected president of the society by universal acclaim, but as he was not present, Steuben served as acting head. At Steuben's insistence, Pierre L'Enfant designed the society's seal and insignia. The basic aims of the society—among other things, to provide charitable assistance to American officers and their families who had fallen on hard times, as so many would—were harmless and above reproach.

Membership in the society was to be hereditary, passed down from father to eldest-born son. Herein lay the source of the controversy that would surround the group in the next few years. The Cincinnati, with its exclusive character and distinctive heraldry, struck many Americans as being too much like a noble order, an innovation that was highly suspect to a people who trumpeted liberty and equality. As a charter member and a titled nobleman himself, Steuben would naturally come to be seen as the author of such an alien and dangerous idea.

WITH MOST OF THE ARMY on the road home, Steuben's formal duties as inspector general had gone from being an unworkable burden to almost nothing overnight. He did not have a family anxiously awaiting his return home, as most of the Continental generals did. Washington therefore selected him for a truly unconventional assignment: a diplomatic mission to General Sir Frederick Haldimand, the British military commander in Canada.

The transfer of British-held military posts to American hands was a potentially tricky matter, not only in New York, where thousands of Loyalists cringed at the thought of retribution by vengeful Patriots, but also in the frontier outposts to the north and west of the thirteen states. Washington wanted to make sure that the British did not abandon their frontier forts until the Americans were prepared to relieve them. This would be Steuben's job—to work out the details of the transfer with the British authorities, and to visit the British forts as far west as Detroit in order to determine what kind of forces were needed to garrison these strongpoints.

It was fortunate for Steuben's health that the mission was an unmitigated failure. The Baron ventured north through Albany into the dense wilderness of northern New York, and via Lake Champlain toward Quebec. Haldimand, alerted to his intended purpose by William North, who had gone ahead to make contact with the British general, intercepted the Prussian at the town of Sorel on August 8. He treated the Baron with kindness and tact, but firmly told him that he could not visit any of the British outposts. Haldimand did not have the authority to allow it, and certainly he had received no orders to evacuate. The mission was over. Steuben reversed course, took some time to recover his strength at Saratoga, and returned to duty.[41]

A LL THAT REMAINED at New Windsor was the pitiful detritus of the army: the sick, the maimed, those too weak to journey home on their own. These he tended to as best he could, arranging hospital care for some, transporting others to West Point so that they could recuperate among the skeleton force guarding the Hudson there.

The Baron wrote very little during the autumn of 1783, keeping his thoughts to himself as he presided over the last lingering, tentative heartbeats of the army he had done so much to create. We can only guess at his emotions as he filled out his last reports, while the days grew shorter in his beloved Hudson Valley, the approaching winter setting the Highlands ablaze with fiery color. The army, the thing that had been his salvation and his home, was passing away before his eyes, and he had nowhere to go.

He did, however, have the advantage of closure of sorts, for since he was compelled to stick it out to the mournful end, he was witness to the final acts of the Continental Army. He rode alongside General

Washington on November 25, 1783, at the head of the procession that reclaimed New York City as the British withdrew to their transports in the harbor, while Patriot crowds thronged the streets to cheer the victors. He returned to Washington's side nine days later, sitting by him and Knox at a table on the second floor of Fraunces Tavern, embracing his general during the round of tear-filled farewells after Washington said his parting words to his officers there. He left New York that day with Washington, and shared with him the barge that took them to the New Jersey shore and the road to Philadelphia.

The general and the Baron parted ways in Philadelphia. The Baron would stay there to tend to his final business as inspector general. But Washington's military career was over. He left for Annapolis, where Congress now sat, to tender his resignation at noon on December 23, 1783. Before Washington quit public life—for good, as he thought at the time—he performed his last act as general-in-chief: he wrote a letter of thanks to the Baron de Steuben.

Altho' I have taken frequent Opportunities both in public and private, of Acknowledging your great Zeal, Attention and Abilities in performing the duties of your Office; yet, I wish, to make use of this last Moment of my public Life, to Signify in the strongest terms, my intire Approbation of your Conduct, and to express my Sense of the Obligations the public is under to you for your faithful and Meritorious Services. . . . I am persuaded you will not be displeased with this farewell token of my Sincere Friendship and Esteem for you.[42]

CHAPTER 12

An Old Soldier in Peacetime

[January 1784—November 1794]

You cannot do a Service to a worthier Man nor to one
to whom we are more obliged. He is certainly the
Father of our Discipline, tho' he had to deal with docile
Children.

RICHARD PETERS TO JACOB READ,
FEBRUARY 23, 1784[1]

EARLY IN 1778, the Baron de Steuben had declared to
John Hancock that he was "an American for life." He
didn't really mean it then, not *exactly*. He can be for-
given a bit of ingratiating talk, perhaps, for at that time he was
a job applicant, and it was important that he demonstrate at-
tachment to the Cause in order to secure a commission. The
Baron did sympathize with the Cause, even if he knew little
about America or Americans. Over time, he grew to form a
strong bond with his hosts and with the land itself.

But he also had the dreams and ambitions of a younger
man, ambitions that made him hope for further martial glory
in Europe, in the French army. Repeated rebuffs from Gérard
and Luzerne squeezed the life from that hope. Yet in December 1782, while he was talking money with Alex Hamilton's
committee in Philadelphia, he made a final appeal to France—
directly to Vergennes. He reminded the foreign minister that "a

peace glorious to France" was in the offing, and that the peace was in part Steuben's doing. "You cannot forget the instruments whose services you have made use of to attain this important object." What he requested, as a token of Louis XVI's favor, was not an actual command in the line, but an honorary commission as major general and a pension—enough to "enable him to end his days at ease in the dominions of the King."[2]

Vergennes had not forgotten his "instrument." He could not, for Steuben's fame in Europe was nearly as great as it was in America. One could buy an engraving of the Baron's likeness at any bookshop in Paris; Lafayette, while traveling through Europe in 1786, found that nearly everyone in Prussia had heard of their native son's exploits in the New World. Yet the French foreign minister felt no pressing obligation to reward him. "The King owes no recompense to the Baron de Steuben," the minister informed Luzerne. He let Steuben down more easily, but not by much. "You have rendered essential services to the United States," Vergennes wrote him in July 1783, "and I have no doubt of your reaping those rewards you have so much right to expect." Steuben would have to seek his fortune through Congress, for France had none to give him.[3]

Steuben's attitude toward the United States might, at first glance, appear to be ambivalent. He showed every sign of adopting America as his home. He bragged about its peculiarities to his friends in Europe; he was driven almost to madness by those Virginians who quailed in the face of peril instead of springing to the call to defend their country. When he wrote out his will in the summer of 1781, he left the bulk of his estate to the eldest son of his sister, the impoverished Baroness von Canitz, but on several conditions: that the young Canitz must move permanently to the United States, reject "the title Baron or any other sign of nobility," and take up American citizenship "as a good republican."[4] Why, then, was Steuben still so eager to leave at the end of the war?

The answer is simple. Steuben was exhausted. His activity in the Revolution drained him, aging him well beyond his fifty-three years.

He felt it in his bones, in his increasingly frequent fevers, in the recur-ring and painful flare-ups of gout that left him unable to ride a horse. His patriotism was not a sham. When he appealed to Vergennes in 1782–83, he did not do so as a mercenary looking to move on to bigger and better things under a different master, but rather as a tired, old man who wanted only to live out his last days in honorable comfort. The Baron suspected that he would not find such tranquility and ease in the United States.

His suspicions would prove correct.

THE BARON DID NOT FLY from public service at war's end. Instead he launched himself into a project that had been very much on his mind since 1779: the creation of a permanent military establish-ment for the new republic. Steuben understood that as much as he fa-vored the armies of Prussia and France, the United States could not and should not imitate them. Congress and indeed most Americans were dead set against a standing army. Aside from its cost, it would also raise the specter of military dictatorship à la Oliver Cromwell. Though the dark days of Cromwell's Protectorate had ended more than a century ago, it was as fresh in the minds of educated Americans as if it had happened the week before.

The major powers of Europe, Steuben therefore argued, should most definitely *not* serve as a model for American military organiza-tion. He turned instead to the few existing republics in Europe for inspiration. One in particular struck him as especially pertinent: Switzerland. Like the fledgling United States, Switzerland was cash-poor and relatively undeveloped. Yet for centuries, even before attain-ing formal independence in 1648, it had managed to shake off the yoke of any foreign prince who laid claim to the land. It did so by rely-ing on a well-organized, home-grown militia of ordinary peasants and woodsmen.

The main reason that the military security of the Swiss rested on their militia was economic: "the Want of the necessary means to maintain a Standing Army." America had even better grounds for such a military system. Switzerland was small and compact; America was expansive, with a long, vulnerable coast and a long, vulnerable frontier. If the United States entrusted its national defense to a standing army, that army would necessarily have to be very large indeed to cover so much territory. "It is to our Militias that We must find the real Strength which we are to oppose to that of Great Britain."[5]

The thought remained on his mind over the next four years, so when Washington—prompted by Hamilton in April 1783—asked his generals for their ideas regarding a peacetime army, Steuben's pen practically flew. He submitted two long memoranda. The first, addressed to Secretary at War Benjamin Lincoln, covered military academies and manufactories. The second, written for Washington five days later, revealed the heart of his vision.

The defense of the United States, Steuben argued, could not be left entirely to impromptu musterings of militia. There would have to be a permanent army no matter what, but it could be kept small—fewer than five thousand men. It was needed to garrison "a chain of small posts along the frontiers," to protect overland trade and to serve as "a check upon the Indians." But five thousand men would not be enough to deter a full-scale assault by a European power. That was where the militia came in. No matter how large the militia was, no matter how it was organized, it would have to be uniform in composition. All units would have to be the same size, and they must be trained in the same manner, using the official *Regulations* already adopted by the Continental Army.

"As long as our Ambition is confined," Steuben concluded, "to promoting the happiness of our citizens within our limits," then a small professional army, supplemented in wartime by the trained militia, would do the trick. "A system of this nature will make us more respectable with the powers of Europe than if we should keep up an army of fifty thousand men." And it could all be done without "the enormous expence which a large land and sea force would subject us to."[6]

Washington approved. Steuben's ideas formed the core of the

general's "Sentiments on a Peace Establishment," which he tendered to Congress in May 1783. It had no immediate effect. Congress was far more worried about how it would rid itself of the army it had than it was about the way it would raise the next army.

Undeterred, Steuben took up the project again in January 1784, with the same fevered intensity with which he had attacked the Blue Book five years earlier. Duponceau reunited with him at Annapolis to work out the details. Both the regular army and the militia, Steuben suggested, should be organized into "legions"—self-contained all-purpose units that included line infantry, light infantry, cavalry, and artillery. Altogether, in wartime, the regular army and the organized militia would number twenty-five thousand men—enough to discourage any would-be invader. Steuben forwarded a draft proposal to Washington, now living as a gentleman farmer at Mount Vernon. The former general endorsed it enthusiastically as a plan calculated "to insure us the blessings of peace."[7]

The Baron formally submitted his proposal to Congress on March 21, 1784, the same day he tendered his resignation. Again, there was no response.[8]

Steuben's passion about the peacetime military establishment would not permit him to let the matter rest. Working from his new residence in New York City, he dispensed with Congress altogether and made a direct appeal to the people. The result was a pamphlet, *A Letter on the Subject of an Established Militia, and Military Arrangements, Addressed to the Inhabitants of the United States*, which he published that summer at his own expense. It was the same plan with a friendlier face. Yes, he admitted to his readership, he *did* advocate a standing army, but it would be unrealistic for militia to constantly guard the immense western frontier against "savages . . . who are unalterably your enemies." A five-thousand-man army should not be the object of fear, for it would be "composed of your brothers and your sons." "Are they not your natural guardians?" he asked his audience. "And shall it be supposed [that] a cockade and feather . . . can alienate either their affections or their interest?"[9]

Though the Baron's body was already beginning to fail him, his mind remained agile, skipping easily from one military topic to another: on the characteristics of practical military clothing (which should definitely *not* follow European fashions), on the establishment of cannon foundries and powder mills, on the training of the militia.[10] His most valuable counsel centered on military education. Steuben had long been an advocate of a national military academy. The regular army would require professionally trained officers, but the militia would need them, too. In wartime, the United States could not risk putting its fortunes into the hands of amateur leaders. "The merchant may read Marshall Saxe, the Mathematician Monsieur Vauban, but it is the soldier alone who regards their lessons and takes up the sword," he wrote in his *Letter.*

In a document he wrote for Secretary at War Lincoln, the Baron laid out the salient characteristics of the American military academy—down to the last detail, including the conduct of cadets in the mess halls. One hundred and twenty cadets would be selected every three years for matriculation, all at least fourteen years of age and with a basic grammar-school education. A faculty of five professors and seven "masters of arts" would instruct them in the vital disciplines: mathematics, history, geography, civil and international law, "natural and experimental philosophy," eloquence, civil engineering, drawing, French, horsemanship, fencing—a classic liberal arts education, with an emphasis on the art of war.

The overriding concern, as with all of Steuben's suggested reforms, was uniformity. Cadets, he argued, should not be forced to take a commission against their will, but no man should ever be promoted to an officer's rank in the army unless he had completed his studies at the academy.

CONGRESS DID NOT ACT IMMEDIATELY on Steuben's plans. They also ignored his claims for money and recognition.

Recognition was still very important to him. Much like his friend

Nathanael Greene, he wanted to be thanked. He harbored a little bit of resentment toward generals who, in his opinion, had done less and been rewarded more than he—such as Lafayette, whose fame in Europe and America was greater than his own. "I know well that in the [French] queen's quarters, the history of the American Revolution has produced only one young hero," he complained to his old army friend, the Freiherr von der Goltz, now the Prussian ambassador in Paris. "But then you know how women always need a little miracle-performing Jesus."[11]

Overall, though, Steuben felt appreciated in his new home. The men whose opinions mattered most to him continued to sing his praises. And he did not dwell excessively on the past. Only in his appeals to Congress did he relive his past glories and achievements, and there his motivation was not mere sentimentality. He wanted, and needed, money.

Granted, the Baron's claims were probably a bit high, considering that Congress was not in a position to be generous. But Steuben was not alone: some of the most powerful men in the republic—Richard Peters, Alexander Hamilton, John Jay, Elbridge Gerry—gave him regular counsel, encouraging him to expect munificence from Congress. "I will forgive many of their Sins," Peters vowed to Horatio Gates, "if they make the Atonement of doing this valuable & worthy Officer Justice."[12] The Baron's friends presented proposals for compensation ranging in amount from $8,000 to $45,000. Even Thomas Jefferson, who apparently nursed no grudge against his former tormentor, moved that Congress grant Steuben $10,000. All failed. At first Congress would agree to give him only $2,000, a gold-hilted sword, and an official vote of thanks, though after much wrangling the amount was increased to $10,000 credit "on account"—still well short of the total back and bonus pay that was already due him.[13]

The emptiness of the Treasury was not the only reason for Steuben's failure to make a positive impression on Congress. The Baron made some powerful enemies, whose collective power outweighed the considerable influence of his friends.

The Baron's high standing in the Society of the Cincinnati was the first thing to attract unflattering attention. Many in Congress viewed the Cincinnati as an insidious cabal "formed in Europe to overturn our happy institutions." One of them was Aedanus Burke of South Carolina. Under the pseudonym "Cassius," Burke wrote a pamphlet attacking the Society as "a Race of Hereditary Patricians or Nobility," singling out the Baron as the "creator" and "Grand Master" of the order. "I have the honor to inform Baron Steuben," he wrote, "that an order of peerage may do well under the petty princes of Germany, yet, in America, it is incompatible with our freedom."[14]

Steuben, who joined the New York chapter of the Cincinnati in 1786 and served for several years as its president, shrugged off the ridiculous accusations. "*À ça, Monsieur le Cincinnatus,*" he wrote in jest to Henry Knox, the real guiding hand behind the Society, in November 1783, "Your pernicious designs are thus revealed. You wish to introduce dukes and peers into our Republic. No, my Lord, no, my Grace, that will not do. . . . Blow Ye the Trumpet in Zion!"[15]

Laugh as he might at the carpings of the "Bostonians and gentlemen of the *Holy Land*" and their "modest and Presbyterian airs," the truth was that the Baron's position damaged his standing with Congress. Massachusetts delegate Rufus King jabbed at him:

> I know that he was a Soldier of Fortune and a mercenary in Europe; and notwithstanding his affected Philanthropy and artificial Gentleness, I hold his character the same in America; the only difference is this: in Europe he received little money and less flattery. . . . He has from this circumstance of preference and from the adulation of sycophants, been buoyed up to the preposterous Belief that his military Talents are superior to those of any Soldier in America.[16]

Once Steuben perceived this prejudice, once he determined that Congress would not deal with him fairly, he dropped any pretense at tact when discussing politics, no matter whom he offended. "As long as I live in this D___ Republic, I will at least have the Liberty of laughing When Ever I feel a disposition for it—wich God knows is very seldom."[17]

In the autumn of 1786, high taxes and forced foreclosures sparked an insurrection among the farmers of the western Massachusetts hill country. The episode came to be known as Shays' Rebellion, after its leader, a former Continental officer named Daniel Shays. Most of the Baron's former comrades in the Continental command spoke out vociferously against the rebels. To people like Henry Knox and Alexander Hamilton, the nearly bloodless uprising highlighted the need for stronger central government.

Steuben lamented the rebellion as a harbinger of bad things to come, the "collapse" of the "edifice we struggled for seven years to build." But as the uprising spread, his sympathies took a surprising shift. Like Thomas Jefferson—a man who in so many ways was Steuben's political opposite—the Baron sided with the rebels. The farmers, many of them Continental veterans, were being forcibly impoverished by a state government dominated by merchants and speculators, men who had profited handsomely from the war. To Steuben, the farmers' plight illustrated what he saw as the central problem with the American republic: those in power had exploited the common man in the War for Independence, and continued to do so after the war was over.[18]

In private, to Billy North, Steuben poured out his contempt for the Massachusetts authorities in letters dripping with vicious, theatrical sarcasm. "This mob," he wrote to North in October 1786, referring to Shays's rebels, "consisted of men of the Vilest principles, Desperate in their fortune etc.—therefor a disgrace to human nature." The leaders of Massachusetts, on the other hand, were "Gentlemen of property & Consideration. This alone gives us a sufficient superiority over these Retches."[19]

The Baron could not restrain himself from making his views public. He published a scathing article in the *New York Daily Advertiser* lampooning the army's efforts to quell the rebellion. He wrote the article under the pseudonym "Bellisarius," but everyone of importance who read the article knew it was the Baron. Many of them were not amused.[20]

Steuben's response to Shays' Rebellion highlights the Baron's conflicted relationship with American government. A republic worked well when its leaders were virtuous, he felt, when they held the common good above all other considerations and interests. But the leading men in American politics after 1783 no longer had the kind of virtue that had made the leaders of 1776 great. "It seems to me that we have neither the virtue nor the wisdom [necessary] to be a democratic republic," he wrote shortly after the end of the war. Government was now in the hands of those who sought only their personal gain, measured in dollars, and cared nothing for the plight of the men who had fought and died for them and for independence.[21] Such a nation could not long survive. When George III's son, Prince William Henry, expressed an interest in visiting the United States in 1786, Steuben wryly remarked, "It doesn't surprise me. Eagles are always about when the scent of carrion is in the air."[22]

The conduct of Congress so sickened the Baron that he contemplated—briefly—supporting the creation of an American constitutional monarchy. He wrote to Prince Henry of Prussia to sound him out: Would the prince care to accept the crown of an American kingdom if it were offered to him? Henry expressed mild and cautious interest, but the Constitutional Convention assembled in Philadelphia before anything could come of the venture.[23]

Congress did not do right by Steuben; the delegates never fully honored the vague promises that had been made to him at York in 1778. But that in itself did not condemn Steuben to poverty. He did that to himself. He would never really moderate his profligate spending habits in his declining years, spending what money he received from Congress as soon as it reached his hands. Worse, he even

spent money *before* it reached his hands. "He is and will be all eter-
nity," North once groused to Walker, "eating the calf in the cow's
belly."[24]

Shortly after the end of the war, the Baron leased a large house in
what was then the countryside of Upper Manhattan. He christened it
"The Louvre," and though it was run down, he was determined that it
should rival Belmont in stately elegance. There he planned to entertain
his friends among the notables of New York society. He lavished nearly
all of the money he squeezed from Congress in 1784 on renovations,
new furniture, and books; he splurged on unsupportable luxuries, including three new carriages. The spending reduced him to penury in
no time at all. He could not afford to entertain his friends, and for
much of 1786 he stayed in the house alone with only Azor—who had
remained faithfully by his side through the war years—to keep him
company. Unable to keep the house up, he relinquished his lease at the
end of 1786. For much of his life thereafter, he failed to maintain a
permanent residence anywhere, drifting from one boardinghouse to
another or living with Ben Walker and his new bride, Polly, in their
Manhattan home.

It was not quite the way he had envisioned his retirement, and
understandably it sometimes brought him to despair and bitterness.
"Vive la liberté!" he wrote to North as his dream of transforming the
Louvre into a gentlemanly gathering place faded before his eyes. "In
this country the laborers are barons and the barons are beggars."[25]
But overall he kept his spirits up. "Whatever be one's circumstances,
the best is to put on a cheerful face," he had once told Henry Laurens, and he stood by that code now. Even though he felt ashamed
of his indigence, so much so that he refused dinner invitations that
he could not reciprocate, he gleefully immersed himself in the social
life of New York City. He was naturalized as a citizen there, on the
Fourth of July 1786, and stayed within the city most of the time.[26]
Besides his position in the local chapter of the Cincinnati, he served
as president of the German Society of New York from 1786 until his

death, and was an active member of the German Reformed congregation.

Plus he had Walker and North. Ben and Billy had families of their own now, but they continued to look after the Baron long after they were no longer being paid to do so. North, who remained in the army as inspector until 1788, fussed incessantly over Steuben and monitored his expenses. He and Walker tried, repeatedly, to put the Baron on a budget, and they admonished him for his extravagance. Regardless of their stern advice, the Baron looked instead to gain easy money as he latched onto one get-rich-quick scheme after another, most of them centering on the financial fad of the moment: land speculation. He pursued several such ventures, all equally fantastical—one of them a plan to create a Spanish "military colony" on the Mississippi, where Continental Army veterans could live free on rich farmland in return for military service. Like all of the Baron's postwar business ventures, this arrangement with "Don Quixote Countrie" never panned out.

North feared that sometimes he pushed the affable old man too hard. "God knows I would as soon wound myself as wound him," he wrote to Walker, "but his sore must be probed." Indeed, the ministrations of his surrogate sons did grate on the Baron sometimes, and he chided North for his miserliness, "the only vice that increases with Age." "'With these Castles in Air, the Old fool goes still on in his extravagant expenses,' So says Billy," the Baron lashed back at North in 1788. "Silence, Mr. Billy, I hear you . . . you are not always in the Right. . . . I live & must live poorer than I ever did." Yet overall he took great comfort in the fact that his "kids" cared so deeply for him. "It is true that he often scolds me," Steuben wrote to North, describing his friend in the third person. "But it is because he wants me to be better than I really am. . . . He wishes that I were one of the seven sages of Greece, but my passions often make a fool of me."[27]

The Baron was not entirely without assets. He was cash-poor but land-rich. Pennsylvania, New Jersey, and New York had all given him substantial tracts of wilderness land in gratitude for his services, and even Virginia—before Steuben made himself persona non grata there—offered him a large, as-yet-unsurveyed plot of land in the Ohio Valley. Steuben sold his New Jersey and Pennsylvania estates, but he stubbornly held on to the sixteen thousand acres promised him by the state of New York and his old ally Governor George Clinton. He chose for himself a remote, completely undeveloped parcel deep in the wilds of the Mohawk Valley, just north of what was then called Fort Schuyler.*

Here, on the estate that he called "Steuben," the Baron intended to live as a country squire. He would build a manor house on the property, invite land-hungry New Englanders to clear the land and set up farmsteads, while he lived off of his share of the harvest from the fecund soil. Proximity to the Mohawk River would facilitate easy export of surplus crops.

Steuben did indeed have a cabin built on the property, though never the grand mansion he had envisioned. A few tenants came to work the land—one of them was Jonathan Arnold Steuben, the Connecticut soldier who had changed his traitor's name at the Baron's suggestion—but few of them stayed for very long. But as Walker and North frequently reminded him, the endeavor took far more effort than it was worth. The costs of developing the land put Steuben deep in debt long before the estate yielded even marginal profits.

T HE BARON RETURNED TO PUBLIC LIFE only once more, when the new constitutional government of the United States took form in New York City in the spring of 1789. His prestige had not entirely faded, and he enjoyed a prominent place near George Washington on the balcony of Federal Hall as the new president took his oath of office on April 30. Soon President Washington called on Steuben for his advice, the two men falling easily into their old roles again—Washington as the commander in chief, the Baron as his military adviser—

---

* Perhaps more familiar as Fort Stanwix, near Rome, New York.

as they discussed the structure and mission of the postwar army and its employment on the western frontier. Steuben was delighted by the gesture. "I have dined with the great man," he told North that May, flattered that his old general still held his opinion in high regard when Congress had consistently ignored him. "I have had a talk with him tête-à-tête for four hours, a horseback ride from nine in the morning until two o'clock."[28]

With Washington at the helm of the new government and Alexander Hamilton as secretary of the treasury, the Baron hoped he would get the recompense he had earned, that he deserved. But their presence in government made little difference. Despite Hamilton's strivings on his behalf, Congress would go no further than to authorize a $2,500 annual pension for him.

Nor did Washington's reconnection with the Baron signal that a new career might be in the offing. Steuben did not expect one, but the president actually gave it some thought. In the winter of 1792, Washington was looking for a new general to lead U.S. forces against the Shawnee-Miami-Delaware confederation in the Ohio country. The confederation had already annihilated the expeditionary force of Steuben's old army friend Arthur St. Clair in a bloody debacle on the banks of the Wabash River. It would stand as the worst defeat ever of United States troops by Native Americans, and Washington was not about to let the matter rest. As he mulled over the possible candidates for the commander's position, he jotted down a few thoughts on the character and abilities of each.

On the Baron, Washington wrote: "Sensible, sober and brave, well acquainted with tactics and with the arrangement and discipline of an army." Not effusive, but accurate. His shortcomings? "High in his ideas of subordination—impetuous in his temper—ambitious" . . . and then the curse: "a foreigner."[29]

Washington's assessment, if it had ever become known to the Baron, would have cut him to the quick. Steuben was well aware of his temper and his ambition, and his insistence on obedience to orders.

But *a foreigner?* Even when he wrote little essays and memoranda for no one's eyes but his own, analyzing the problems of American government and the "military constitution," Steuben always referred to Americans as *we*, not *they*.

The Baron himself, however, would have conceded that in 1792 he was no longer the soldier, no longer the man, he had been ten years before. He was too old and feeble, his tired frame incapable of weathering the physical demands of leading an army into the Ohio country. As it was, his activities in New York after 1790 wore him out more and more each year. He moved with the season, wintering in New York City, summering on his Mohawk Valley estate, exhausting himself with the arduous journey and the constant worries that accompanied the development of his tract. But the bullheaded Steuben stuck it out to the end. He would not admit defeat.

In 1794, Steuben decided to spend the winter at his wilderness estate, residing in his two-room log cabin while still contemplating the construction of a far more elaborate house on the property. There were few diversions to entertain the sociable if ailing man. In July he presided over the dedication of the Hamilton Oneida Academy, a grammar school for local whites and Oneidas that later would form the basis of Hamilton College. But mostly he whiled away the long, dreary, lonely hours in his cabin, playing chess with his new secretary, John Mulligan, reading Montesquieu and his beloved Cervantes. Mulligan, a learned young graduate of Columbia College, would be Steuben's only companion that winter. The Baron celebrated his sixty-fourth and final birthday in the gray solitude of his cabin.

In the wee morning hours of November 25, 1794, Mulligan was startled from his sleep by loud cries from the Baron. It was an unnatural sound, for the stoic gentleman usually grumbled and cursed over physical pain, but the Baron was in "extreme agony." His entire left side was paralyzed; he appeared to have had "suffered long," and he yelped to Mulligan that he was dying. Mulligan, frantic at the unexpected sight of the helpless Baron, roused a hired hand and sent him to summon help. Steuben was in great pain, "retching violently," and remained in bed for the next two days. On Wednesday, the twenty-sixth, he lost consciousness, and though a physician arrived the following day, there was little he could do. At about half past noon on Friday, November 28, 1794, the Baron de Steuben passed from this world.[30]

Billy North arrived at the cabin a day or two later, just in time to preside over his mentor's funeral. It was a very simple ceremony, in keeping with Steuben's wishes and his Calvinist faith, a faith that he kept almost entirely to himself. "Wrapped in his cloak, encased in a plain coffin," the body of the Baron de Steuben was interred in an unmarked grave while North, Mulligan, and a few tenants and neighbors stood glumly by.

A decade later the grave site had been all but forgotten. Ben Walker, fortunately, happened to be in the vicinity when a new post road was laid over the Baron's grave. To the faithful aide, this was nothing short of sacrilege. At his own expense, he had Steuben's remains disinterred and moved to a new grave in a nearby grove of trees.

IN THE NEXT CENTURY, the state of New York would memorialize its adopted son, erecting a a simple but massive granite monument atop his grave, a bronze plaque saluting the Baron as *indispensable*. But few people visit the site. Even today, even in the spring and summer months when it is open to the public, there is something inexpressibly sad and mournful about the Baron's last resting place.

Elsewhere Steuben is commemorated more ostentatiously. There are statues of him at Valley Forge, Monmouth, and Lafayette Square, in Washington, DC. New York and Indiana each have a Steuben County; Ohio, a Steubenville, named for the frontier outpost of Fort Steuben, itself christened in honor of the Baron by Billy North in 1786. He has become a symbol for German American friendship, his name gracing German cultural festivals throughout the United States, notably the "Steuben Day" parades held annually on his birthday in New York, Chicago, and Philadelphia.

The lasting image of the Baron, though, is that of the blustering, foul-mouthed drillmaster of Valley Forge. Yet that legend, the very thing that has kept Steuben's name alive in American history texts, has also overshadowed his other contributions to American military victory in the Revolutionary War, to the point that those contributions have become little more than a footnote to the story of the Baron shouting his *"Goddams"* at awkward citizen-soldiers in the snows around the Schuylkill.

And that is unfortunate, for the Baron's significance goes far beyond the fruit of his first three months' labor in 1778. The Blue Book would survive as the official regulations of the U.S. Army through the War of 1812; its rationale—that European military practice could be integrated into a uniquely American way of war— would last for much longer. His notion of a small peacetime army, supplemented in times of war with a national militia, would likewise serve as the underlying foundation of the American military establishment for many decades to come. West Point, and indeed all of the American service academies, are products of the Baron's agile mind. Above all other contributions tower the concepts of discipline and professionalism in the army as a whole and in the officer corps in particular.

The Baron de Steuben's contribution to American independence and, more important, to the history of the American way of war was fundamental. Although he did not gain the glory of his more fortunate European comrades in the Continental Army—Lafayette comes to mind—he brought more of value to that army than any of them did. No one deserves sole credit for the creation of the American army— that was a team effort, by many individuals over many years—but if anyone ranks at the head of that team, it was assuredly the tempestuous Baron.

The Baron de Steuben's is the classic "coming to America" story writ large. Like so many immigrants before or since, he cut himself

loose from the Old World and journeyed to the New intending to re-
invent himself. He did just that. Although he blurred a few details of
his past in order to seek preferment in the United States, somewhere
between his arrival and the achievement of American independence,
the Baron became something very much like the man he had pretended
to be.

Steuben's cabin, near present-day Rome, New York. Here Steuben
administered his unprofitable wilderness estate after the war, while
he made plans to build a much more elaborate manor house on his
property. He died here in November 1794. *(Emmet Collection, Miriam
and Ira D. Wallach Division of Art, Prints and Photographs, The New York Public
Library, Astor, Lenox and Tilden Foundations)*

Notes

Regarding the Notes

For this book, I have relied primarily on the vast collection of Steubeniana contained in *The Papers of General Friedrich Wilhelm von Steuben, 1777–1794*. This collection, assembled through the considerable labors of Edith von Zemenszky in the late 1970s and early '80s, brings together not only the largest single grouping of Steuben manuscripts (at the New-York Historical Society, New York City), but also nearly all known correspondence to or from Steuben, or even mentioning Steuben, from dozens of archival repositories and libraries worldwide. Largely in order to save ink, I have indexed these documents in the notes that follow by their location in the Zemenszky collection on microfilm. The actual location of the individual manuscripts can be found by consulting the Zemenszky collection.

Abbreviations

CHS: Chicago Historical Society, Chicago, IL

PAH: Syrett, Harold C., and Jacob E. Cooke, eds., *The Papers of Alexander Hamilton*, 25 vols., New York, 1961.

PHL: Hamar, Philip M. et al., eds., *The Papers of Henry Laurens*, 16 vols., Columbia, SC: 1968–2003.

SP: Zemenszky, Edith von, ed., *The Papers of General Friedrich von Steuben, 1777–1794*, Microfilm, 7 reels, Millwood, NY, 1976–84.

Chapter 1: The Finest School of Warfare in the World

1. Friedrich Kapp, *Life of Frederick William von Steuben* (New York: 1859), 49–50.
2. Gordon Craig, *The Politics of the Prussian Army, 1640–1945* (New York, 1955), 1–21.
3. Christopher Duffy, *The Army of Frederick the Great* (New York, 1974), 54–68. By "foreigners" I mean non-Prussians, which includes German men from other territorial states within the Holy Roman Empire.

4. Otto Büsch, *Militärsystem und Sozialleben im alten Preußen. Die Anfänge der Militarisierung der preußisch-deutschen Gesellschaft* (Berlin, 1962); Gerhard Ritter, *The Sword and the Scepter: The Problem of Militarism in Germany*, trans. Heinz Norden (4 vols., Coral Gables, FL, 1969–73), 1:15–42.

5. On the details of Steuben's ancestry, early life, and service record, see: "Zuverlässige Nachrichten von dem Geschlecht und Herkommen des Nordamerikanischen Generals, Friedrich Wilhelm Ludolf Gerhard Augustin von Steuben," *Historisches Portefeuille zur Kenntniss der gegenwärtigen und vergangenen Zeit* 4 (Berlin, 1785), 447; Daniel Heinrich Hering, *Beiträge zur Geschichte der evangelisch-reformirten Kirche in den preußisch-brandenburgschen Ländern* (2 vols., Breslau, 1784–85), 312–13; Anton B. C. Kalkhorst, "Neuen Daten über Steubens Dienstzeit im Heere Friedrichs des Grossen," in the Kalkhorst/Steuben Papers, Box 336, Folder 14, CHS.

6. Edgar Melton, "The Junkers of Brandenburg-Prussia, 1600–1806," in H. M. Scott, ed., *The European Nobilities in the Seventeenth and Eighteenth Centuries*, 2nd ed. (Basingstoke, 2007), 118–70.

7. For the latest research on the noble status of the Steuben family, which effectively refutes the work of earlier prosopographers, see: Theodor Albrecht, *Friedrich Wilhelm von Steuben: Des Generals unbekannte Ahnen: ein Forschungsbericht* (Berlin, 1983). The details of the controversy over Steuben's genealogy are also available online, on the Steuben family genealogy website: http://www.steuben.de. My thanks to Henning Hubertus von Steuben for this reference.

8. Christopher Duffy, *Russia's Military Way to the West: Origins and Nature of Russian Military Power 1700–1800* (London, 1981), 42–55.

9. Christopher Duffy, *The Military Life of Frederick the Great* (New York, 1986), 21–75; John MacAuley Palmer, *General von Steuben* (New Haven, 1937), 23–28.

10. Duffy, *Army of Frederick the Great*, 160; Kapp, *Steuben*, 49–50.

11. Ibid., 31.

12. Ibid., 24–53.

13. In his own writings, especially on American political life, Steuben quoted extensively from *Don Quixote* and Montesquieu's *L'Ésprit des Lois*. The inventory of his personal library from 1784–86 includes an even mixture of works on military theory, political theory, history and fiction. Steuben also enjoyed a few bawdier comedies, such as Laurence Sterne's *Tristram Shandy*. "Catalogue de ma Bibliotheque," 1786, *SP* 7:489.

14. Kapp, *Steuben*, 49.

15. Duffy, *Military Life*, 101–21; Johannes Kunisch, *Das Mirakel des Hauses Brandenburg: Studien zum Verhältnis von Kabinettspolitik und Kriegsführung im Zeitalter des Siebenjährigen Krieges* (Munich, 1978).

16. Duffy, *Army of Frederick the Great*, 69–92, 165; Hans Delbrück, *Geschichte der Kriegskunst im Rahmen der politischen Geschichte* (7 vols., Berlin, 1921–28),

4:230–49; Hew Strachan, *European Armies and the Conduct of War* (London, 1983), 18–22.

17. Duffy, *Army of Frederick the Great*, 76–78.

18. Steuben's correspondence with the king is preserved in the Steuben/Kalkhorst Papers, Box 336, Folder 14, CHS.

Chapter 2: Courtier and Supplicant

1. Steuben to undisclosed recipient, June 16, 1764, Kalkhorst/Steuben Papers, Box 336, Folder 11, CHS.

2. Ibid.

3. Prince Henry of Prussia to Steuben, November 18, 1764; Friederike of Württemberg to Steuben, December 31, 1764, Kalkhorst/Steuben Papers, Box 336, Folder 11, CHS.

4. Steuben to Daniel Marianus Frank, May 17, 1773, Kalkhorst/Steuben Papers, Box 336, Folder 11, CHS.

5. Steuben to Daniel Marianus Frank, February 1, 1772, Kalkhorst/Steuben Papers, Box 336, Folder 11, CHS.

6. Steuben to Daniel Marianus Frank, February 12, 1772, Kalkhorst/Steuben Papers, Box 336, Folder 11, CHS.

7. Steuben to Daniel Marianus Frank, January 29, 1772, Kalkhorst/Steuben Papers, Box 336, Folder 11, CHS.

8. Palmer, *General von Steuben*, 79–81. Copies of Steuben's correspondence with Baden, and with the Baron de Hahn in the Strasbourg garrison, are preserved in the Kalkhorst/Steuben Papers, Box 336, Folder 11, CHS. In 1771, the former margraviates of Baden-Durlach and Baden-Baden were united as the margraviate of Baden, under the rule of the former margrave of Baden-Durlach.

9. Palmer, *General von Steuben*, 79–80.

10. Peter Burdett to Benjamin Franklin, June 1777, *SP* 1:1.

11. Stacy Schiff, *A Great Improvisation: Franklin, France, and the Birth of America* (New York, 2005), 7–45; Brian N. Morton and Donald C. Spinelli, *Beaumarchais and the American Revolution* (Lanham, MD, 2003), 53–112.

12. Benjamin Franklin to James Lovell, October 7, 1777, *SP* 1:12.

13. Lee Kennett, *The French Armies in the Seven Years' War* (Durham, NC, 1967), 22–26, 139–43.

14. Morton and Spinelli, *Beaumarchais*.

15. Beaumarchais to Steuben, June 26, 1777, SP 1:2; Thomas J. Schaeper, *France and America in the Revolutionary Era: The Life of Jacques-Donatien Leray de Chaumont, 1725–1803* (Providence, RI, 1995), 96–103; Silas Deane, *The Deane Papers, 1774–1790* (5 vols., New York, 1887–91), 5:439.

16. Beaumarchais to the Comte de Vergennes, December 7, 1777, in Gunnar von Proschwitz, ed., *Pierre Augustin Caron de Beaumarchais: Lettres de combat*

(Paris, 2005), 176–77. On Deane's activity in Paris, see: Coy Hilton James, *Silas Deane—Patriot or Traitor?* (East Lansing, MI, 1975).

17. Morton and Spinelli, *Beaumarchais*, 80.
18. Ibid., 56–58, 79–80, 168; Deane, *Deane Papers*, 5:439.
19. Palmer, *General von Steuben*, 105–106.
20. Unknown to Prince Josef Friedrich Wilhelm, August 13, 1777, Kalkhorst/Steuben Papers, Box 336, Folder 13, CHS.
21. Paul Wentworth to the Earl of Suffolk, September 24, 1777, *SP* 1:11; Steuben to Vergennes, December 30, 1782, *SP* 6:56.
22. Silas Deane to Robert Morris, September 3, 1777, *SP* 1:5; Benjamin Franklin and Silas Deane to George Washington, September 4, 1777, *SP* 1:6; Louis de L'Estarjette to Henry Laurens, September 5, 1777, *SP* 1:7.

Chapter 3: This Illustrious Stranger

1. *SP* 1:15.
2. "The Autobiography of Peter Stephen Du Ponceau," *The Pennsylvania Magazine of History and Biography* 63 (1939), 216; Morton and Spinelli, *Beaumarchais*, 139.
3. Morton and Spinelli, *Beaumarchais*, 7–8, 79–80, 137.
4. Philander Dean Chase, "Baron von Steuben in the War of Independence" (Ph.D. dissertation, Duke University, 1972), 271–72.
5. Duponceau diary, *SP* 1:9; "Autobiography of Peter Stephen Du Ponceau," 199–200, 216–17.
6. "Autobiography of Peter Stephen Du Ponceau," 201–202; Steuben to Daniel Marianus Frank, July 4, 1779, *SP* 1:432.
7. Palmer, *General von Steuben*, 105–109.
8. Steuben to Daniel Marianus Frank, July 4, 1779, *SP* 1:432; "Autobiography of Peter Stephen Du Ponceau," 199–200.
9. Palmer, *General von Steuben*, 117–19.
10. Samuel Adams to James Lovell, January 10, 1778, *SP* 1:27; to Horatio Gates, January 13 and 14, 1778, *SP* 1:30, 33.
11. "Autobiography of Peter Stephen Du Ponceau," 21.
12. Steuben to John Hancock, January 6, 1778, *SP* 1:22; Palmer, *General von Steuben*, 119.
13. William Gordon to George Washington, January 9, 1778, *SP* 1:26.
14. Francy to Beaumarchais, January 11, 1778, *SP* 1:28; Steuben to Beaumarchais, January 12, 1778, *SP* 1:29; Washington to Steuben, January 9, 1778, *SP* 1:24; Henry Laurens to Steuben, January 14, 1778, *SP* 1:31.
15. John Ferling, *Almost a Miracle: The American Victory in the War of Independence* (Oxford, 2007), 282; Thomas Fleming, *Washington's Secret War: The Hidden History of Valley Forge* (New York, 2005), 69–128.
16. "Autobiography of Peter Stephen Du Ponceau," 202.
17. Morton and Spinelli, *Beaumarchais*, 167; Louis Gottschalk, *Lafayette Joins the American Army* (Chicago, 1937), 17–20.

18. "Autobiography of Peter Stephen Du Ponceau," 202–203.

19. Duponceau diary, *SP* 1:9.

20. "Autobiography of Peter Stephen Du Ponceau," 212.

21. Duponceau diary, *SP* 1:9; Robert Morris to Henry Laurens, February 4, 1778, *SP* 1:39.

22. Steuben to the Continental Congress, Henry Laurens, and George Washington, December 6, 1777, *SP* 1:15, 16, 17.

23. Steuben to Horatio Gates, December 27, 1777, *SP* 1:21.

24. Duponceau diary, *SP* 1:9; "Autobiography of Peter Stephen Du Ponceau," 204–206.

25. L'Enfant accepted the offer; Romanet could not be persuaded to stay in America. Like most of the French officers then waiting at Boston, he was "very unhappy," and had a "poor impression of the character of the inhabitants of this part of the world, and their conduct towards strangers." He left Boston for France on March 12. Pierre Landais to Steuben, March 11, 1778, *SP* 1:64.

26. Steuben to John Hancock, February 9, 1778, *SP* 1:44, 45; to Samuel Adams, February 10, 1778, *SP* 1:47; Horatio Gates to Henry Laurens, February 17, 1778, *SP* 1:49; Continental Congress resolution, February 18, 1778, *SP* 1:51; Henry Laurens to George Washington, February 19, 1778, *SP* 1:52.

27. Richard Peters to Steuben, October 30, 1785, *SP* 6:465.

28. Steuben to John Hancock, February 9, 1778, *SP* 1:44.

29. Henry Laurens to George Washington, February 19, 1778, *SP* 1:52.

CHAPTER 4: A MAN PROFOUND IN THE SCIENCE OF WAR

1. Friedrich Kapp, *Leben des amerikanischen Generals Friedrich Wilhelm von Steuben* (Berlin, 1858), 662.

2. Charles Lee to Mrs. Sidney Lee, June 22, 1782, in Edward Langworthy, *The Life and Memoirs of the Late Major General Lee* (New York, 1813), 349–52.

3. Thomas Conway to Horatio Gates, April 21, 1778, *SP* 1:98.

4. Lafayette to Henry Laurens, January 5, 1778, *PHL* 12:257; Steuben to Henry Laurens, November 28, 1778, *SP* 1:268.

5. Duponceau diary, *SP* 1:9; William North, *Baron von Steuben* (Utica, NY, 1990), 11.

6. Steuben to Daniel Marianus Frank, July 4, 1779, *SP* 1:432.

7. Fleming, *Washington's Secret War*, 174.

8. Ibid., 129–205.

9. Ibid., 155; Steuben to Horatio Gates, March 21, 1778, *SP* 1:71.

10. Henry Laurens to Steuben, January 14, 1778, *SP* 1:31. The actual location of Steuben's headquarters at Valley Forge is still very much a matter of speculation. We know from Duponceau's diary (*SP* 1:9) that he moved quarters at least once while at the Forge. Jacqueline Thibaut, *In True Rustic Order: Historic Resource Study and Historical Base Maps of the Valley Forge Encampment, 1777–1778* (*The Valley Forge Report*, vol. 3; Valley Forge National

Historical Park, 1982), 146–48. In his postwar memoirs, Duponceau noted that Steuben's quarters were located very near to those of Maj. Gen. William Alexander, Lord Stirling. "Autobiography of Peter Stephen Du Ponceau," 207–208.

11. Henry Laurens to John Laurens, February 18, 1778, *PHL* 12:462.
12. John Laurens to Henry Laurens, February 27, 1778, *SP* 1:57.
13. Duponceau diary, *SP* 1:9.
14. "A few Observations made on my reconnaitring the Camp," March 5, 1778, Kalkhorst/Steuben Papers, Box 336, Folder 10, CHS.
15. Henry Laurens to John Laurens, March 1, 1778, *PHL* 12:491.
16. John Laurens to Henry Laurens, February 27, 1778, *SP* 1:57.
17. The Baron de Kalb to Henry Laurens, January 7, 1778, *PHL* 12:267.
18. North, *Baron von Steuben*, 15.
19. John Laurens to Henry Laurens, February 28, 1778, *PHL* 12:483–84.
20. John Laurens to Henry Laurens, February 27, 1778, *SP* 1:57.
21. John Laurens to Henry Laurens, March 9, 1778, *PHL* 12:532–33.
22. Francis Dana to Henry Laurens, March 2, 1778, *SP* 1:59.
23. North, *Baron von Steuben*, 27.
24. Ibid., 26; Duponceau diary, *SP* 1:9.
25. "Autobiography of Peter Stephen Du Ponceau," 208; Harry Ammon, *James Monroe: The Quest for National Identity* (New York, 1971), 18–22.
26. John Laurens to Henry Laurens, February 27, 1778, *SP* 1:57.
27. John Laurens to Henry Laurens, March 9, 1778, *PHL* 12:532–33; Steuben to Henry Laurens, March 12, 1778, *PHL* 12:552–53.
28. Joseph H. Jones, ed., *The Life of Ashbel Greene, V.D.M.* (New York, 1849), 109.
29. North, *Baron von Steuben*, 11.
30. A good discussion of the experience of combat in the Revolution can be found in Michael Stephenson, *Patriot Battles: How the War of Independence Was Fought* (New York, 2007).
31. Steuben to the Board of War, December 1778, *SP* 1:271.

Chapter 5: On the Parade-Ground at Valley Forge

1. *SP* 1:79.
2. Steuben to the Board of War, December 1778, *SP* 1:271.
3. General Orders, March 17, 1778, *SP* 1:68.
4. Ibid.
5. Henry Beekman Livingston to Robert R. Livingston, March 25, 1778, *SP* 1:79.
6. Steuben to the Board of War, December 1778, *SP* 1:271.
7. North, *Baron von Steuben*, 13.
8. "Autobiography of Peter Stephen Du Ponceau," 219; North, *Baron von Steuben*, 12–14.

9. Steuben to the Baron de Gaudy, 1787–88, in Kapp, *Leben des amerikanischen Generals Friedrich Wilhelm von Steuben*, 662.

10. George Washington to Peter Scull, March 19, 1778, *SP* 1:69; to James Varnum, March 19, 1778, *SP* 1:70; General Orders, March 22, 1778, *SP* 1:73.

11. Horatio Gates to Steuben, March 25, 1778, *SP* 1:77.

12. General Orders, March 24, 1778, *SP* 1:75.

13. North, *Baron von Steuben*, 12–13; "Autobiography of Peter Stephen Du Ponceau," 210–11.

14. George Washington to William Smallwood, May 1, 1778, *SP* 1:107.

15. General Orders, March 28, 1778, *SP* 1:82.

16. "Instructions for elementary Manœuvres," March 28–April 29, 1778, *SP* 1:76; Steuben to the Continental Congress, May 27, 1778, *SP* 1:144.

17. Henry Beekman Livingston to Robert R. Livingston, March 25, 1778, *SP* 1:79.

18. Horatio Gates to Steuben, March 25, 1778, *SP* 1:77.

19. "Instructions for elementary Manœuvres," March 28–April 29, 1778, *SP* 1:76.

20. Steuben to the Board of War, December 1778, *SP* 1:271.

21. Joseph Plumb Martin, *Private Yankee Doodle*, (Boston, 1962) 118.

22. John Laurens to Henry Laurens, March 25, 1778, *PHL* 13:36; Steuben to Henry Laurens, April 2, 1778, *PHL* 13:68–69; John Laurens to Henry Laurens, April 18, 1778, *PHL* 13:139–40.

23. Alexander Scammell to John Sullivan, April 8, 1778, *SP* 1:91.

24. North, *Baron von Steuben*, 14.

25. Alexander Scammell to Timothy Pickering, April 21, 1778, *SP* 1:99.

26. George Washington to the Continental Congress, April 30, 1778, *SP* 1:105.

27. Instructions for the feu de joie, May 5, 1778, SP 1:113.

28. John Laurens to Henry Laurens, May 7, 1778, *PHL* 13:264–65.

29. "Autobiography of Peter Stephen Du Ponceau," 209.

CHAPTER 6: JEALOUSIES AND HINDRANCES

1. *PHL* 13:68–69.

2. Some historians have argued against this, claiming that the kind of training Steuben imparted—while typical for the period—did not actually prepare the troops for the physical conditions of combat. See, for example, Wayne K. Bodle, *The Valley Forge Winter: Civilians and Soldiers in War* (University Park, PA, 2004), 189–220. To make such an argument, however, is to misconstrue the nature of infantry tactics in eighteenth-century warfare; the maneuvers Steuben taught to the troops were precisely those used to form line of battle from column, and vice versa, and were therefore highly practical on the battlefield.

3. George Washington to his generals, April 20, 1778, in John C. Fitzpatrick, ed., *The Writings of George Washington* (39 vols., Washington, DC, 1931–44), 11:282–83; Steuben to George Washington, April 25, 1778, *SP* 1:101.

4. Stephen R. Taaffe, *The Philadelphia Campaign, 1777–1778* (Lawrence, KS, 2003), 188–89, 206–208.

5. Thomas Ewing, ed., *George Ewing, Gentleman: A Soldier of Valley Forge* (Yonkers, NY, 1928), 53–54.

6. Joseph Plumb Martin, *Private Yankee Doodle* (Boston, 1962), 83–84.

7. Ibid., 84.

8. Theodore Thayer, *The Making of a Scapegoat: Washington and Lee at Monmouth* (Port Washington, NY, 1976), 10; Taaffe, *Philadelphia Campaign*, 206–208; Henry Laurens to Francis Hopkinson, May 27, 1778, PHL 13:346–47; Gottschalk, *Lafayette Joins the American Army*, 186–93.

9. Lloyd A. Brown and Howard H. Peckham, eds., *Revolutionary War Journals of Henry Dearborn, 1775–1783* (Freeport, NY, 1969), 121.

10. William Gordon, *History of Rise, Progress, and Establishment of the Independence of the United States of America* (3 vols., New York, 1801), 3:192; Palmer, *General von Steuben*, 169–70; Henry Laurens to Richard Caswell, May 26, 1778, PHL 13:344–45.

11. Drill instructions from Steuben and William Davies, May 15, 1778, *SP* 1:134; General Orders, June 1, 1778, *SP* 1:153.

12. Jacob Morgan, Jr., to George Bryan, May 30, 1778, in Samuel Hazard, ed., *Pennsylvania Archives* (12 vols., Philadelphia, 1852–56), 6:568–69.

13. William Henry Drayton to Steuben, May 21, 1778, *SP* 1:140.

14. Richard Peters to Timothy Pickering, June 9, 1778, *SP* 1:160; Henry Laurens to Louis du Portail, May 20, 1778, *PHL* 13:336.

15. Steuben to the Continental Congress, May 27, 1778, *SP* 1:144.

16. By a curious coincidence, one member of Steuben's staff already knew Conway very well: Duponceau. While in the French army, Conway had been stationed for a time on the island of Rhé. Indeed, young Duponceau owed much of his knowledge of spoken English to his early conversations with Conway. "Autobiography of Peter Stephen Du Ponceau," 204.

17. Thayer, *Making of a Scapegoat*, 16.

18. Alexander Hamilton to Elias Boudinot, July 26, 1778, *PAH* 1:528–29.

19. "Instructions for elementary Manœuvres," March 28–April 29, 1778, *SP* 1:76.

20. James Mitchell Varnum to Washington, May 5, 1778, *SP* 1:112.

21. Michael Ryan to Steuben, June 11, 1778, and Steuben to Ryan, June 12, 1778, *SP* 1:161–62; John Laurens to Henry Laurens, June 14, 1778, *PHL* 13:458.

22. Steuben to the Board of War, May 27, 1778, *SP* 1:144.

23. General Orders for June 15, 1778, *SP* 1:164.

24. Steuben to Washington, June 17, 1778, *SP* 1:165.

25. Washington to Steuben, June 18, 1778, *SP* 1:166.
26. Washington to Henry Laurens, June 18, 1778, *SP* 1:168; Alexander Hamilton to William Duer, June 18, 1778, *PAH* 1:497–500.

Chapter 7: Trial by Combat

1. *SP* 1:432.
2. Steuben to George Washington, June 18, 1778, *SP* 1:169.
3. Johann Ewald, *Diary of the American War: A Hessian Journal*, ed. and trans. by Joseph P. Tustin (New Haven, 1979), 132–33.
4. On the preliminaries to Monmouth, see: Taaffe, *Philadelphia Campaign*, 197–211; David G. Martin, *The Philadelphia Campaign: June 1777–July 1778* (Cambridge, MA, 1993), 197–208; William Stryker, *The Battle of Monmouth* (Port Washington, NY, 1970), 47–112.
5. Steuben's opinion at council of war, June 24, 1778, Fitzpatrick, ed., *Writings of George Washington*, 12:115–17; Lafayette to George Washington, June 24, 1778, in Louis Gottschalk, ed., *The Letters of Lafayette to Washington, 1777–1799* (Philadelphia, 1976), 47.
6. Steuben to Charles Scott, June 25, 1778, Steuben to George Washington, June 25, 1778, and Col. Stephen Moylan to George Washington, June 25, 1778, *SP* 1:173–75.
7. Steuben to George Washington, June 27, 1778, *SP* 1:176.
8. On the course of the battle itself, see: Taaffe, *Philadelphia Campaign*, 212–21; Martin, *Philadelphia Campaign*, 209–34; Stryker, *Battle of Monmouth*, 117–233.
9. Kapp, *Steuben*, 159; John Laurens to Henry Laurens, July 2, 1778, *PHL* 13:545.
10. Steuben's official—and only accurate—account of his actions at Monmouth is to be found in the testimony he presented at the court-martial of Charles Lee on July 18, 1778, printed in Charles Lee, *The Lee Papers* (4 vols., New York, 1871–74), 3:95–97.
11. Testimony of Lt. Col. Robert Harrison, in Lee, *Lee Papers*, 3:71–73.
12. John U. Rees, *"What is this you have been about to day?" The New Jersey Brigade at the Battle of Monmouth* (2003), Internet resource (http://revwar75.com/library/rees/monmouth/Monmouth.htm).
13. Steuben's testimony at the Lee court-martial, July 18, 1778, *SP* 1:190.
14. Alexander Hamilton to Elias Boudinot, July 5, 1778, *PAH* 1:513.
15. North, *Baron von Steuben*, 14.
16. Steuben to Daniel Marianus Frank, July 4, 1779, *SP* 1:432.

CHAPTER 8: THE BLUE BOOK

1. *PHL* 14:370–72.
2. Charles Lee to Henry Laurens, October 30, 1778, in Langworthy, *Life and Memoirs of Major General Lee*, 342–43.
3. General Orders, July 2, 1778, and July 5, 1778, *SP* 1:182, 184.
4. André-Michel de Choin to the Chevalier de Luzerne, July 22, 1778, *SP* 1:192.
5. John Laurens to Henry Laurens, July 6, 1778, *SP* 1:186.
6. George Washington to Henry Laurens, July 24, 1778, *SP* 1:198.
7. Testimony from court-martial of Reuben Lipscomb, July 5–9, 1778, *SP* 1:183; General Orders, July 12, 1778, *SP* 1:188.
8. General Orders, July 22, 1778, *SP* 1:193.
9. Alexander Hamilton to Elias Boudinot, July 26, 1778, *PAH* 1:528–29.
10. Louis-Pierre de La Neuville to Horatio Gates, July 1778, *SP* 1:179; Steuben to George Washington, July 24, 1778, *SP* 1:194.
11. Steuben to George Washington, July 24, 1778, *SP* 1:194.
12. George Washington to Henry Laurens, July 24, 1778, *SP* 1:198.
13. George Washington to Gouverneur Morris, July 24, 1778, *SP* 1:199.
14. George Washington to Henry Laurens, July 26, 1778, *SP* 1:202.
15. Alexander Hamilton to Elias Boudinot, July 26, 1778, *PAH* 1:528–29.
16. Steuben to Richard Peters, October 1, 1778, *SP* 1:242.
17. Steuben to George Washington, August 7, 1778, *SP* 1:208.
18. The Baron d'Arendt to Steuben, July 24, 1778, *SP* 1:195; the Chevalier de Crénis to Steuben, July 24, 1778, *SP* 1:196–97.
19. Gouverneur Morris to George Washington, August 2, 1778, *SP* 1:204.
20. Henry Laurens to George Washington, August 20, 1778
21. Conrad-Alexandre Gérard to Steuben, September 12, 1778, *SP* 1:228; Henry Laurens to Steuben, September 17, 1778, *PHL* 14:323–24.
22. Opinion of the Board of General Officers, September 11, 1778, *SP* 1:227.
23. George Washington to Henry Laurens, September 12, 1778, *SP* 1:229.
24. Steuben to Conrad-Alexandre Gérard, September 25, 1778, *SP* 1:236.
25. Steuben to Conrad-Alexandre Gérard, September 24, 1778, *SP* 1:235.
26. Steuben to Richard Peters, October 1, 1778, *SP* 1:242; Steuben to Joseph Reed, October 5, 1778, *SP* 1:244; Steuben to Henry Laurens, October 1, 1778, *PHL* 14:370–72.
27. Henry Laurens to Steuben, October 12, 1778, *PHL* 14:400–401; C. F. William Maurer, *Dragoon Diary: The History of the Third Continental Light Dragoons* (Bloomington, IN, 2005), 129–47, 465–97.
28. Steuben to Henry Laurens, October 1, 1778, *PHL* 14:370–72.
29. Ibid.
30. Steuben's opinions on a British expedition against Boston, and on American winter quarters, October 18, 1778, *SP* 1:248.

31. George Washington to Henry Laurens, November 13, 1778, *SP* 1:264; Steuben to Henry Laurens, November 26, 1778, *SP* 1:265.
32. Steuben to the Continental Congress, November 28, 1778, *SP* 1:267.
33. Remarks on the Prussian and French armies, November 1778–February 1779, *SP* 1:251; remarks on French infantry regulations, November 1778–February 1779, *SP* 1:252; remarks on duties of staff officers in the French army, November 1778–February 1779, *SP* 1:253; instructions for maneuvers, November 1778–February 1779, *SP* 1:257; instructions for baggage on the march, November 1778–February 1779, *SP* 1:258.
34. Francy to Beaumarchais, November 24, 1778, in Brian N. Morton, ed., *Correspondance de Beaumarchais* (4 vols., Paris, 1969–78), 4:275–76.
35. Steuben to Charles Lee, December 2, 1778, *SP* 1:273; Alexander Hamilton to Steuben, December 19, 1778, *PAH* 1:601.
36. Lord Stirling to George Washington, February 26, 1779, *SP* 1:298; comments of Lord Stirling and Arthur St. Clair, February 26, 1779, *SP* 1:299; George Washington to William Galvan, March 11, 1779, *SP* 1:308.
37. Memorial of Baron de Knoblauch to Congress, May 4, 1779, *SP* 1:337.
38. Richard Peters to Henry Laurens, January 22, 1779, *SP* 1:286; Charles Carré to Steuben, July 12, 1780, *SP* 2:388; Palmer, *General von Steuben*, 201–202.
39. Chapter outline for regulations, November 1778–February 1779, *SP* 1:255; George Washington to Steuben, February 26, 1779, *SP* 1:297; Steuben to George Washington, March 5, 1779, *SP* 1:303; Steuben to the Continental Congress, March 25, 1779, *SP* 1:312; Timothy Pickering to John Jay, March 27 and 29, 1779, *SP* 1:314, 315; Congressional resolutions on *Regulations*, March 29, 1779, *SP* 1:316.
40. Kapp, *Steuben*, 660–61.
41. Steuben to the Continental Congress, March 25, 1779, *SP* 1:312.
42. Robert S. Quimby, *The Background of Napoleonic Warfare: The Theory of Military Tactics in Eighteenth-Century France* (New York, 1957), 113–33. Guibert's book, *Essai général de tactique* (Paris, 1772), was perhaps the most important book on tactical theory to appear in the eighteenth century. Among other things, it advocated a much simplified "manual exercise," as Steuben did. The Baron, in fact, owned a copy, as well as copies of books by most of Guibert's rivals—Mesnil-Durand, Puységur, and Folard. "Catalogue de ma Bibliotheque," 1788, SP 7:489.
43. Lord Stirling to George Washington, February 26, 1779, *SP* 1:298; Lord Stirling's and Arthur St. Clair's comments, February 26 and March 10, 1779, *SP* 1:299, 306; George Washington to Steuben, March 11, 1779, *SP* 1:307.

CHAPTER 9: THE TRUE MEANING OF DISCIPLINE

1. *SP* 2:212.
2. George Washington to James Duane, January 8, 1779, *SP* 1:281; remarks on formation of the army, March 1779, *SP* 1:301; report of Board of War, January

21, 1779, *SP* 1:285; James Duane to George Washington, January 24, 1779, *SP* 1:287.

3. Henry Laurens to John Laurens, April 18, 1779, *SP* 1:329; Steuben to Richard Peters, June 12, 1779, *SP* 1:404.

4. Palmer, *General von Steuben*, 314.

5. Lord Stirling's and Arthur St. Clair's comments, February 26, 1779, *SP* 1:299.

6. Richard Peters to Steuben, June 19, 1779, *SP* 1:411.

7. Steuben to William North, October 23, 1788, *SP* 7:205.

8. Steuben to Benjamin Walker, February 23, 1780, *SP* 2:212; Steuben to August-François Des Epiniers, November 1, 1779, *SP* 2:80; Des Epiniers to Steuben, January 1780, January 12, and April 14, 1780, *SP* 2:152, 157, 257; Francy to Steuben, January 12 and March 4, 1780, *SP* 2:156, 226; Francy to Beaumarchais, November 10 and 24, 1778, in Morton, ed., *Correspondance de Beaumarchais*, 4:262–63, 275–76.

9. Steuben to Daniel Marianus Frank, July 4, 1779, *SP* 1:432.

10. Kapp, *Steuben*, 641.

11. Conrad-Alexandre Gérard, May 6, 1779, *SP* 1:340.

12. Timothy Pickering to Steuben, June 19, 1779, *SP* 1:412.

13. Richard Peters to Steuben, June 19, 1779, *SP* 1:411.

14. Steuben to John Jay, June 12, 1779, *SP* 1:403.

15. Steuben to Richard Peters, June 12, 1779, *SP* 1:404; Steuben to Timothy Pickering, June 12, 1779, *SP* 1:405.

16. Richard Peters to Steuben, June 19, 1779, *SP* 1:411.

17. Chase, "Baron von Steuben," 134.

18. North, *Baron von Steuben*, 16–17; "Autobiography of Peter Stephen Du Ponceau," 218–19.

19. Remarks on the formation of the army, March 1779, *SP* 1:301.

20. William B. Reed, ed., *Life and Correspondence of Joseph Reed* (2 vols., Philadelphia, 1847), 2:115.

21. Steuben to Benjamin Franklin, September 28, 1779, *SP* 2:57.

22. Remarks on the formation of the army, March 1779, *SP* 1:301; Steuben to Benjamin Franklin, September 28, 1779, *SP* 2:57.

23. See, for example, the following inspection returns: *SP* 2:104, 106, 108, 113, 118, 135, 137, 140, 145.

24. George Washington to Steuben, January 22, 1780, *SP* 2:163.

25. Steuben to Joseph Reed, October 5, 1778, *SP* 1:244; instructions on the formation of the army, November–December 1778, *SP* 1:261.

26. Ferling, *Almost a Miracle*, 349.

27. Steuben to George Washington, March 28, 1780, *SP* 2:245.

28. The Board of War to Steuben, January 25, 1780, *SP* 2:166; Steuben to Washington, January 26–30, 1780, *SP* 1:167; Timothy Pickering to Steuben, January 29 and January 31, 1780, *SP* 2:171, 173.

29. Steuben to George Washington, February 23, 1780, *SP* 2:213.

30. Steuben to Benjamin Walker, February 23, 1780, *SP* 2:212.

31. Terry Golway, *Washington's General: Nathanael Greene and the Triumph of the American Revolution* (New York, 2005), 215–17.

32. Chase, "Baron von Steuben," 154–55.

33. Steuben to George Washington, April 6, 1780, *SP* 2:250; Congressional resolution and committee instructions on army formation, April 6–11, 1780, *SP* 2:251.

34. Steuben to Duponceau, May 5, 1780, *SP* 2:299; Duponceau to Steuben, July 7, 1780, *SP* 2:381.

35. Instructions for review of troops, April 24, 1780, *SP* 2:260; General Orders, April 25, 1780, *SP* 2:261; Martin, *Private Yankee Doodle*, 187–88.

36. "Disposition for the Manœuvre," May 29, 1780, *SP* 1:325.

37. Golway, *Washington's General*, 220–25.

38. General Orders, June 7, 1780, *SP* 2:337.

39. General Orders, June 9, 1780, *SP* 2:340.

40. Steuben to William Livingston, June 20, 1780, *SP* 2:363; Steuben to George Washington, June 20, 1780, *SP* 2:364; George Washington to Steuben, June 20, 1780, *SP* 2:365.

Chapter 10: Tormenting the Governor

1. *SP* 5:169.

2. Joseph Beatty Doyle, *Frederick William von Steuben and the American Revolution: Aide to Washington and Inspector General* (Steubenville, OH, 1913), 185–88.

3. Act of Connecticut Assembly, ca. January 30, 1783, *SP* 6:78.

4. Kapp, *Steuben*, 231.

5. Steuben to Daniel Marianus Frank, July 4, 1779, *SP* 1:432.

6. Steuben to Joseph Reed, May 24, 1780, *SP* 2:320.

7. James Thacher, *A Military Journal during the American Revolutionary War, from 1775 to 1783* (Boston, 1827), 207.

8. "Plan for the Formation of the Light Infantry," July 14, 1780, *SP* 2:390; Steuben to George Washington, July 18, 20, 22, and 28, 1780, *SP* 2:405, 411, 418, 432; George Washington to Steuben, July 18 and 22, 1780, *SP* 2:408, 420; Henry Knox to Steuben, January 16, 1780, *SP* 2:160; Steuben's notes on distribution of orders, June 1780, *SP* 2:327.

9. Steuben to George Washington, October 23, 1780, *SP* 3:4.

10. George Washington to Nathanael Greene, October 22, 1780, *SP* 3:2; George Washington to Samuel Huntington, October 22, 1780, *SP* 3:3.

11. George Washington to Steuben, October 22, 1780, *SP* 3:1.

12. "Autobiography of Peter Stephen Du Ponceau," 227.

13. Ibid., 312–13.

14. Nathanael Greene to Steuben, November 20, 1780, *SP* 3:43.

15. Steuben to George Washington, November 24, 1780, *SP* 3:57; Steuben to Nathanael Greene, November 27–28, 1780, *SP* 3:68.
16. John E. Selby, *The Revolution in Virginia, 1775–1783* (Williamsburg, VA, 1988), 254–55.
17. Steuben to Thomas Jefferson, December 15, 1780, *SP* 3:154.
18. Edward Carrington to Nathanael Greene, January 5, 1781, *SP* 3:278.
19. John Christian Senf to Steuben, January 9, 1781, *SP* 3:326.
20. Steuben to Thomas Jefferson, January 6, 1781, *SP* 3:280.
21. Steuben to Nathanael Greene, January 8, 1781, *SP* 3:308.
22. George Gibson to Steuben, January 5, 1781, *SP* 3:276.
23. William North to Nathanael Greene, February 23, 1781, *SP* 4:117.
24. Nathanael Greene to Steuben, January 7, 1781, *SP* 3:293.
25. William North to Nathanael Greene, February 23, 1781, *SP* 4:117.
26. Steuben to George Washington, February 18, 1781, *SP* 4:54.
27. Thomas Jefferson to Steuben, February 16, 1781, *SP* 4:27.
28. William Davies to Steuben, February 18, 1781, *SP* 4:55.
29. Steuben to Thomas Jefferson, February 11, 1781, *SP* 3:590.
30. Steuben to George Washington, February 18, 1781, *SP* 4:54.
31. Ibid.
32. Armand le Gardeur de Tilly to Steuben, February 17, 1781, *SP* 4:46.
33. Richard Claiborne to Nathanael Greene, May 2, 1781, *SP* 5:12.
34. John Walker to Thomas Jefferson, March 9, 1781, *SP* 4:278.
35. Steuben to Thomas Jefferson, March 9, 1781, *SP* 4:274.
36. Thomas Jefferson to Steuben, March 10, 1778, *SP* 4:287.
37. Steuben to the Board of War, March 23, 1781, *SP* 4:379.
38. Steuben to Nathanael Greene, March 27, 1781, *SP* 4:404; Steuben's draft plan, March 27, 1781, *SP* 4:412.
39. Richard Henry Lee to Thomas Jefferson, March 27, 1781, *SP* 4:409; George Weedon to Thomas Jefferson, March 27, 1781, *SP* 4:411; Lafayette's comments, March 27, 1781, *SP* 4:412.
40. Virginia State Council resolution, March 29, 1781, *SP* 4:427; Steuben to Lafayette, March 29, 1781, *SP* 4:419; Steuben to George Weedon, March 29, 1781, *SP* 4:421.
41. George Weedon to Steuben, April 1, 1781, *SP* 4:446; Steuben to Nathanael Greene, April 2, 1781, *SP* 4:448.
42. Nathanael Greene to Steuben, April 2, 1781, *SP* 4:449.
43. Steuben to Peter Gabriel Muhlenberg, April 1, 1781, *SP* 4:441.
44. Steuben to Lafayette, April 10, 1781, *SP* 4:498; Lafayette to Steuben, April 21, 1781, *SP* 4:606.
45. General Orders, April 22, 1781, *SP* 4:627.
46. Selby, *Revolution in Virginia*, 270–72; Robert P. Davis, *Where a Man Can Go: Major General William Phillips, British Royal Artillery, 1731–1781* (Westport, CT, 1999), 125–61.

47. Steuben to Nathanael Greene, April 25, 1781, *SP* 4:644.
48. Thomas Jefferson to Steuben, April 26, 1781, *SP* 6:656.

CHAPTER 11: FROM VIRGINIA TO FRAUNCES TAVERN

1. *SP* 6:37.
2. William Davies to Steuben, March 10, 1781, *SP* 4:283; North, *Baron von Steuben*, 18–20.
3. Steuben to Nathanael Greene, May 15, 1781, *SP* 5:57.
4. Steuben to Nathanael Greene, May 15, 1781, *SP* 5:23; Nathanael Greene to Steuben, May 1, 1781, *SP* 5:3.
5. Steuben to Lafayette, May 28, 1781, *SP* 5:108.
6. Steuben to Lafayette, June 3, 1781, *SP* 5:134; Steuben to Archibald Cary, June 3, 1781, *SP* 5:133.
7. Steuben's account of events before the retreat from Point of Fork, June 1781, *SP* 5:132.
8. Steuben to George Washington, June 11, 1781, *SP* 5:169.
9. Richard C. Bush III, "The End of Colonel Gaskins's War, May–October 1781," internet resource (http://www.wscottsmith.com/VirginiaCampaign/gaskins/history.html).
10. Quoted in Joseph Jones to George Washington, June 20, 1781, *SP* 5:210.
11. Archibald Cary to Thomas Jefferson, June 19, 1781, *SP* 5:209.
12. Lafayette to George Washington, June 18, 1781, *SP* 5:206.
13. Stanley J. Idzerda, ed., *Lafayette in the Age of the American Revolution: Selected Letters and Papers, 1776–1790* (Ithaca, NY, 1977), 2:9, 385.
14. William Davies to Nathanael Greene, June 17, 1781, *SP* 5:199.
15. Steuben to Richard Peters, July 23, 1781, *SP* 5:251.
16. Nathanael Greene to Steuben, July 19, 1781, *SP* 5:248; Steuben to Nathanael Greene, August 13 and September 9, 1781, *SP* 5:276, 293.
17. Steuben to Benjamin Walker, September 9, 1781, *SP* 5:294.
18. Steuben to Nathanael Greene, September 19, 1781, *SP* 5:298.
19. Nathanael Greene to George Washington, September 17, 1781; George Washington to Nathanael Greene, October 6, 1781, in Richard K. Showman et al., eds., *The Papers of Nathanael Greene*, 16 vols (Chapel Hill, NC, 1976–98), 9:363, 429.
20. North, *Baron von Steuben*, 21–22; Richard M. Ketchum, *Victory at Yorktown* (New York, 2004), 245.
21. North, *Baron von Steuben*, 22.
22. Account from Henry Winfree, April 28, 1781, *SP* 4:676; North, *Baron von Steuben*, 25.
23. North, *Baron von Steuben*, 24–25.
24. Steuben to Nathanael Greene, November 5, 1781, *SP* 5:334.
25. North, *Baron von Steuben*, 25.

26. Steuben to Johann Christoph von Hövel, January 5, 1781, *SP* 5:361.
27. Steuben to George Washington, January 1782, February 4 and 6, 1781, *SP* 5:357, 379, 381.
28. Robert K. Wright, Jr., *The Continental Army* (Washington, DC, 1983), 175.
29. North, *Baron von Steuben*, 23–24; "Disposition for the Manœuvre of the Army," August 1782, *SP* 5:530; "Order of Review," September 7, 1782, *SP* 5:545.
30. Evelyn M. Acomb, ed., *The Revolutionary Journal of Baron Ludwig von Closen, 1780–1783* (Chapel Hill, NC, 1958), 242.
31. Thacher, *Military Journal*, 312.
32. Steuben to Nathanael Greene, January 26, 1783, *SP* 6:73.
33. Steuben to Elias Boudinot, December 5, 1782, *SP* 6:37.
34. Remarks on claims submitted to Congress, December 9, 1782, *SP* 6:40; Steuben to Benjamin Walker, December 27, 1782, *SP* 6:50; report of the Congressional Committee on Claims, December 30, 1782, *SP* 6:60.
35. Thomas Fleming, *The Perils of Peace: America's Struggle for Survival After Yorktown* (New York, 2007), 259–74.
36. William North to Benjamin Walker, February 16, 1783, *SP* 6:84.
37. North, *Baron von Steuben*, 27.
38. Steuben to George Washington, April 26, 1783, *SP* 6:141.
39. Chase, "Baron von Steuben," 280–81.
40. Philip van Cortlandt et al. to Steuben, June 9, 1783, *SP* 6:165.
41. George Washington to Elias Boudinot, June 30, 1783, *SP* 6:183; Washington's instructions for Steuben, July 12, 1783, *SP* 6:199; Nicholas Fish diary, July 20–August 4, 1783, *SP* 6:211; Steuben to George Washington, August 23, 1783, *SP* 6:236.
42. George Washington to Steuben, December 23, 1783, *SP* 6:279.

Chapter 12: An Old Soldier in Peacetime

1. *SP* 6:330.
2. Steuben to Luzerne, December 30, 1782, *SP* 6:54; Steuben to Vergennes, December 30, 1782, *SP* 6:56; Luzerne to Vergennes, January 2, 1783, *SP* 6:65.
3. The Baron von Bouwinghausen to Steuben, 1782, *SP* 5:494; Lafayette to Henry Knox, February 11, 1786, *SP* 7:14; Vergennes to Luzerne, July 21, 1783, *SP* 6:212; Vergennes to Steuben, July 21, 1783, *SP* 6:213.
4. Steuben's will, 1781, *SP* 5:115. Steuben's two Canitz nephews, August and Wilhelm, had been living with their elderly grandfather, Wilhelm August von Steuben. They visited Steuben in the United States shortly after the war; according to Steuben, they cheated one of his friends of some $300. The Baron cut August von Canitz from his will, and told the two brothers never to visit him again or he would have them arrested. Steuben to August and Wilhelm von Canitz, January 24, 1789, *SP* 7:222, 223.
5. Steuben to Jeremiah Powell, April 1779, *SP* 1:330.

6. "Pro memoria," April 1783, *SP* 6:121; Steuben to George Washington, April 15, 1783, *SP* 6:129; "Projet pour l'établissement des academies et manufactures militaires," April 16, 1783, *SP* 6:132; Steuben to George Washington, April 23, 1783, *SP* 6:134.

7. "Thoughts on a National Militia," February–March 1784, *SP* 6:303; George Washington to Steuben, March 15, 1784, *SP* 6:336.

8. Steuben to Thomas Mifflin, March 21, 1784, *SP* 6:340.

9. *A Letter on the Subject of an Established Militia, and Military Arrangements, Addressed to the Inhabitants of the United States* (New York, 1784), 2–16.

10. "Pensées sur L'Habillement militaire," February–March 1784, *SP* 6:300.

11. Kapp, *Leben des amerikanischen Generals Friedrich Wilhelm von Steuben*, 660–61.

12. Richard Peters to Horatio Gates, February 23, 1784, *SP* 6:329.

13. Continental Congress resolution and vote on claim, April 13, 1784, *SP* 6:351.

14. Aedanus Burke, *Considerations on the Society or Order of Cincinnati* (Philadelphia, 1783); John C. Meleney, *The Public Life of Aedanus Burke: Revolutionary Republican in Post-Revolutionary South Carolina* (Columbia, SC, 1989), 84–96.

15. Steuben to Henry Knox, November 11, 1783, *SP* 6:267.

16. Rufus King to Elbridge Gerry, November 5, 1786, quoted in Chase, "Baron von Steuben," 301.

17. Steuben to William North, November 15, 1786, *SP* 7:68.

18. Steuben to William North, September 13 and 17, 1786, *SP* 7:46, 48.

19. Steuben to William North, October 18, 1786, *SP* 7:57.

20. Steuben to William North, October 27, 1786, *SP* 7:59.

21. Steuben's thoughts on American government, February–March 1784, *SP* 6:297; "Observations sur les Etats Unies et leurs Gouvernement," February–March 1784, *SP* 6:299.

22. Steuben to William North, October 29, 1786, *SP* 7:60.

23. Prince Henry of Prussia to Steuben, April 1787, *SP* 7:92.

24. William North to Benjamin Walker, August 25, 1792, *SP* 7:408.

25. Palmer, *General von Steuben*, 333.

26. Steuben's record of naturalization, July 4, 1786, *SP* 7:32. He had already been made an honorary citizen of Pennsylvania in 1784.

27. Steuben to William North, November 24, 1778, Kalkhorst/Steuben Papers, Box 336, Folder 1, CHS; Steuben to William North, July 11, 1786, and October 23, 1788, *SP* 7:35, 205.

28. Steuben to William North, May 30, 1789, *SP* 7:324.

29. Washington's notes on potential army commanders, March 9, 1792, *SP* 7:376. Actually, virtually none of the generals Washington considered met with his unreserved approval. The command ultimately went to Anthony Wayne, though he was not Washington's first choice for the position, but Wayne's dramatic victory at Fallen Timbers on August 20, 1794, certainly proved the wisdom of the selection.

30. John Mulligan to Benjamin Walker, November 29, 1794, *SP* 7:480.

INDEX